TAP OUT TEXTBOOK
The Ultimate Guide to Submissions for Grappling

TAP OUT TEXTBOOK
The Ultimate Guide to Submissions for Grappling

By
Steve Scott

Turtle Press   **Santa Fe, NM**

To contact the author or to order additional copies of this book:

Turtle Press
PO Box 34010
Santa Fe NM 87594-4010
1-800-778-8785
www.TurtlePress.com

ISBN 9781934903148
LCCN 2009010166
Printed in the United States of America

Warning-Disclaimer

This book is designed to provide information on specific skills used in submission grappling, mixed martial arts, judo, jujitsu, sambo, catch wrestling and other martial arts. It is not the purpose of this book to reprint all the information that is otherwise available to the authors, publishers, printers or distributors, but instead to compliment, amplify and supplement other texts. You are urged to read all available material, learn as much as you wish about the subjects covered in this book and tailor the information to your individual needs. Anyone practicing the skills presented in this book should be physically healthy enough to do so and have permission from a licensed physician and be under the supervision of a qualified instructor before participating.

Every effort has been made to make this book as complete and accurate as possible. However, there may be mistakes, both typographical and in content. Therefore, this text should be used only as a general guide and not as the ultimate source of information on the subject presented here in this book on judo, jujitsu, sambo, grappling, martial arts or any skill or subject. The purpose of this book is to provide information and to entertain. The authors, publisher, printer and distributors shall neither have liability nor responsibility to any person or entity with respect to loss or damages caused, or alleged to have been caused, directly or indirectly, by the information contained in this book. If you do not wish to be bound by the above, you may return this book to the publisher for a full refund.

10 9 8 7 6 5 4 3 2 1 0

Library of Congress Cataloguing in Publication Data
Scott, Steve, 1952-
Tap out textbook : the ultimate guide to submissions for grappling / by Steve Scott.
    p. cm.
ISBN 978-1-934903-14-8
1. Martial arts--Holding. 2. Hand-to-hand fighting. I. Title.
GV1102.7.H64S39 2009
796.81--dc22
                    2009010166

Contents

SECTION TWO: CHOKES & STRANGLES 175

This section emphasizes strangles and chokes aimed directed against the carotid arteries on the sides of the neck as well as against the trachea (windpipe) and front of the check and throat. In some cases, neck cranks and shoulder locks are also shown when relevant to a choking technique. A wide variety of ways to break down an opponent, roll an opponent into a choke, flatten out an opponent for a choke or apply chokes from a variety of positions.

SECTION THREE: LEGLOCKS   343

This section includes all submission techniques directed toward the lower body, including the ankles, knees, legs and hips. A large number of toeholds and ankle locks are featured. Both straight and bent knee leglocks are shown in this section as well. The use of position, breaking an opponent down, set ups, rolling techniques to gain momentum and controlling your opponent are featured.

ACKNOWLEDGEMENTS

Thanks to Becky Scott, Mark Lozano, Jorge Garcia, Bill West, Eric Millsap, Bob Rittman, Bret Holder, Alan Johnson, Sharon Vandenberg, Mike Thomas, Victoria Thomas, Jamie Millsap, Holly Weddington, Ellen Wilson and Jake Purcell for the photographs used in this book. Thanks to all the athletes and coaches at Welcome Mat for posing for the photographs in this book as well as their technical input, advice and ideas. Thanks to John Saylor and the Shingitai Jujitsu Association, Dave Barth and the Parkville Athletic Complex in Parkville, Missouri and Bill Brown and Bill Brown's Karate in Kearney, Missouri.

FOREWORD BY SEAN WHEELOCK

As the television play-by-play commentator for the M1 Challenge, I have the opportunity to travel the world and see some of the best and most talented fighters in mixed martial arts. Above all else, these outstanding professional athletes all posses outstanding fundamentals in a wide array of combat sports. It has become not just clear—but obvious to me—that success in MMA begins with the ability to do the little things right. And of course, doing the little things right comes from a firm grasp of the fundamentals.

Groundfighting and submission techniques are considered by many to be the backbone of mixed martial arts. Being skillful as a groundfighter is vital to winning in this sport. I have yet to meet anyone in my work as an MMA television commentator who understands how to teach groundfighting better than Steve Scott.

Steve immediately impressed me because he values technique above all else. Steve knows that to be a success in any combat sport or martial art, including MMA, one must learn how to do things right and one must learn the fundamentals. He is a master educator with the ability to impart world-class knowledge to everyone from an MMA champion to an absolute beginner.

I am proud to call Steve Scott my coach as well as my friend. Not only has he made me a much better competitor in all aspects of groundfighting, he has made me a vastly better MMA commentator through his ability to truly explain to me the most complex submissions, holds, takedowns and throws.

No matter your level as a fighter and athlete, or what combat sport you practice, you will learn something new from Steve Scott. You'll also learn how to do something better and improve upon your technique. And most of all, you'll learn the fundamentals--the starting point for all champions.

Sean Wheelock

INTRODUCTION

If you force your opponent to submit and tap out, most likely, he'll never forgive you, and most certainly, he'll never forget you. You will always be the one who made him give up and he'll always have that in the back of his mind if he ever fights you again. It's a psychological edge that you gain and that edge is necessary for success in this rough and tumble world we live in.

This textbook is intended to be a handy, thorough and practical reference for every athlete, coach, student or follower of grappling, jujitsu, judo, MMA, sambo, wrestling, self-defense or any martial art. There are a lot of different techniques in this book using a lot of different situations, positions and set ups. While I make no claim that every move ever invented is shown in this book, there are a lot of moves on these pages and this book features a variety of ways to ruin any opponent's day. I'm sure you'll find what is on these pages to be useful, informative and, most of all, effective. This textbook covers both fundamental and advanced applications of many techniques. Some of the skills presented in this textbook are common and some are not. Whether you're a serious grappler or fighter, a newcomer to the world of grappling, a coach, or a fan interested enough to learn more about what it takes to make an opponent tap out, I'm sure you'll find something useful for your particular needs in this book. In all cases, take what is presented on these pages, experiment with it and make it work for you. Function dictates form. I'm a firm believer in cross-training and it's my intention that this book is something that can be used by anyone interested in submission techniques whether you're an MMA fighter, judo athlete, submission grappler, self-defense athlete or anyone who sees the value in functional skill training.

I've written several other books on specific subjects of submission grappling, jujitsu, judo and sambo. Each book specializes in a particular area of techniques. In this book, we jump right in and show lots of different submission moves. I recommend that this book be used along with my other books that Turtle Press has published on each specific area. Each of my other books explores various core and fundamental positions and set-ups in an introductory section. If you want a comprehensive and exhaustive study of all phases of groundfighting, throws and takedowns, you might want to get my other books to complete the series. Later on, there will be a description of each book for your reference.

In almost all forms of sport and self-defense personal combat, submission techniques aimed at the arms, neck and legs are common. These are what I call the "primary" submission techniques. Many primary submission techniques of armlocks, strangles (and chokes) and leglocks are presented in this textbook. The armlocks shown on these pages focus on the elbow and shoulder joints and are allowed in most forms of sport grappling and MMA. The strangles shown in this book are both "gi" and "no gi" and can be applied in just about every form of sport combat and well as self-defense. The leglocks shown here are aimed primarily at the knee and ankle, but in some cases, hip locks are shown as well. Smaller joint locks, shoulder locks or neck cranks aren't the focus of this book, although in some cases, you'll see some of these techniques used in association with an armlock, choke or leglock.

This book offers both the Welcome Mat and Shingitai Jujitsu perspective on a variety of submission techniques: armlocks, strangles and leglocks, a number of which haven't appeared in other books as well as, in some cases, books previously written by me. However, I've included some skills on these pages that have been presented in several of my other books but have looked at them from a different perspective and offered some different advice and information, and hopefully, made it all instructive for you as the reader. My background is in Shingitai jujitsu, judo and sambo, but I am a serious student and fan of old-time legitimate professional wrestling and its modern form of catch wrestling. I encourage you to take the open-ended approach we take in Shingitai Jujitsu and do as much cross training as possible to develop your skills, tactics and fighting heart so that you can compete on any mat or be prepared to fight anyone.

The great thing about books, DVDs and other forms of information is that each of us can take something of value from these sources, alter them as necessary and expand the body of knowledge, not only for ourselves, but also for others. If you're like me, you may read the same book many times and discover something a bit different about a particular technique or move since the last time you looked at it and wonder how you missed that point or aspect. What's happening is that you're growing in your appreciation and knowledge, and what may not have worked for you in the past now seems natural and skillful when you try it. I hope this book can help you in this way as well as the more obvious way of giving you information that you can use right now.

This book is organized into three sections. The first section is about armlocks, the second section covers strangles and chokes and the last section shows leglocks. The techniques aren't sub-categorized into specific sections, but generally tend to "flow' from one move to the next, however that's not always the case. There are a lot of skills presented in this book and every one of them can be applied in a variety ways in a variety of situations in a variety of different grappling and fighting sports. What may not be allowed in one sport can be used in another, and what may not be allowed presently in a sport may be allowed at a later time. Sport rules may change, but a good move only gets better because you've been practicing it and perfecting it.

As with all my other books, the photos appearing on these pages are of the men and women who train with me. The photos you see on these pages were taken during workouts, tournaments or training sessions. A good, hard workout is often a creative event and the mind works as hard as the body. With this philosophy, we've tried to capture these creative ideas with a camera lens and present them in this book. I simply can't give enough credit to the athletes and coaches at Welcome Mat whose skill, enthusiasm and input made this book possible, so thanks go to all these athletes and coaches at Welcome Mat Judo, Jujitsu and Sambo Club as well as the Barn of Truth where John Saylor has his headquarters for the Shingitai Jujitsu Association. I am very fortunate to be associated with such talented people. My sincere thanks also go to Turtle Press and Cynthia Kim for their professional support and encouragement. As always, a special thanks goes to my wife Becky Scott for her ideas, patience and support in the development, writing and production of this book.

I encourage you to visit my web site at www.WelcomeMatJudoClub.com or visit www.TurtlePress.com to look at my other books and DVDs. Included after this Introduction is a list of my other books that you can use to compliment this textbook.

Steve Scott
Kansas City, Missouri

Other Books WRITTEN BY STEVE SCOTT and Published by TURTLE PRESS that Complement this Textbook:

Armlock Encyclopedia

This book specializes in the armlocks used in all forms of submission grappling, jujitsu, judo, MMA, sambo, martial arts and any other combat sports of fighting. The specifics of why armlocks work are examined in depth.

Grappler's Book of Strangles & Chokes

This is a comprehensive study of both "gi" and "no gi" strangles and chokes. The differences between strangles and chokes are explained as well as the physiological reasons why these techniques work, and why they are dangerous.

Vital Leglocks

Ankle, knee and other lower body submissions are presented in this book. Taken from sambo, jujitsu, old-time legitimate professional wrestling and catch wrestling, the theory and technique of lower body submissions are presented in this book.

Groundfighting Pins & Breakdowns

This book is a comprehensive and thorough presentation of many positions and situations and how to set an opponent up, break him down and get him on his back to pin him. A huge number of hold-downs and pins used in judo, jujitsu, sambo, submission grappling and MMA are shown in this book. This book serves a dual purpose in that it not only shows how to break an opponent down to hold him, but it is also one of the most comprehensive studies of position grappling on the market.

Throws And Takedowns

You have to get your opponent to the mat or ground before you can apply a submission technique on him and this book shows many ways to do it. How and why a throwing technique works as well as the difference between a throw and a takedown are examined. Both common and unique throwing techniques and takedowns are shown in this book.

Drills For Grapplers

If you want to master a move, you have to drill on it. This book shows many drills, games and exercises that you can use on the mat. Drills for all ages and skill levels are presented. This book was written for both coaches and athletes.

Championship Sambo: Submission Holds and Groundfighting

If you're interested in the Russian sport of sambo, this book offers a history of sambo, its technical basis and a variety of groundfighting techniques used in all levels of competition. One of the few books on sambo published in the United States, it has a variety of armlocks, hold-downs and leglocks commonly seen in sambo.

Championship Sambo: The DVD

This DVD, about 2 ½ hours in length, shows a variety of groundfighting skills as well as numerous throws and takedowns native to Russian sambo.

To order the books and DVD listed above, visit Turtle Press at www.TurtlePress.com.

SECTION ONE: ARMLOCKS
MAKE HIM TAP OUT AND HE'LL NEVER FORGIVE YOU AND NEVER FORGET YOU

IT DOESN'T MATTER WHAT YOU CALL IT, JUST CALL IT A WIN

Years ago, as one of my athletes, Donnie Bunch, came off the mat after beating his opponent, a teammate asked him what move he used to win. Donnie said he didn't remember the technique's name and tried to describe how he worked it on his opponent. His teammate listened to Donnie's explanation and then told him the name of the move. Donnie, still pumped up after his win, replied, "It doesn't matter what you call it, just call it a win!"

That pretty well sums it up. Most techniques go by several names, depending on what grappling sport or martial art you practice or where you learned it. The bottom line is that a good move is a good move, no matter what you call it or where you learned it. The name of the technique can be in English, Japanese or any other language, but if the name of the move provides a common description that everyone in your gym or group understands, then the name serves its purpose. The terminology and names for techniques used in this book reflect what we call them at Welcome Mat and what they're commonly called in most dojos or gyms.

YOU HAVE TO GET HIM DOWN FIRST

It's true that most fights end up on the ground, but it's just as true that most fights start standing up. If you can't get him to the ground with control and force, all the groundfighting in the world won't help you. I encourage you to become a complete grappler or fighter. Don't limit yourself to only one aspect of grappling or fighting. If you have holes in your game, a good opponent will spot them quickly and use them against you, whether it's standing or on the ground. Learn how to throw your opponent, use punches and kicks and other skills that will get him to the ground so you can finish him off. I recommend you read my book THROWS AND TAKEDOWNS (published by Turtle Press) to get some solid, effective and functional ideas on how to throw or take your opponent to the ground or mat.

SAFETY FIRST: WHEN IN DOUBT, TAP OUT

When you apply a submission technique on your opponent and he taps out, let off the pressure and avoid hurting him. Likewise, if you get caught, tap out and live to fight another match. Everybody gets caught once in a while, especially in training. Whether it's tapping out with a hand, foot, knee, elbow or any other body part, yelling "uncle" or some other audible phrase, or any other way of signaling surrender or submission, it's important to respect it. Let's look at it realistically. If you don't tap out of an armlock or leglock, you could sustain severe and (in many cases) permanent injury or damage to the joints, muscles or other tissue. If you don't tap out of a strangle and get choked out cold, you will definitely incur brain damage or other neurological impairment. It's a fact.

Which brings us to the next subject.

WARNING: THE TECHNIQUES IN THIS BOOK ARE DANGEROUS

The techniques, skills and other moves in this book are dangerous. If you don't take them or your training seriously, you may get hurt or hurt someone else. Respect your training partners, opponents and anyone who you may come in contact with and be careful when you study, practice and perform the skills in this book. You should be physically healthy enough to practice the techniques presented in this book and should study, practice and perform them under the guidance of a qualified coach or instructor. Like I always tell my athletes, "Respect your partner. Remember, it's his turn next!"

This section will focus in on the four primary armlocks used in every style of grappling practiced in just about every culture on earth. There are a lot of ways of stretching, bending, twisting, cranking, pulling and generally abusing somebody's arm, but there are pretty much four primary, fundamental ways to make all that happen and that are often used in jujitsu, submission grappling, sambo, catch wrestling, MMA or any form of wrestling practiced around the world. These four methods are: 1. Juji Gatame (Cross-body Armlock), 2. The Bent Armlock, 3. The Armpit Lock, 4. The Straight Armlock. Let's get at it. There are a lot of armlocks to do, so here we go.

JUJI GATAME Cross-Body Armlock

It's pretty safe to say that anytime you trap your opponent's arm and shoulder between your legs and pull on it, it's a Juji Gatame. I prefer to use the Japanese name for this move and will call this armlock Juji Gatame or simply Juji throughout the entire book.

ARMPIT LOCK Waki Gatame

This is a powerful armlock. The idea is to trap the arm while applying pressure on his shoulder. It's a shoulder lock with an elbow lock and best done from the position shown above. Anytime you pull on an opponent's arm and hug it to your armpit or chest, it's an Armpit Lock

BENT ARMLOCK Ude Garami, the "Kimura" Arm Entanglement

I prefer to call this armlock the Bent Armlock, so that's what it will be called in this book. There are a lot of ways to bend or crank your opponent's arm and a wide variety of techniques, grips and set ups to manipulate your opponent's arm and shoulder will be shown in this book. Many people in MMA call this armlock the "Kimura" in honor of Masahiko Kimura, the great judo champion.

STRAIGHT ARMLOCK Ude Gatame, The "Armbar"

There are a lot of variations and ways of grabbing your opponent's arm when applying the Straight Armlock and Jarrod is doing one of them on Chad in this photo. It's a safe bet that anytime you straighten out your opponent's arm and not have it hugged in against your side (as in the Armpit Lock) or have it trapped between your legs (as in the Juji Gatame), it's a Straight Armlock.

SPINNING JUJI GATAME

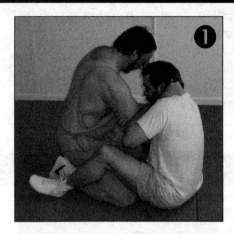

This is one of the most fundamental armlock skills to master and is used in every form of grappling or fighting. Bill, sitting on his buttocks, scoots in close to Steve so that Bill's buttocks are jammed up against Steve's knees. This puts Bill close enough to make this move work. Bill uses his left arm to trap Steve's right arm as shown.

Bill starts to lean to his right and this shows how important it is for Bill to be close to Steve.

Bill "shrimps" or curls tight as he rolls to his right side, putting body ing close and tight. Bill wants to "stay round" so he can roll Steve easier. Bill uses his right hand to hook under Steve's left leg and this helps pull him in closer to Steve. Bill makes it a point to place his head as close as possible to Steve's left knee and uses his right leg to drive against Steve's left side. Notice that Bill still has his left hand trapping Steve's right arm.

TECHNICAL TIP: My athletes drill this armlock every practice. It not only teaches you a lot about how to lock someone's arm, it also teaches essential skills in position and mobility. If you drill on this armlock every practice (and I mean every practice), your skill level in all armlocks will increase dramatically.

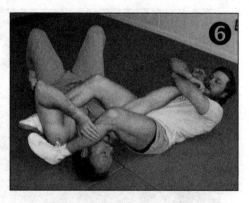

Bill swings his left leg up over Steve's neck and head, hooking it hard against Steve's neck. As he does this, Bill continues to drive with his right leg against Steve's side. Notice how round and compact Bill is here, which makes rolling Steve over onto his back easier.

Bill rolls Steve over onto his back. Look at how close Bill's buttocks and hips are to Steve's right shoulder. Bill now uses both hands to trap Steve's right arm to Bill's chest and body as shown. Bill will roll back and apply the armlock.

Bill rolls back to stretch Steve's arm out, but notice how Bill is crossing his arms to hug Steve's arm tight to Bill's chest. Sometimes, you'll use this "cross arm" or "hug" method of trapping your opponent's arm to secure the Juji Gatame.

BELLY DOWN JUJI OUT THE BACK DOOR

Derrick has John on his back and is about to roll back to apply Juji Gatame.

John defends against the armlock by pulling his right arm and shoulder in and "stealing his arm back" from Derrick. Often, the bottom grappler will also attempt to roll up and into his opponent and get onto his knees for stability.

As John rolls up onto his knees, Derrick makes sure to hug John's right arm tight to his chest. Derrick uses the momentum of John coming up onto his knees to roll back over his own right shoulder. Notice that Derrick is "staying round" so he can roll easier.

Derrick rolls over his right shoulder making sure to keep John's arm tightly against his chest and belly.

Derrick rolls over onto his front and can finish the armlock right here if he arches his body and drives his hips down against John's outstretched right arm.

Derrick can also continue to roll over and pull on John's arm as shown getting the tap out. Sometimes, Derrick's rolling action will actually force John to roll over his head and right shoulder and onto his back. If this happens, Derrick can apply the Juji Gatame with John on his back.

TECHNICAL TIP: Being able to do Juji Gatame from a variety of positions will make you a dangerous grappler or fighter. The "belly down" position happens a lot. Remember, if you lock on with a Juji Gatame (or any armlock), don't let go if it until you absolutely have to! Keep his arm, steal it away from him and stretch it, bend it or crank it, but use it to make him tap out.

TAP OUT TEXTBOOK

THE DIFFERENCE BETWEEN ARMLOCKS AND ARMBARS

Really, it's more a matter of nomenclature, but the word "armlock" is generic and refers to any joint lock involving the arm. An "armbar" describes the action of placing something behind your opponent's elbow as a fulcrum and bending or stretching it against that fulcrum causing pain. This "bars" your opponent's arm.

BELLY DOWN JUJI WHEN OPPONENT STACKS YOU

Chris is trying a spinning Juji Gatame on Jarrod and Jarrod stands or kneels and moves to his right (toward Chris's head) to nullify the rolling action and "stack" Chris onto his back.

Chris does a backward roll over his head and shoulders (or if necessary, just the shoulder closest to Jarrod, in this case, his left shoulder). Chris makes sure to pull Jarrod's arm in tight to his chest and body as he does the backward roll and stretches Jarrod's arm in this belly down Juji Gatame.

Jarrod is stacking Chris and pushing him high onto his shoulders to ease the pressure on his elbow.

GOING OUT THE BACK DOOR JUJI GATAME WHEN OPPONENT STACKS YOU

Bill's spinning under Josh for the Juji Gatame.

Josh pulls back and away from Bill to avoid the armlock. Bill keeps holding tight onto Josh's right arm with his left arm as Bill rolls back high on his shoulders and head.

Bill keeps spinning high on his shoulders as shown and uses his left leg to hook hard against Josh's head and neck. Look at how Bill "anchors" or locks his right foot against Josh' left upper leg and hip to keep it from moving away further.

Bill rolls over the back of his left shoulder and "out the back door" and ends up on his left side as shown. Bill keeps pulling hard on Josh's right arm.

Bill drives hard and arches with his hips as he stretches Josh's right arm and gets the tap out. Bill West used this move a lot during his competitive career in judo and is a real master of this technique.

BELLY DOWN JUJI GATAME

You don't always have to have your opponent on his back to get Juji Gatame and this basic (but effective) move proves it. Jon is on his elbows and knees and Rusty gets his back and positions his body across Jon's back as shown. Rusty uses his head to post on the mat for stability. Rusty's right leg is under Jon's body and parallel to it.

Rusty uses both hands and arms to scoop Jon's right arm and as he does this, Rusty hooks his left leg under Jon's head as shown.

TECHNICAL TIP: This is a good, basic way to learn how to do the belly down Juji Gatame but just because it's a basic move, don't think for a minute that it won't work on an elite grappler or skilled opponent. It will!

Rusty pulls on Jon's arm, drives his hips hard downward and flattens Jon onto the mat stretching Jon's right arm.

JUJI GATAME WITH OPPONENT ON KNEES (BOTH LEGS ACROSS BODY)

Bret is over on his right side with both of his leg across Scott's body in this variation of this armlock.

TECHNICAL TIP: This proves that you can get a Juji Gatame on your opponent from any position!

BELLY DOWN JUJI GATAME USING A KNEE PUSH

Trevor goes from a rodeo ride to the belly down Juji by using both hands to scoop Chris's left arm. As he does this, Trevor uses his right leg to hook under Chris's head and uses his left foot to push on Chris's left knee.

Trevor uses his left foot to push Chris's left knee back as shown. As he does this, Trevor really starts to use both hands to pull on Chris's left arm.

Trevor flattens Chris out and drives with his hips into Chris's outstretched left arm to get the armlock.

LEG JAM JUJI GATAME

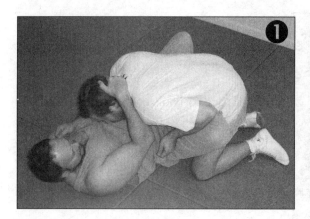

Steve is using the cross-leg or belt line defense with his right shin across Bill's waist. The belt line defense from the guard is a good one and allows you to set your opponent up for a variety of submission techniques.

Steve rolls to his right side and uses both his arms to hug Bill's right arm to his chest as shown.

Steve kicks his left leg over Bill's head.

Steve pulls hard with both hands as he arches his hips driving them into Bill's right elbow and outstretched arm.

Steve stretches Bill's right arm to get the tap out. Look at how Steve is using his right knee to jam in Bill's hips area as he uses his left leg to hook over Bill's head.

THE BALL BAT GRIP: THE STANDARD GRIP FOR JUJI GATAME

Jon is grabbing Travis' outstretched arm the same way he would grab a baseball bat. This is the basic, no frills and all-around best way to grab your opponent's arm to apply Juji Gatame. Not everybody grabs the arm this way and not everybody uses only this, or any one, way of grabbing an opponent's arm. You'll see several different ways to grab your opponent's arm in this book and all of them work. Everyone develops his own preference, but I recommend that you learn Juji Gatame using this grip initially and experiment with other grips as you improve on the armlock.

TECHNICAL TIP: THE LEG PRESS
This shows Jon controlling Travis with the leg press. This is an important position where you control your opponent before you apply the Juji Gatame. You'll see this position often in this book and it's used to control your opponent for more than only the Juji Gatame. There are many ways of using the leg press to control your opponent. Try what's shown in this book and experiment with it on your own.

JUJI GATAME WITH OPPONENT ON KNEES WITH LEG TRIANGLE

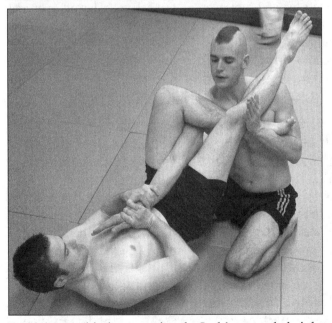

Derrick uses his legs to triangle Josh's extended right arm for more control and pressure.

JUJI GATAME WITH OPPONENT ON KNEES USING LEG ACROSS NECK

Notice how Derrick is using his right leg and foot to hook Josh around the waist for more control of the body.

LEG JAM ROLL TO JUJI GATAME USING BELT LINE DEFENSE FROM GUARD

Derrick has his right knee pointed out with his right shin jammed in Jarrod's midsection.

Here's another view of how Derrick has his right leg positioned across Jarrod's hip area or midsection.

Derrick shrimps to his right as he uses his right hand to hook under and grab Jarrod's left leg as shown. Derrick is sideways to Jarrod.

Derrick swings his left leg and foot over Jarrod's head, hooking it. Derrick lifts Jarrod's left leg with his right hand and drives his right knee into Jarrod's midsection as he uses his left leg to hook hard on Jarrod's head, causing Jarrod to roll over.

Derrick rolls Jarrod over and has him in a leg press. Derrick will roll back to apply the Juji Gatame.

TECHNICAL TIP: Derrick hasn't placed his right leg over and across Jarrod's torso because he didn't need to do that to apply the armlock. The basic application of Juji Gatame teaches to place your legs in this way. Derrick's right shin is jammed hard up and under Jarrod's leg and upper back. The top of Derrick's left foot is placed on the back of Jarrod's left leg as well and Derrick is squeezing his knees together to trap Jarrod's outstretched right arm. Derrick is using his left foot and lower leg to draw in and control Jarrod's head. Your leg placement in Juji Gatame is important and like every other body part, use your legs to control your opponent.

STRAIGHT ARMLOCK WITH FOOT OR KNEE ASSIST FROM THE GUARD

Kirk has Eric in his guard and uses his left arm to hook over Eric's right arm. Kirk uses his left hand to grab Eric's left lapel as shown.

Kirk uses his right foot to push on Eric's left knee as he uses his right hand to grab Eric's right collar.

Kirk uses his right foot to push Eric's left knee back and forces Eric to his front as shown. Notice how Kirk has used his hands to trap Eric's extended right arm. Kirk is applying his straight armlock on Eric's right arm now.

Kirk uses his left foot (or sometimes left knee) to drive down on Eric's body as shown. This adds to the pressure on Eric's right elbow and gets the tap out. This is a good choke as well, so this is a "double trouble" move that can work for you.

DOUBLE TROUBLE TRIANGLE

If your opponent scoops up under your leg as Chance is doing, thank him for the opportunity to slap on your triangle choke. Steve can quickly place his right leg on Chance's left shoulder and start to work his triangle.

Chance uses his left arm and hand to scoop under Steve's right leg as shown.

Steve quickly places his right leg across Chance's left shoulder and moves to his right side. Steve pulls Chance's right arm to cinch him in tighter and control the arm. Steve hooks his right hand and arm under Chance's left leg, pulling Steve to his right.

Steve closes his triangle on Chance by placing the top of his right foot under his left knee.

Steve uses his right hand to lift Chance's left knee and leg and roll Chance over. Steve has the triangle on tight and is using his left hand to pull on Chance's right arm.

Steve rolls Chance to his side and applies the triangle choke and armlock. This is what we call "double trouble."

STRAIGHT ARMLOCK DOUBLE TROUBLE WITH THE TRIANGLE

Instead of using Juji Gatame, Bret is using the straight armlock on Chuck along with the triangle choke.

Bret is using the figure 4 variation of the straight armlock. Often, it's a good idea to go for the "double trouble" using an armlock when you trap your opponent in with your triangle.

TECHNICAL TIP: POINTING THE PINKIE
I don't worry as much about where the little finger of an opponent's outstretched arm points as some people do. It's more important to have your hips in as close as possible to your opponent so that you can use your pelvic girdle as the fulcrum against his elbow. Too many people try to apply the Juji Gatame when they don't have their opponent's arm in tight enough or they are not in close enough with their hips. They spend more time trying to move an opponent's arm around so that his little finger points upward than they do making sure they're in close enough for the hips and pelvis to be a fulcrum. Your close hip placement is more important than where his little finger points. Mike is pulling on Bjorn's arm and has his hips in close. Bjorn's small (pinkie) finger isn't pointing up and the armlock is effective anyway.

JUJI GATAME WHEN OPPONENT IS ON ONE KNEE OR POPS UP

Derrick has Jarrod in his guard and Jarrod steps up on his right leg. He may be setting Derrick up to start to control Derrick's left leg and foot for a heel hook or other type of ankle or leglock. In some cases, an inexperienced opponent may simply feel more comfortable propping his foot up like this. Either way, this gives Derrick a good opportunity to get a tap out with Juji Gatame.

Derrick shrimps to his left and uses his left hand and arm to hook under Jarrod's right bent knee as shown. Derrick uses his left hand to pull himself in really close to Jarrod's right foot and knee. Look at how close Derrick's head is to Jarrod's right foot. Derrick also places his left leg across Jarrod's midsection.

Derrick swings his right leg over Jarrod's head and neck as shown to start the spinning Juji. Derrick uses his right hand to trap Jarrod's left arm to his body.

Derrick rolls Jarrod over. Look at how Derrick hooks his right leg over Jarrod's neck and head to drive him down harder and with a lot of control. Derrick is using his left hand and arm to scoop Jarrod's bent right leg at the knee.

Derrick rolls Jarrod over and the momentum of the roll brings Derrick to a seated position. This rolls Derrick in really close to Jarrod for maximum control. Look at how close Derrick's hips and legs are to Jarrod. Derrick is also using both hands to pull Jarrod's left arm in tight to his body and chest.

Derrick rolls back and stretches Jarrod's arm to get the Juji Gatame and the tap out.

SPINNING JUJI FINISH IF YOUR OPPONENT POPS UP ON BOTH FEET

Sometimes, a skilled opponent my pop up off his knees onto both of his feet as Derrick is doing. Jarrod shrimps to his right and uses his right hand to grab Derrick's left leg. Jarrod's right leg is placed across Derrick's left side and he uses his left hand to grab Derrick's right arm and pull it to his chest to trap it.

Jarrod swings his left leg over Derrick's head and neck and uses both of his legs to drive Derrick over. Jarrod uses his right hand to grab Derrick's left lower leg to help pull Derrick over into the roll.

Jarrod rolls Derrick over. Derrick is forced to roll over his right shoulder. The momentum of the roll will put Derrick on his back and Jarrod will roll up into a sitting position.

The momentum of the roll puts Derrick flat on his back and Jarrod rolls up onto his buttocks. This puts Jarrod's hips really close to Derrick's right arm and shoulder and puts Jarrod's hips in close enough and in the right position to provide him with a great fulcrum to apply the armlock against Derrick's elbow. Jarrod can immediately roll back, stretch out Derrick's right arm and get the tap out.

STRAIGHT ARMLOCK FROM GUARD WITH DOUBLE TROUBLE TRIANGLE CHOKE

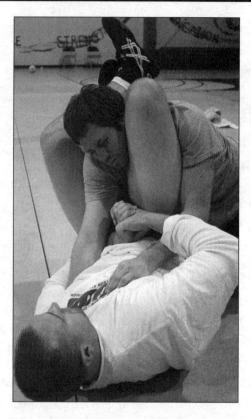

Sometimes, if you have your opponent in your guard and you apply the straight-on triangle choke from this position, you can give him some "double trouble" and catch him with a straight armlock. Bret is using the square lock grip for the straight armlock on Chuck. He'll tap out from one or the other.

QUICK CATCH STRAIGHT ARMLOCK FROM THE GUARD

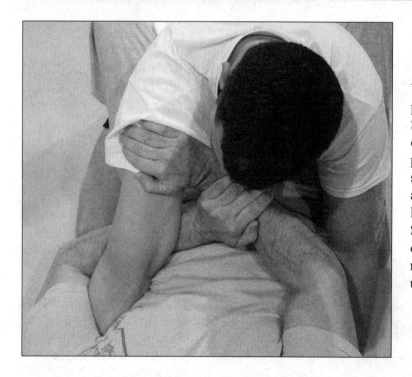

You can get a "quick catch" on your opponent when he's on top in your guard. Scott has used his right arm to hook under Steve's left shoulder or may have placed his right hand on the mat for stability by Steve's left hip. Steve takes advantage of this opportunity by quickly slapping a straight armlock on Scott. Steve is applying the figure 4 armlock on Scott in this photo. This is a surprise move and can catch even good grapplers unaware.

SPINNING JUJI GATAME WHEN OPPONENT STANDS UP

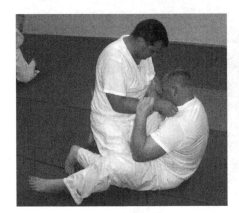

Nick has Kirt in his guard.

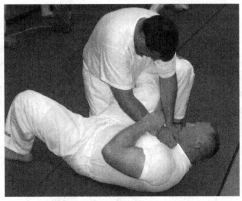

As Kirt starts to stand up on his left foot, Nick shrimps to his right and uses his right hand to hook under Kirt's left ankle or lower leg. Nick's right leg is placed across Kirt's left ribcage.

As Kirt tries to stand, Nick keeps pulling himself in tight to Kirt's left leg as shown and hooks his left leg over Kirt's head.

Nick pulls himself in tight to Kirt as Kirt stands. Nick uses his left leg to hook over Kirt's head hard.

Nick uses his right hand and arm to scoop Kirt and drives Kirt over and rolls him to the mat.

Nick applies Juji Gatame for the tap out.

JUJI GATAME WITH LEGS EXTENDED FROM GUARD

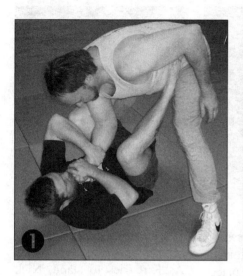 

1. Bill has both of his feet in Steve's hips with Steve standing.

2. Bill uses his right hand to grab Steve's left ankle and pull himself in close to Steve as shown.

 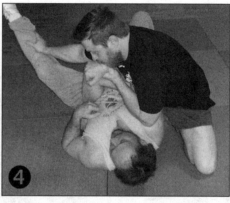

3. Bill drives with both of his feet in Steve's hips and scoops Steve's left leg with his right hand to roll Steve to the mat.

4. Bill rolls over on top of Steve.

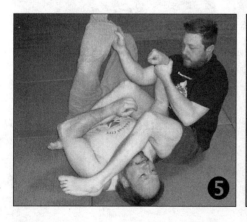 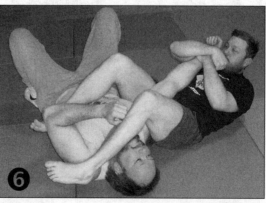

5. Bill kicks his left leg over Steve's head and makes sure his hips are close in tight to Steve's right shoulder for more control of the right arm.

6. Bill rolls back and stretches the arm.

JUJI GATAME AGAINST STANDING OPPONENT

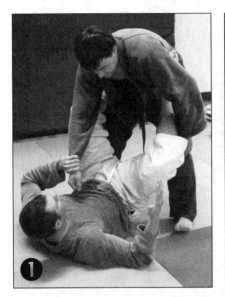

Josh is on his back and Nikolay is standing attempting to get past Josh's guard.

Josh makes sure to place his right foot in Nikolay's left hip and spins to his right. Josh uses his right hand to hook under Nikolay's left leg to help pull Josh in close.

Josh spins to his right and has his head close to Nikolay's left leg and foot. Josh uses his left hand to pull Nikolay's right arm to him.

Josh uses his left leg to hook over Nikolay's head.

As Josh uses his left leg to hook over Nikolay's head, Josh places his right leg against Nikolay's left side at the rib cage.

Josh grabs Nikolay with both arms and pulls Nikolay's arm close to him as he arches his back, driving his pelvis into Nikolay's extended right arm and elbow to get the Juji Gatame.

BENT ARM TRIANGLE FROM THE GUARD

From the guard, Josh uses his right hand to pull on Kyle's right hand drawing it across Josh's body. Josh moves his left hand under Kyle's bent right arm. Josh's left leg is up and ready.

Josh uses his right hand to push Kyle's right hand in toward Kyle's chest as Josh uses his left hand to hook and pull Kyle's bent right arm.

Josh swings his left leg over Kyle's bent right arm as shown as he continues to use his right hand to push Kyle's right hand back toward Kyle.

Josh closes the triangle by hooking his left foot in his right knee. Josh uses his right leg to push down to tighten the triangle and get the armlock.

TECHNICAL TIP: Josh really applies a lot of pressure on Kyle's right arm by placing his left foot under his right knee as shown and driving his right foot down toward the mat. This triangle with the legs adds a lot of pain to the armlock. This particular armlock is a good example of the "arm hug" or "elbow hug" method of doing a bent armlock.

STRAIGHT ARM SCISSORS

Derrick (on the bottom) uses his left hand to trap Josh's right arm to his chest as shown. As he does this, Derrick, lifts his left leg over Josh's right shoulder. Derrick uses his right hand to grab his left ankle to pull his leg over.

Derrick moves his body to the left as he pulls his left leg and foot over Josh's right shoulder.

Derrick swings his left leg over Josh's right shoulder and arm and forms a triangle with his legs trapping Josh's right arm.

Derrick sits up and drives the weight of his body into Josh's right shoulder and extended arm. Derrick can use his left hand to grab Josh and pull his body up as he sits up to add pressure to the armlock.

JUJI GATAME TO STRADDLE PIN TO JUJI GATAME

Jake rolls Josh over with a spinning Juji.

Jake rolls up and controls Josh with a leg press. As he does this, Jake uses his right arm and hand to hook Josh's left (far) leg. Jake uses his left arm and hand to hook Josh's right (near) arm.

Jake kicks his left leg back and places his left knee behind and under Josh's head as shown. Jake squeezes his legs and feet together and straddles Josh with the straddle pin.

Josh realizes he's stuck there and will move away from Jake to escape.

TECHNICAL TIP: You can see how Jake leans back to stretch Josh's arm and Jake is using a "high and low" grip on Josh's arm. Jake is using his right hand to hold Josh's wrist and hand to his upper chest and is using his left hand and arm to trap Josh's arm to his chest.

Jake kicks his left leg back over Josh's head and rolls back for the Juji Gatame.

STRAIGHT ARM LOCK FROM THE TOP AGAINST OPPONENT'S GUARD

Jarrod has Chad in a chest hold or a half guard.

Jarrod pulls his body back a bit and uses his hands and arms to pull Chad into him as he pulls back.

> **TECHNICAL TIP:** Trapping your opponent's arm with your head and shoulder is an effective way of controlling his arm to set him up for the elbow or shoulder lock.

Jarrod gets to his left knee and posts with his right foot as shown. Jarrod uses his right arm to rake across the back of Chad's right upper arm as shown. Jarrod uses his left hand to continue pulling on Chad's right shoulder. Jarrod starts to trap Chad's right arm with his head and right shoulder.

Jarrod grabs his hands together in a square lock. Jarrod is using his head and right shoulder to trap Chad's extended right arm. Doing this causes pain in Chad's right elbow and shoulder.

BELLY DOWN JUJI GATAME FROM THE GUARD

Steve has Chance in his guard and is using his right foot to push Chance's left knee.

Steve pushes Chance back with his right foot and as he does, Steve starts to roll to his right side.

As Steve pushes with his right foot, he flattens Chance onto his front side. Steve uses his left hand to trap Chance's right arm to his chest as Steve starts to move his left leg up and over Chance.

Steve rolls over onto his front side and pulls Chance's right arm in tight. Steve arches with his hips against Chance's outstretched right arm at the elbow. Steve gets the tap out with the Juji Gatame.

Steve swings his left leg over Chance as he grabs Chance's arm and pulls on it with both hands. Steve continues to roll over his right side.

NORTH OF THE BORDER JUJI GATAME

When you are in your opponent's guard (as Derrick is, on his knees), make sure you stay "south of the border." In other words, you should stay below his belt line or below his hip line and not extend forward, which puts you off balance and vulnerable to a variety of techniques. If your opponent makes the major mistake of reaching too far forward toward you when you have him in your guard, you can work in a quick Juji Gatame (or many other moves). Derrick has made the mistake of going "north of the border" and Jarrod will apply a Juji Gatame from the guard.

Jarrod uses both hands to control and pull Derrick's right arm to his chest as Jarrod rolls onto his right side.

Jarrod swings his left leg over Derrick as he pulls with both hands on his outstretched right arm.

Jarrod makes sure to jam his right knee downward on Derrick's right elbow as he pulls with both hands on Derrick's right arm. Jarrod can finish the armlock from this position or continue to roll over onto his front side. World Judo Champion AnnMaria (Burns) DeMars got a lot of opponents to tap out from this finish position.

Jarrod rolls over onto his front pulling with both hands on Derrick's right arm and arching his hips to get the armlock.

DOUBLE STRAIGHT ARM PUSH

Out of the guard position, Bret uses both feet to push against Scott's hips. As he does this, Bret traps Scott's shoulders with his knees as shown. At the same time, Bret pulls on Scott's wrists to extend Scott's arms.

Bret uses his legs and knees to trap Scott's shoulders and squeezes his knees together to form the fulcrum against Scott's elbows. Bret hooks his ankles together to form a scissors to trap Scott's body.

If he needs to, Bret can shift to his left and kick his left leg over Scott's right shoulder as Bret pushes with his left foot on Scott's left hip.

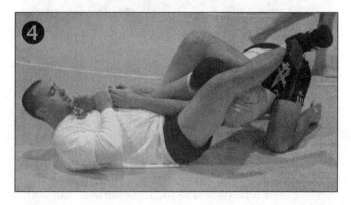

Bret can form a leg triangle from this position and trap Scott's right arm in a straight armlock.

STRAIGHT ARM HEAD HOOK WITH LEGS

A variation of this armlock is for Bret to jam his left shin in the left side of Scott's neck and head and place his right leg over the top of Scott's head to trap it.

STRAIGHT ARM SHOULDER TRIANGLE

Bret can place his left leg over Scott's right shoulder and form a leg triangle trapping Scott's right shoulder and arm. Bret can apply a straight armlock by pulling on Scott's right wrist and moving Scott's extended right arm into Bret's right thigh.

STRAIGHT ARMLOCK IF OPPONENT STANDS

Bret's not done with poor Scott yet. If Scott manages to stand, Bret continues to pull on Scott's extended right arm and form a leg scissors on Scott's head and shoulders as shown. Bret is locking both Scott's right elbow and shoulder in this lock.

BENT ARMLOCK FROM THE BOTTOM OR GUARD

This is a great technique and is used in every form of grappling and fighting known to mankind. I recommend you drill on this as often as possible and have it as part of your arsenal.

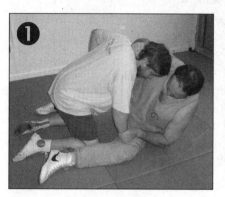

Steve has Bill in his guard and uses his left hand to grab Bill's right wrist. Steve has rolled onto his left hip and leg as shown.

Steve uses his right hand and arm to loop over Bill's right shoulder.

Steve forms a figure 4 with his arms on Bill's right arm.

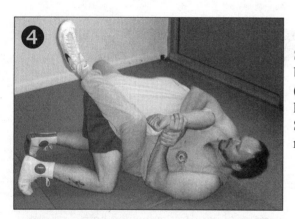

Steve quickly swings his body back in toward Bill (to Steve's right and onto his back at this point). Steve clamps Bill's bent right arm in tight.

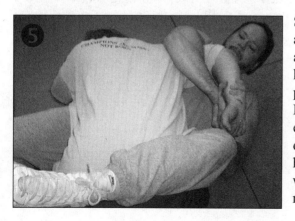

Steve places his left leg across Bill's lower back and pins Bill's body with his legs. Steve's right upper leg is wedged under Bill's body and his right elbow drives Bill's shoulder down while his left hand drives the wrist upward causing pain in Bill's right shoulder and elbow.

TECHNICAL TIP: Steve traps Bill with his legs as shown. Steve has placed his right foot on the mat and is using his right knee to jam under Bill's body. Steve uses his left leg that is placed over the top of Bill's body to squeeze Bill. As he does this, Steve cranks on Bill's arm and drives him forward onto his head and face.

JUJI GATAME COUNTER TO CAN OPENER

Erik is using the can opener on Mike from the guard position as shown.

Mike shrimps to his right in a spinning Juji Gatame.

Mike uses his left leg to hook over Erik's head to start to roll Erik over.

Mike rolls Erik over with a good example of how the spinning Juji Gatame works.

Mike rolls onto his back to apply the Juji Gatame.

BENT ARM KICKOVER LOCK USING A CROSS GRIP FROM THE GUARD

This is an old armlock from the early days of judo and is popular in MMA and BJJ as the omo plata.

Josh has Kyle in his guard and has used both hands to pull Kyle's right arm across Josh's body as shown.

Josh uses his right hand to keep Kyle's right arm across his body. Josh uses his left hand to reach under Kyle's right armpit and grab Kyle's left lapel. Josh moves his left leg up on Kyle's right shoulder and upper back.

Josh uses his right hand to push Kyle's right arm away as Josh moves his body to his right.

Josh uses his right hand to grab Kyle's right shoulder and lapel as shown. Josh swings his left leg up and over Kyle's right shoulder.

Josh swings his left leg over Kyle's right shoulder trapping Kyle's right arm.

BENT ARM KICKOVER LOCK USING A CROSS GRIP FROM THE GUARD

Josh moves his right leg up to start his leg triangle as he loops his left leg and foot over Kyle's right arm.

Josh forms a leg triangle as shown. This traps Kyle's right shoulder and arm.

Josh can finish the armlock by using his left leg to drive down on Kyle's extended right arm and use his right hand to push up on Kyle's right lower arm and wrist.

Josh swings his body into Kyle and starts to sit up. Doing this forces Kyle's right elbow to bend.

Josh sits up onto his left hip as shown and drives Kyle forward onto his front. Kyle's right arm is bent back and Josh is applying pressure on Kyle's right shoulder and elbow to get the tap out.

BENT ARM KICKOVER LOCK TO CHICKEN WING

Alan has Scott in the bent arm kickover.

Alan rolls his body forward placing his left knee on Scott right shoulder. Alan uses his left hand to grab Scott's left hip, forcing Scott's left hip to come off the mat some more.

Alan uses his left hand to hook under Scott's left arm and shoulder.

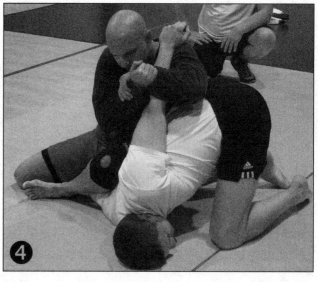

Alan continues to drive down with his left knee on Scott's right shoulder pinning it to the mat. Alan grabs his hands together as shown and lifts and drives Scott's left arm up and forward in a chicken wing.

BENT ARM HUG AND LEG PRESSURE FROM THE LEG PRESS

Josh has Kyle on his back in the leg press, defending against the armlock by hooking his hands together. Josh uses his right arm to hook under Kyle's bent right arm. Josh hugs Kyle's right arm in tight to his body.

Josh rolls his right hand in with his palm up causing his forearm to act like a knife blade and cut into Kyle's bent right elbow.

Josh places his right hand on his left forearm to isolate Kyle's right arm.

Josh uses his right leg to push down on Kyle's right wrist and hand.

TECHNICAL TIP: Josh can use his leg that's closer to Kyle's head (in this case, Josh's left leg) to apply pressure on Kyle's bent right arm.

BENT ARM HUG AND TRIANGLE FROM THE LEG PRESS

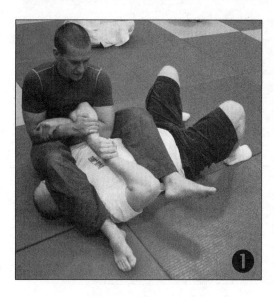

Jarrod has Nick in a leg press and uses his left arm to scoop Nick's left arm in tight to his body.

Jarrod jams his left leg over and onto Nick's bent left wrist and lower forearm as shown.

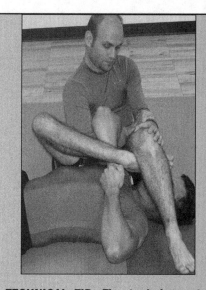

TECHNICAL TIP: The techniques to lever your opponent's arm free are powerful bent armlocks that put him in double trouble. If the bent armlock doesn't get him, stretch his arm out for the Juji Gatame. Kelly is showing another view of the "arm hug" technique of applying the bent armlock. He adds pressure with a leg triangle on Mark's bent right arm.

Jarrod forms a triangle with his legs.

Jarrod drives his right foot downward toward the mat causing pressure on Nick's left arm to get the tap out.

ARM HUG BENT ARMLOCK

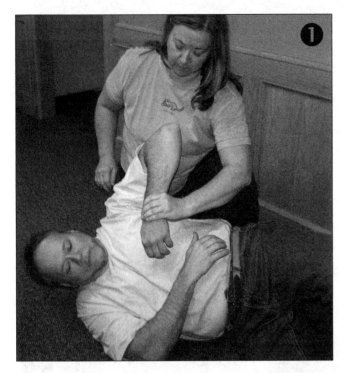

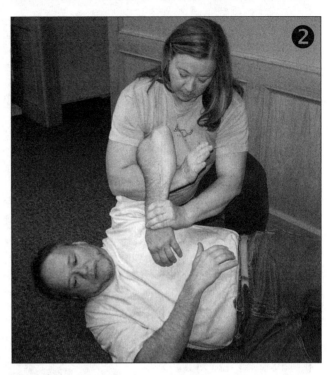

Becky and I were doing some self-defense photos and this bent armlock series is a good one. This application is effective as a follow-up from a throw or takedown. Becky uses her left hand to grab Steve's left wrist as shown.

Becky swings her right arm under Steve's left arm as she uses his left hand to push Steve's left wrist downward toward Steve's chest.

Becky uses her right hand to grab her left forearm to form the figure 4 as she uses her left hand to continue to push downward on Steve's left wrist. This forms a wedge under Steve's elbow joint and causes pain. I know who the boss is in our house!

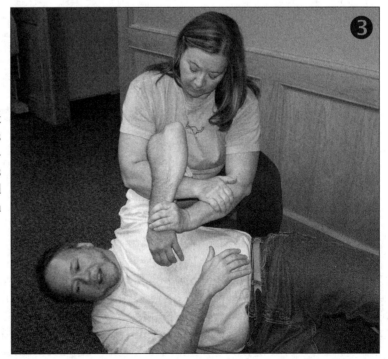

BENT ARMLOCK FROM LEG PRESS

Josh has Roy in a leg press and uses his left hand to grab Roy's right wrist. Josh forms a figure 4 with his hands by grabbing his left wrist with his right hand.

Josh leans hard to his left (in the direction of Roy's head). This forces Roy to release his grip.

This is a good move if the bottom man is strong and won't easily release his grip when defending his arms.

ALTERNATE VIEW

Look at how Josh is pushing on Roy's right wrist and bending his arm. Josh's body is angled about 45 degrees above Roy's shoulder to take much of Roy's upper body strength away.

Josh sits back up, makes sure that Roy's bent right elbow is tucked firmly in his chest and uses his left hand to push on Roy's right wrist. This causes a bent arm crank and gets the tap out.

TECHNICAL TIP: Josh makes sure to keep Roy held to the mat by using his left leg to drive down hard on Roy's head. Look at how close Josh's buttock is to Roy's head, leaving Roy no room for movement and escape.

THE HENGES HANGER BENT ARMLOCK AND FIGURE 4 CHOKE FROM LEG PRESS

Josh has Nikolay in the leg press and uses his left hand to grab Nikolay's right wrist. Josh forms a figure 4 with his arms by using his right hand to grab his right wrist.

Josh uses his right arm, which is hooked under Nikolay's right bent elbow, to pull the right elbow close and tight to Josh's body as shown.

After Josh forms his figure 4 with his hands and arms, he loops his left arm over Nikolay's head and places it behind Nikolay's head as shown.

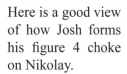

Here is a good view of how Josh forms his figure 4 choke on Nikolay.

ALTERNATE VIEW

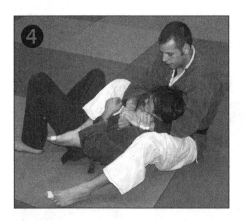

Josh applies a lot of pressure with his right hand across Nikolay's neck. Josh uses his left leg to drive Nikolay's left shoulder upward driving Nikolay's upper body into the choking action.

Josh rolls to his right side and forms a triangle with his legs as shown. Adding this leg pressure adds more pressure to the choke. This is a good choke from this position and Josh can get the tap out from this move if he wants.

Josh applies the Juji Gatame from his right side getting the tap out.

NEAR BENT ARM TRIANGLE FROM THE LEG PRESS

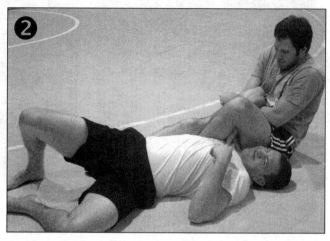

Chuck has Scott in a leg press position and grabs his hands to form a figure 4 lock on Scott's right arm as shown.

Chuck kicks his left leg over Scott and forms a triangle with his right leg. This traps Scott's bent right arm and causes pain.

This photo shows how Chuck's hand formed his leg triangle to trap Scott's bent right arm. This is a double trouble triangle move!

ALTERNATE VIEW

LAPEL GRIP LEVER TO JUJI GATAME FROM LEG PRESS

Steve has Shawn in the leg press. Shawn has crossed his arms tightly to keep Steve from prying or "levering" them free. Steve uses his right hand to hook under Shawn's right arm and will grab his left lapel.

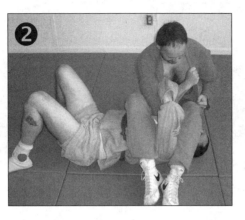

Steve grabs his left lapel.

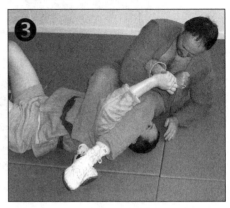

Steve rolls to his left side (toward Shawn's head). This starts to pry Shawn's arms from each other.

Steve uses his left hand and arm to hook under Shawn's right forearm and wrist in much the same way a boxer would do an upper cut punch.

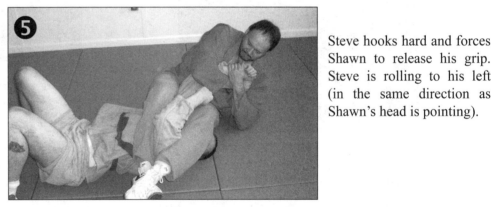

Steve hooks hard and forces Shawn to release his grip. Steve is rolling to his left (in the same direction as Shawn's head is pointing).

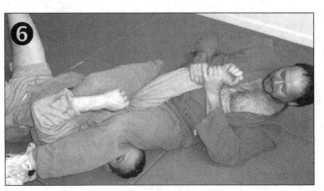

Steve applies Juji Gatame for the tap out.

LEG AND ARM LEVER TO JUJI GATAME FROM LEG PRESS

Steve has Bill in the leg press. Bill is gripping his arms in tight so Steve can't pull them straight for a Juji Gatame.

Steve rolls to his left (toward Bill's legs) and uses his left hand to hook under Bill's near (left) leg.

Steve uses his right leg to hook hard against Bill's head. Steve grabs his hands together as shown.

Steve hooks hard with his right leg against Bill's head. This forces Bill to release his grasp of his hands as shown.

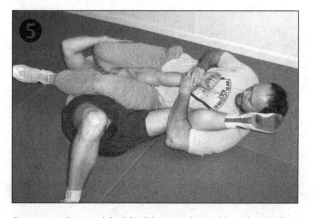

Steve arches with his hips and applies the Juji Gatame.

Steve can add more pressure to the armlock by rolling back. Steve continues to hold his hands together controlling Bill's leg and arm.

THIGH LEVER AND UPPERCUT LEVER FROM LEG PRESS

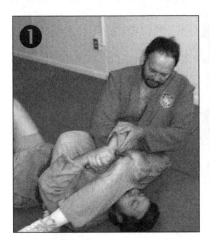

Steve has Bill in the leg press. Steve uses his right hand to grab his left thigh immediately above his left knee.

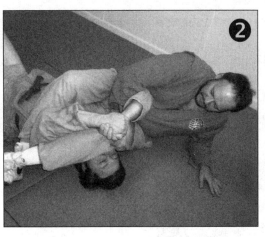

Steve rolls to his left (toward the same direction as Bill's head). This torques Bill's right shoulder and forces his right arm up.

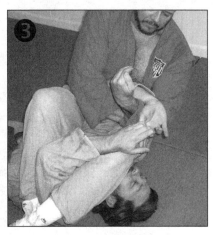

Steve uses his left hand to scoop upward very hard. This forces Bill to release his grasp.

Steve rolls to his left pulling Bill's extended right arm out and hugging it to his chest.

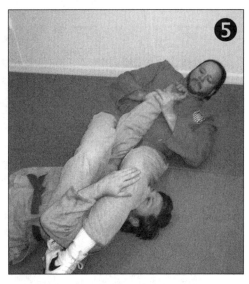

Steve rolls back and applies Juji Gatame.

FAR ARM DRAG LEVER TO JUJI GATAME

Eric has Ben in the leg press and uses both hands to scoop Ben's far (left) arm toward Eric. Eric is grabbing with both hands at Ben's left elbow.

Eric drags his arms and hands up and over Ben's left arm and eventually catches Ben's right arm as well. Eric hugs Ben's arms in tight to his chest.

Eric keeps dragging his hands up Ben's arms and uses both of his hands to grab Ben's right arm as shown.

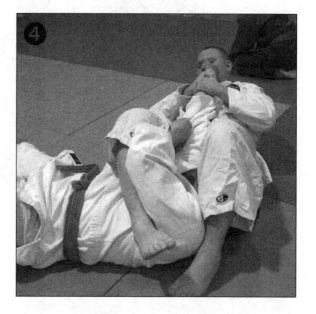

Eric rolls back and applies the Juji Gatame.

STRAIGHT ARMLOCK WHEN OPPONENT SHRIMPS INTO YOU

Mike had Derrick in the leg press attempting to do Juji Gatame but Derrick shrimped into Mike to steal his left shoulder back to prevent Mike from getting the Juji Gatame. Mike uses his left hand to scoop Derrick's right elbow in toward him. Mike uses his left hand to grab Derrick's right wrist and forearm and pull it toward Mike's right shoulder.

Mikes uses both hands to pull Derrick's right arm to him and places Derrick's right wrist at Mike's right shoulder. Mike traps Derrick's right wrist with the right side of his head and his right shoulder as shown. Mike traps Derrick's right elbow with both hands as shown and pulls it into his chest. This places a lot of stress on Derrick's elbow and outstretched right arm and Mike gets the tap out.

DOUBLE ARM HOOK LEVER

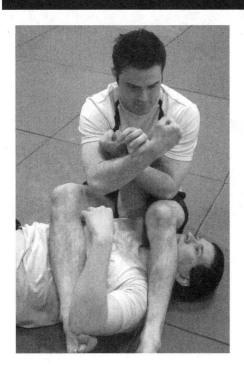

As soon as Derrick rolls Jarrod onto his back, Derrick can use both of his forearms to hook Jarrod's right arm and lever it back to straighten it. Derrick's left arm is hooked into the inside of Jarrod's right elbow and Derrick's left forearm is hooking up toward Jarrod's right wrist. Derrick is getting "high and low" control points on Jarrod's right arm and will immediately scoop Jarrod's right arm to Derrick's body as he rolls to his back and straightens Jarrod right arm to get the tap out.

BENT ARM TWIST LEVER TO JUJI GATAME

Ken has Bjorn in the leg press and uses his left hand (the one closest to Bjorn's head) to hook under Bjorn's arms as shown.

Ken grabs his hands together as shown with his left wrist close to Bjorn's right wrist. Ken's right elbow is pressed against the outside of Bjorn's right elbow. Ken forcefully drives his right elbow into Bjorn's right elbow and pulls back with his left hand on Bjorn's wrist. This causes Bjorn's elbow to twist causing pain and forcing Bjorn to release his grip.

TECHNICAL TIP: If Bjorn doesn't release his grip, Ken can keep twisting Bjorn's arms causing him to tap from the bent armlock.

When Bjorn lets go of his grip, Ken rolls back and stretches Bjorn's right arm for the tap out.

LEG KICK ARM LEVER TO JUJI GATAME

While this is one of the most basic ways to lever an opponent's arm free, it still works! Josh uses his arms to hook Jon's right elbow and arm as Josh uses his right foot to jam or kick Jon's far (left) arm at the elbow.

TECHNICAL TIP: Josh keeps his left leg and foot over Jon's head to control his upper body as he uses the leg and foot closest to Jon's hips and legs (in this case, the right foot and leg) to kick Jon's arm loose.

Josh kicks Jon's arms loose and applies the armlock.

TRIANGLE ARM LEVER AND GRIP FOR JUJI GATAME

Jarrod is using an arm triangle of figure 4 grip on Derrick's arm as he applies the Juji Gatame. This is also a good way to lever your opponent's arm free to secure the armlock.

TOP SPIN TO JUJI GATAME FROM MOUNT

This is pretty much the standard spin from the mount to apply Juji Gatame. Tom has Ed on his back. Tom uses his right hand to grab Ed's left arm.

Tom uses his right arm to grab Ed's left forearm and wrist and pulls it into his chest. Tom uses his left hand to push against Ed's chest and he springs up on both feet to a squat.

Tom spins to his right and kicks his right leg over Ed's head. Tom hugs Ed's left arm tight to his chest.

Tom rolls back and gets the tap out with Juji Gatame.

JUJI GATAME FROM A HIGH MOUNT

Scott has Chuck in a high mount with his legs up close to Chuck's arms. You can see how Scott is using his legs to trap Chuck's shoulders to keep him from moving.

Scott jams his right leg under Chuck's head, using his left hand to lift up on Chuck's head.

Scott starts his spin over Chuck as he uses his left hand to pull Chuck's arms to his chest.

Scott spins over Chuck to the Juji Gatame.

TECHNICAL TIP: The high mount is really useful because it crunches your opponent's shoulders and arms together and puts him in a weak position. Not only that, the top grappler has more mobility when using this mount position than in the normal mount position when you are sitting back on his torso more.

Scott rolls back and secures the Juji Gatame.

TOP TURN TO JUJI GATAME

This is a variation of the topspin set up, but the bottom man has managed to turn to his side. Jarrod uses his left arm to hook under Jeff's left arm and shoulder.

Jarrod rides Jeff with Jeff on his left side. Jarrod sinks in a half nelson with his left hand and arm on Jeff's left shoulder and uses his right hand to post on the mat for stability.

Jarrod moves to his right toward Jeff's head and uses his right hand to scoop Jeff's left shoulder and arm. Jarrod's left leg is straddling Jeff's torso and his left foot is on the mat.

Jarrod still has his left leg across Jeff's torso and quickly kicks his right leg over Jeff's head.

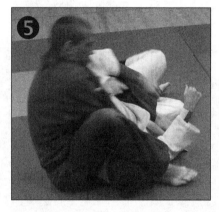

Jarrod moves his right leg over Jeff's head and starts to roll back to apply the Juji Gatame. Jarrod is using both hands to scoop Jeff's right arm in tight to his body.

Jarrod rolls back and applies the armlock.

STRAIGHT ARMLOCK FROM THE HIGH MOUNT

Bret has Chuck in the mount. Bret uses his right hand to grab Chuck's left wrist. There are a lot of straight armlocks from the top position in the mount and this is a quick one that can catch your opponent by surprise.

Bret quickly yanks back on Chuck's right hand with both hands as shown and "bars" Chuck's right extended arm across his right thigh and hip. Bret pushes downward on Chuck's extended right arm to get the tap out. This is a fast, sudden action and can catch your opponent by surprise.

TAP OUT TEXTBOOK

BENT ARMLOCK TO JUJI GATAME

Drew forms a figure 4 lock on Mike's right arm as Mike is laying flat in the "chicken" position.

Drew sits back and pulls Mike's right arm with him as he does.

Drew uses his right knee to block behind Mike's head as he jerks Mike's right shoulder up off the mat as shown. Drew pulls Mike's right elbow close to his chest.

Drew rolls back and applies the Juji Gatame.

Drew moves his left foot over Mike's head as he moves around to Mike's back.

ALTERNATE VIEW

Here's a back view of how Drew is positioned behind Mike. Look at how Drew has his right knee placed on Mike's back.

BENT ARMLOCK FROM BELT AND NELSON

Chad has a belt and nelson on Jarrod. The belt and nelson is a great breakdown to get your opponent on his back to pin him, and is also a great way to control your opponent for an armlock. Chad's right hand is grabbing Jarrod's belt (be sure to grab palm down as shown for better control). Chad uses his left arm to hook under Jarrod's right arm and shoulder and uses his left hand to grab his right wrist.

Chad moves to his left and drives his upper chest and shoulders up and under Jarrod's right shoulder. This drives Jarrod over onto his back. Notice that Chad continues to hold onto Jarrod's belt and he keeps his hand grip.

Chad has Jarrod on his back and immediately uses his left hand to grab Jarrod's right wrist. Chad's right arm is tightly scooping Jarrod's right shoulder.

Chad forms a figure 4 with his hands on Jarrod's bent right arm and applies the bent armlock.

BENT ARMLOCK ROLL TO JUJI GATAME

Mike gets a figure 4 lock on Kirk's right arm as shown. Mike is positioned at the top of Kirk's head with his right knee behind Kirk's head to block it.

Mike pulls Kirk's right arm in tight to his chest as shown.

Mike moves around to Kirk's backside, scooping his right arm to his chest. Mike has pulled Kirk onto his left side.

Mike jams his right knee across Kirk's right ribcage as Mike starts to roll forward over his right shoulder.

BENT ARMLOCK ROLL TO JUJI GATAME

Mike rolls over his right shoulder as shown.

Mike continues his roll. Mike wants to "stay round" so he can better control Kirk.

Mike finishes his roll and rolls Kirk over onto his back.

Mike immediately applies Juji Gatame.

BELT AND NELSON TO JUJI GATAME

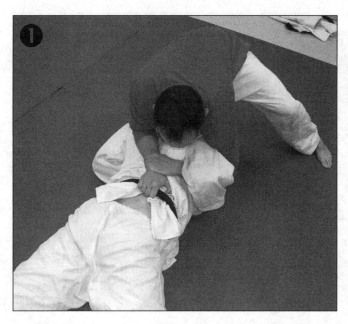

Chad sets Jarrod up with the belt and nelson. It doesn't matter if Jarrod is flat on his front (shown) or on all fours.

> This breakdown to Juji Gatame really stretches your opponent's entire arm, shoulder and pectoral area in addition to being a good elbow lock.

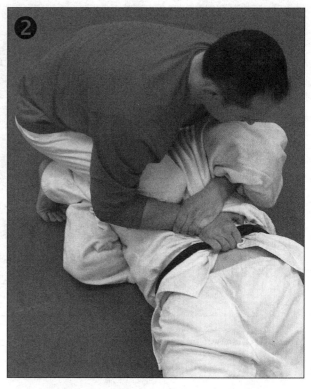

Chad moves around Jarrod's head (to Chad's right) keeping his hand and arm hold on Jarrod's belt. Chad places his right knee across Jarrod's left shoulder and upper back as shown.

Chad places his left foot over Jarrod's head and jams his left heel close to Jarrod's head as shown.

Chad rolls backward using his arms to pull Jarrod back with him. This stretches Jarrod out in a very uncomfortable way and Chad can apply the Juji Gatame for the tap out.

ADAMS JUJI GATAME

World Judo Champion Neil Adams used a variation of this move with great success. Often you can start this from a rodeo ride with your opponent on all fours and roll him over to this seated rodeo ride position.

TECHNICAL TIP: The rodeo ride shows how important it is to get your opponent's back. Whenever possible, get behind your opponent, control him with good leg control and leg wrestling (get your hooks in) and dominate him!

Ken scoots back slightly to give himself some working room. Look at how he moves his left leg and hip away from Eric. Ken is using his right hand to hook under Eric's right shoulder.

This shows the view from the other side. Ken uses his left hand to push Eric's head away and has his right leg across Eric's right hip for control.

ALTERNATE VIEW

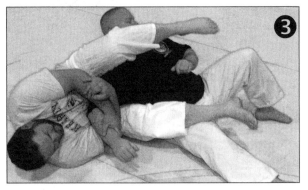

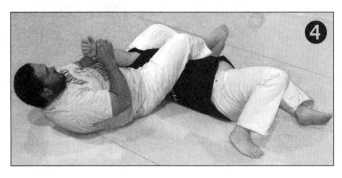

Ken rolls to his right side and uses his left leg to hook over Eric's head. Ken uses both arms to scoop Eric's right arm in tight to his chest.

Ken uses his left leg to hook over Eric's head and drives Eric onto his back. Ken applies the Juji Gatame.

JUJI GATAME FROM THE SINGLE WING CHOKE

Eric is behind Kirk in a seated rodeo ride and trying to apply the single wing choke, but Kirk fights it off.

Eric rolls to his left (in the direction he has Kirk's arm winged) and starts to kick his right leg up and over.

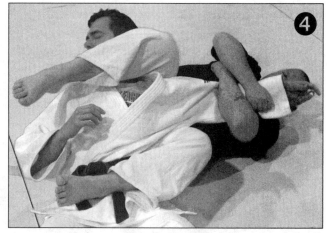

Eric applies the Juji Gatame.

Eric continues to roll to his left hip and side and uses both arms to pull Kirk's left arm tight to his chest as he uses his right leg to hook over Kirk's head and neck.

BENT ARMLOCK WITH KNEE TRAP WHEN OPPONENT IS FLAT

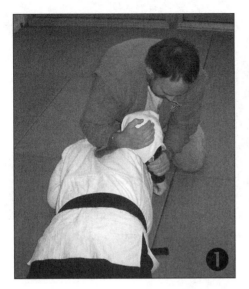

Steve forms a figure 4 with his hands and arms on Eric's right arm.

Steve uses his right hand to pull up on Eric's right elbow as he uses his left hand to grab Eric's right wrist. This pulls Eric's right arm up off the mat.

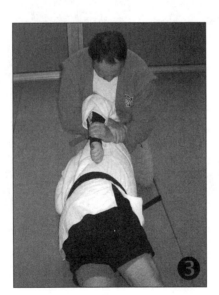

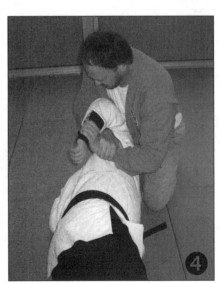

Steve uses his knees to trap Eric's head and pulls Eric's right arm to his chest as shown.

Steve cranks Eric's right arm back using the bent armlock.

BENT ARMLOCK FROM TRIANGLE CHOKE

Drew has Roy in a triangle choke from the side.

Drew forms a figure 4 on Roy's left arm.

Drew rolls to his left and slightly onto his front side as he uses his right hand to push downward on Roy's left wrist.

Drew moves over onto his front as he applies the bent armlock on Roy's left arm.

BENT ARMLOCK FROM THE KNEE ON CHEST POSITION

Jarrod had Chad in a knee on chest position with his right knee on Chad's midsection. Jarrod is posting his left foot wide for support.

Jarrod uses both of his hands to grab Chad's left wrist and arm at the elbow.

Jarrod lowers his body as he uses his right hand to pull in on Chad's left elbow and uses his left hand to push on Chad's left wrist.

Jarrod forces Chad's left arm back as Jarrod forms a figure 4 with his hands on Chad's left bent arm.

Jarrod secures the figure 4 lock and applies the bent armlock on Chad.

JUJI GATAME FROM THE KNEE ON CHEST POSITION

Jarrod has his right knee on Jeff's chest or torso and is controlling him.

Here's a another view of how Jarrod is using the knee on chest position to control Jeff

Jarrod uses his right hand to reach under Jeff's left arm and starts to scoop up with it.

Jarrod uses his right arm to trap Jeff's left arm as shown. Jarrod uses his right knee to jam in hard on Jeff's torso and uses his left foot to step over Jeff's head.

JUJI GATAME FROM THE KNEE ON CHEST POSITION

Jarrod uses his right arm to pull Jeff's left arm in tight and starts to move his body over Jeff's head and around to the back of Jeff.

Jarrod moves around to the backside of Jeff as shown.

Jarrod moves all the way behind Jeff and jams his left shin in the left side of Jeff. Jarrod uses both arms to scoop Jeff's left arm in to his chest as he rolls back.

Jarrod rolls back and secures the Juji Gatame.

BENT ARMLOCK (BASIC) UPWARD POSITION FROM THE MOUNT

Steve is on Bill's chest in the mount position and uses his left hand to grab Bill's left wrist.

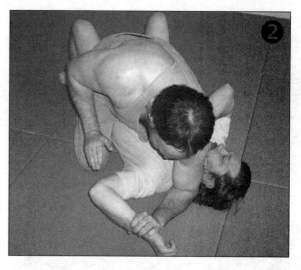

Steve jams his left elbow in the left side of Bill's neck and places his elbow on the mat as shown.

TECHNICAL TIP: Steve is using the figure-4 arm position with the bent armlock. This is the most often used position when doing the bent armlock (Ude Garami). Steve is using his left hand to grab Bill's left wrist and is drawing Bill's left arm in toward Bill's left shoulder. As he does this, Steve is using his right hand to grab his left wrist and is using his right elbow to lift up on Bill's left elbow. This action cranks both the elbow and shoulder!

BENT ARMLOCK (BASIC) DOWNWARD POSITION FROM THE MOUNT

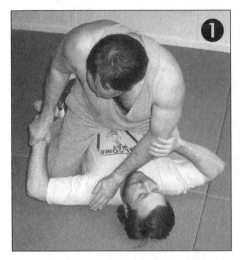

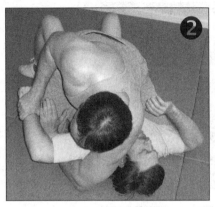

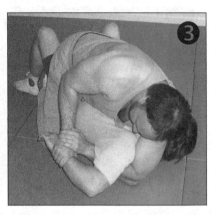

Steve uses his right hand to grab Bill's left wrist and pulls it downward.

Steve uses his left hand and arm to hook over Bill's left shoulder and then under the left upper arm.

Steve forms a figure 4 and uses his hands to pull Bill's left wrist to the left side of Bill's body. Steve uses his left elbow to jam against the mat for leverage as he cranks upward on Bill's wrist.

2-ON-1 BENT ARM GRIP

1-ARM GRIP

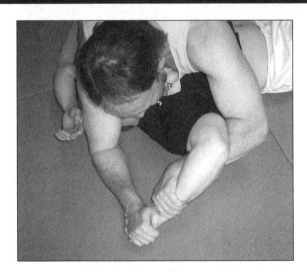

Steve is using both hands to grab on Bill's wrist and forearm to crank upward on Bill's elbow. This is a powerful bent armlock grip and is a good one to know if you don't like the figure 4 grip or can't use it for some reason.

This isn't a "show-off" move, but one that really works! Steve is using his right hand to reach under Bill's left upper arm and is using his right hand to grab Bill's left wrist as shown.

BENT ARMLOCK (UPWARD) FROM THE CHEST HOLD OR SIDE POSITION

Bryan has Chris is a chest hold or a side position.

Bryan uses his left hand to pull in on Chris's right elbow.

Bryan uses his right hand to grab Chris's right wrist as Bryan slides his left hand upward on Chris's bent right arm.

Bryan forms a figure 4 with his hands on Chris's bent right arm and gets the armlock.

BENT ARMLOCK (UPWARD) WITH WRIST CONTROL FROM THE SIDE POSITION

Jarrod had Jeff in a side hold and is using his left hand to hook under Jeff's right arm, bending it and hugging it in tight.

Jarrod uses his right hand to grab Jeff's right hand fingers and knuckles.

Jarrod uses his right hand to drive Jeff's bent right wrist downward to the mat.

Jarrod starts to form a figure 4 lock.

Jarrod finishes the bent armlock and traps Jeff's bent wrist on the mat.

TAP OUT TEXTBOOK

FIGURE 4 BENT ARM CRANK FROM THE SIDE POSITION

Chuck has Scott is a chest hold or side position. Chuck loops his left hand over Scott's right arm. As he does this, Chuck uses his left hand to grab Scott's right wrist. Chuck uses his left hand to grab his right wrist to form the figure 4. After doing this, Chuck uses his right hand to push Scott's right wrist upward toward Scott's head to get the bent arm crank.

BENT ARM SQUARE LOCK FROM SCARF HOLD OR HEAD AND ARM PIN

Drew has Roy in a scarf hold is using the bent arm square lock to crank Roy's right arm as shown. This move traps Roy's right arm and cranks the elbow up and forward causing pain.

BENT ARMLOCK FROM THE SCARF HOLD

Jarrod has Drew in a scarf lock or modified chest hold and is using his right arm to hook under Drew's left arm for control. Jarrod is placing his right hand on the back of his head for more control.

Jarrod uses his left hand to grab Drew's left wrist and arm and is using his right hand to drive Drew's left arm forward.

Jarrod forms a figure 4 hold with his hands to secure the bent armlock.

Jarrod rolls over to his front and applies pressure with the bent armlock

TECHNICAL TIP: Jarrod is using his left hand to grab Kelly's wrist at the joint. Jarrod squeezes Kelly's hand as hard as he can to squeeze his thumb and fingers together and bends his wrist inward as shown. This wristlock helps distract Kelly's attention from Jarrod working the armlock on him.

BENT ARMLOCK (DOWNWARD) FROM CHEST HOLD (SIDE POSITION)

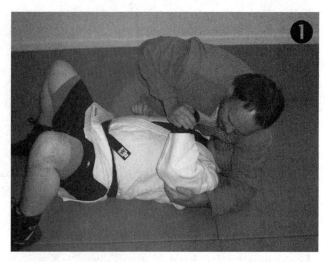

Steve uses his left hand to scoop and control Eric's left elbow as shown.

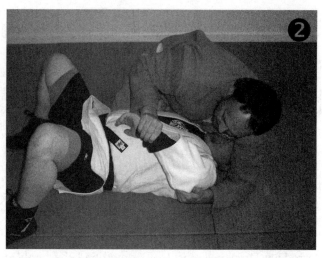

As Steve uses his left hand on Eric's left elbow to trap it, he uses his right hand to push downward on Eric's left wrist.

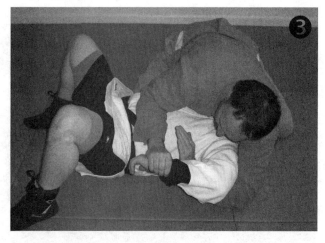

Steve uses his left arm to scoop under Eric's bent left arm.

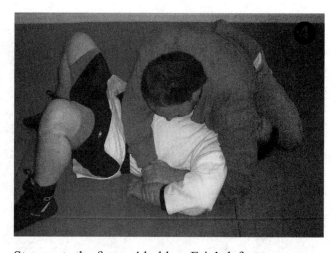

Steve gets the figure 4 hold on Eric's left arm.

Steve cranks on Eric's bent left arm using his left arm to pull up on Eric's left shoulder to add to the pressure.

BENT ARMLOCK SIT THROUGH FROM SIDE POSITION

Jarrod is controlling Mike from the side and has a figure 4 to trap Mike's left arm as shown.

Jarrod uses both hands to grab Mike's left wrist and forearm as shown.

Jarrod uses his right elbow to jam back into Mike's left side. Notice how Jarrod traps Mike's left wrist with his right elbow.

Jarrod uses his left hand to grab his right biceps.

Jarrod moves around to the top of Mike's head. Jarrod hugs Mike's bent left arm tightly to keep it in place.

Jarrod sits through with his right leg as shown.

TECHNICAL TIP: Jarrod uses his left hand to grab his right upper arm as shown. Doing this isolates Mike's left arm and keeps it bent. Jarrod uses his right hand to hook under Mike's left bent elbow as shown and will use his right hand and forearm to lift up on Mike's left elbow causing pain.

BENT ARMLOCK ELBOW LIFT FROM SIDE POSITION

BENT ARM SQUARE LOCK FROM SIDE

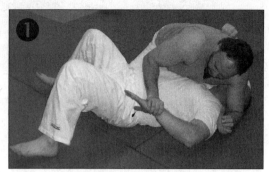

Steve has Nick in the chest hold or side position. This can also be done from the half guard as well. Steve uses his right hand to grab Nick's left wrist.

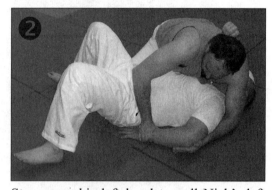

Steve uses his left hand to pull Nick's left arm in close to Nick's left hip. As he does this, Steve uses his left hand to scoop under Nick's left upper arm as shown.

Steve uses his left hand and forearm to scoop under Nick's left bent arm. As Steve scoops and pulls up with his left hand, he uses his right hand to grab Nick's left wrist and isolate it by pushing it downward

Drew has the side position on Roy and jams his left elbow in the left side of Roy's neck for an anchor. Drew places his right arm under Roy's left elbow and places his left wrist over Roy's left wrist as shown. Drew grasps his hands together in a square lock.

Drew gets the armlock by lifting up with his right elbow forcing Roy's left elbow up and forward. Drew also uses his left elbow to push downward causing Roy's left bent elbow to get cranked.

ROLLING BENT ARMLOCK

Steve is trying to do a bent armlock in the downward direction on Bill from a top mount position. Bill fights it off and starts to sit up.

Steve moves to his right and hooks his left leg under Bill's head as shown.

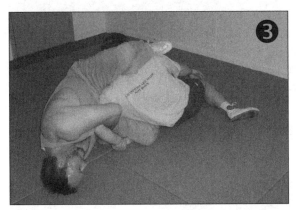

Steve rolls over his right shoulder as he hooks Bill's head with his left leg forcing Bill to roll forward.

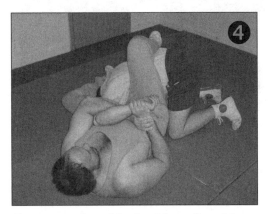

Steve completes his shoulder roll and turns Bill over onto his knees. Steve has continued to keep his figure 4 grip on Bill's left arm.

Steve cranks on Bill's bent arm getting the tap out.

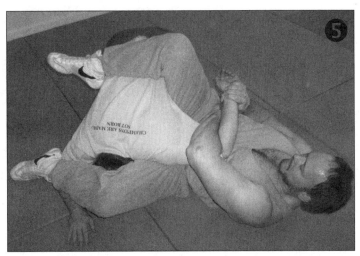

BENT ARMLOCK FROM THE GUARD BELT LINE DEFENSE

Derrick has Sean in his guard and jams his right leg across Sean's midsection. Derrick's right shin is jammed across Sean's hip area and stomach. Derrick rolls to his right side a bit and uses his right hand to grab Sean's left wrist. Derrick uses his left hand to grab slightly behind Sean's left shoulder and pull it toward Derrick to set Sean's left arm up for the armlock to come.

Derrick places his left leg across the back of Sean's head and hooks Sean's head down toward the mat. As he does this, Derrick forms a figure 4 with his hands and arms on Sean's left bent arm.

Derrick applies the bent armlock on Sean as shown.

BENT ARMLOCK FROM THE GUARD BELT LINE DEFENSE & OPPONENT POSTS ON HIS HAND

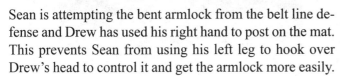

Sean is attempting the bent armlock from the belt line defense and Drew has used his right hand to post on the mat. This prevents Sean from using his left leg to hook over Drew's head to control it and get the armlock more easily.

Sean uses his left leg to wrap around Drew's body as shown to pull Drew in closer as he applies the bent armlock from this position. Instead of using his left leg to hook over Drew's head, Sean uses his left leg to hook around Drew's body for control.

BENT ARM CRANK

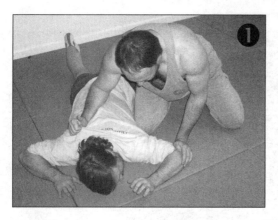

This is a surprise move that can work sometimes. Steve is riding Bill who is flat on his front.

Steve jams his right knee close in to Bill's left side at Bill's armpit as he grabs Bill's left arm. Steve's right arm is grabbing Bill's left wrist, palm up.

Steve sits forward and hugs Bill's left elbow tight to his waist and hips as shown. As he does this, Steve uses his right forearm to drive down on Bill's left upper arm and shoulder and pulls up on Bill's left wrist with his left hand. Steve uses his left hand to scoop under Bill's left elbow for support.

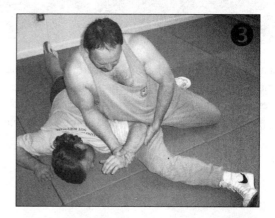

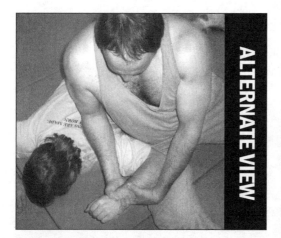

ALTERNATE VIEW

Here is a close up view of how Steve controls and cranks Bill's left bent arm.

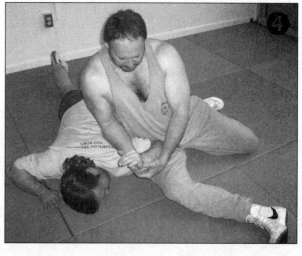

Steve puts on the pressure by using both hands (in the palm up position) to pull up on Bill's left wrist. Bill's left elbow is trapped in Steve's hips and waist. It's kind of a sucker move, but as P.T. Barnum once said, "There's a sucker born every minute."

KICK BACK BENT ARMLOCK

Jeff is riding Erik who is flat on his front. Jeff uses his right hand to grab Erik's right wrist. This is the near wrist hold.

Jeff uses his right knee to block Erik's right elbow as shown.

Jeff moves to his right and to Erik's right side.

Jeff uses his right knee as a fulcrum against Erik's right elbow as he starts his kick back with his left leg.

Jeff completes his kick back and pulls Erik's right hand up and out. As he does this, Jeff uses his right forearm to drive down on Erik's upper right arm.

Look how Jeff pulls Erik's right arm up and out, using both hands to scoop and control it as he uses his right forearm to drive down on Erik's upper right arm. This causes pain in the shoulder and elbow.

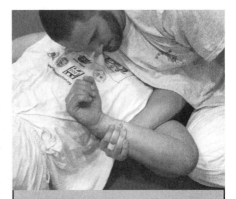

TECHNICAL TIP: Jeff has his right forearm jammed against Erik's right upper arm. Jeff's right hand is palm up, pulling up on Erik's wrist, to create a lot of pressure and pain on Erik's right arm. Jeff will quickly use his left hand to grab Erik's right wrist and pull up.

KICK BACK TO ARMPIT LOCK

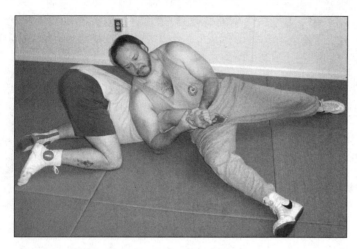

Steve has used the kick back on Bill, but is using the armpit lock instead of the bent armlock to get the tap out.

TECHNICAL TIP: Steve is pulling up with both of his hands on Bill's wrist and is using the right side of his body to drive into the back of Bill's upper right arm as he pulls up on it. Steve is pulling Bill's right arm up and toward Bill's body and this keeps Bill's right arm bent, both of which cause more pain than pulling it straight out for a straight armlock.

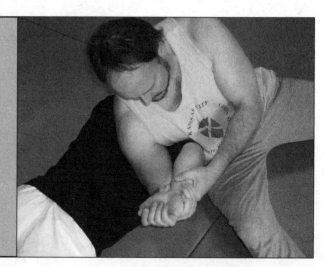

FRONT SIT THROUGH TO BENT ARMLOCK

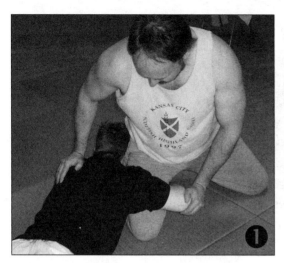

Bill is grabbing Steve's right leg with both of his arms as shown. Bill might have shot in with a single leg and it didn't work, or may be grabbing Steve's leg to set him up for a go behind to get the ride.

Steve uses his right elbow to drive into Bill's armpit as he uses his left hand to grab Bill's right elbow for control. Steve posts out with his left leg and foot.

Steve sits through shooting his right leg forward and pulls Bill's right arm free. As he does this, Steve uses his left hand to grab Bill's right wrist.

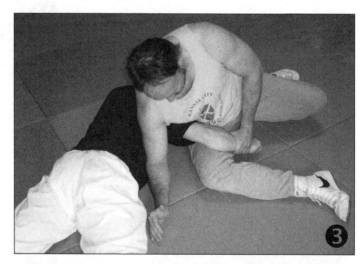

Steve uses both hands to grab Bill's right wrist and he traps Bill's right elbow in his hip and waist. Bill's arm is bent.

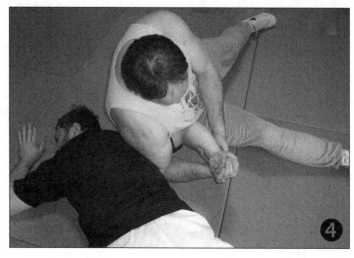

FRONT SIT THROUGH TO ARMPIT LOCK

TECHNICAL TIP: I recommend learning the armpit lock initially from this position. The armpit lock is under-rated in my opinion and should be a ready weapon in your arsenal of moves.

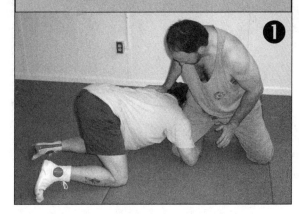

Bill is grabbing Steve's leg as shown.

Steve uses his right arm and elbow to wedge into Bill's right armpit. As he does this, Steve posts out with his left leg for stability.

Steve uses his left hand to grab Bill's right wrist.

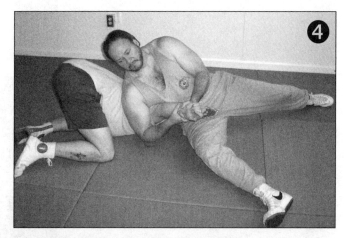

Steve pulls Bill's right arm out straight as he drives forward and uses his upper body to drive into the back of Bill's upper right arm. This causes a lot of strain on Bill's right shoulder and elbow.

BENT ARM CRANK IF OPPONENT ROLLS OVER FROM SIT THROUGH

Drew starts his sit through for the armpit lock but Brian bends his right arm and starts to escape by rolling over his right shoulder. This is a common escape from the sit through to the armpit lock.

Brian rolls over his right shoulder (the one closest to Drew) to avoid the armpit lock.

Brian completes his somersault but Drew makes sure to keep Brian's right arm trapped with his right leg as shown. Drew uses his left hand to control Brian's right elbow to keep it from escaping.

Drew pushes up with his left hand on Brian's bent right arm as he bends his right knee to trap Brian's right wrist to get the tap out. Drew can form a triangle with his legs to add to the pressure.

ALLEN SWITCH TO ARMPIT LOCK

This move is named for World Sambo Champion Maurice Allen, who taught it to me years ago. Ken is on all fours with Eric riding him. Eric has his right arm around Ken's waist. Ken uses his right hand to grab Eric's right hand and pull it tight to his chest.

Ken moves his lower body to his right as he continues to use his right hand to control Eric's right hand. Ken starts to dip his head and shoulders and will move to his left. Ken will spin to his right and move under Eric's right arm and armpit.

Ken continues to spin under Eric and sits through shooting his right leg out as shown. As he does this, Ken keeps pulling on Eric's right hand and arm.

Ken completes his sit through and pulls Eric's right arm out straight to apply the armpit lock and get the tap out.

HEAD ROLL BENT ARMLOCK

Erik is using a rodeo ride on Jeff and uses his right hand to hook Jeff's right arm as shown.

Erik posts on the top of his right head for stability.

Erik gets a figure 4 grip on Jeff's right arm.

Erik jams his left knee and shin on the back of Jeff's head as shown.

Erik forcefully jams his left knee down on Jeff's head and rolls onto his left hip as shown. Erik's left knee is pointing toward Jeff's feet.

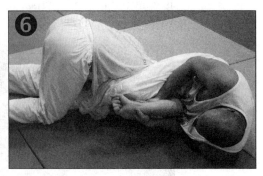

As Erik rolls onto his left hip and side, he scoops Jeff's bent arm up, using his left hand to push the right wrist up and his right arm to push down on the right upper arm, causing pain in both Jeff's shoulder and elbow.

JUJI GATAME FROM THE HIP

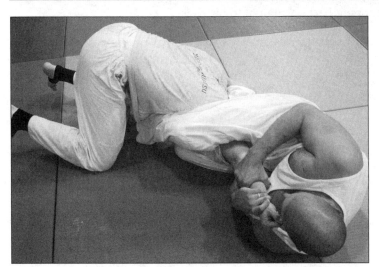

Erik can also pull Jeff's right arm out straight and apply Juji Gatame from here as well.

HEAD ROLL JUJI GATAME WHEN OPPONENT IS FLAT

Mike has Kirt in a rodeo ride and is controlling Kirt's wrists with a wrist ride.

Mike flattens Kirt onto his face.

Mike moves his body to his right and jams his left knee and shin against the back of Kirt's head.

Mike leans to his left driving his knee hard down against Kirt's head, while scooping Kirt's arm tight to his chest.

Mike rolls hard to his left side and drives his left knee in the direction of Kirt's feet. As he does this, Mike pulls Kirt's right arm in tight to his chest and applies Juji Gatame.

WATSON POWER HALF TO JUJI GATAME

Shawn Watson used this set up for Juji Gatame on a lot of opponents in his judo and sambo career.

Shawn is using a power half on Kelvin.

Shawn has control of Kelvin's left shoulder and uses his left leg to jam under Kelvin's left hip as shown. Shawn is putting a lot of pressure on Kelvin's head and neck with the power half at this point.

Shawn moves behind Kelvin and places his left knee behind Kelvin's head to keep it from moving.

Shawn rolls back (mainly over to his left hip to allow his right knee to kick over Kelvin's head) and pulls Kelvin's left arm in tight to his chest to get the Juji Gatame.

DOUBLE CHICKEN WING

This is an old wrestling move that's hard on your opponent's shoulders.

Dave breaks Caleb down onto his front and uses his right arm to hook under Caleb's right arm as shown.

Dave uses his left hand to hook under Caleb's left arm as shown and squeezes Caleb's elbows together.

Dave walks Caleb over by working his body around toward Caleb's head and turns Caleb over as shown.

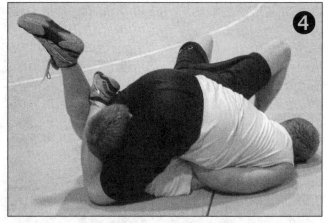

Dave turns Caleb over onto his back, still keeping the chicken wing and forms a leg triangle on Caleb's head. To add to the shoulder pressure, Dave rocks his body forward and uses his legs to pull up on Caleb's head.

BELLY DOWN JUJI GATAME WITH FOOT PUSH ON HIP FROM GUARD

Bill has Josh in his guard and moves his body away from Josh to gain some working room. Notice how Bill uses his left hand to cinch Josh's right arm in tight to his chest.

Bill rolls over his left hip and side and jams his left knee and shin on the back of Josh's head.

Bill jams his left leg under Josh's head and finishes with a belly down Juji Gatame.

FLAT ROLL JUJI GATAME

Jake is flat on his face in the "chicken" position. Steve positions himself as shown.

Steve pulls up on Jake's collar with his left hand up on Jake's hips with his left hand. As he does this, Steve jams his right leg in Jake's right hip.

Steve jams his right leg under Jake and uses his left leg and foot to post out wide.

Steve uses both hands to hook Jake's right arm and pull it tight to his chest.

Steve jams his left leg and foot under Jake's head as shown.

FLAT ROLL JUJI GATAME

Steve does a right shoulder roll and uses his left leg to hook Jake's head, forcing Jake to roll as well.

Steve rolls Jake over onto his back.

Steve rolls Jake over and into the leg press position.

Steve rolls back and applies Juji Gatame.

HEAD ROLL JUJI GATAME

The head roll is one of the most effective and important ways of getting an opponent into Juji Gatame. No matter what kind of grappling or fighting you do, the head roll Juji Gatame is one of the most often used and effective set ups ever done. If you master the basic method shown here you will definitely have a major weapon in your armlock arsenal. I've seen this set up used often in international judo and sambo, and from time to time in MMA.

Derrick starts the move by using a standing ride on Jarrod as shown.

Derrick hooks his right leg and anchors it on Jarrod's left upper leg and hip. As he does this, Derrick posts on the top of his head over to the side of Jarrod. It's important for Derrick to be sideways of Jarrod like this.

As Derrick posts on his head and anchors his right leg on Jarrod's left hip, he uses his left arm to hook Jarrod's left arm as shown.

Derrick uses his left knee and shin to jam against the back of Jarrod's head. Derrick's right foot is still anchored on Jarrod's left hip for control.

HEAD ROLL JUJI GATAME

Derrick jams down with his left knee and shin on the back of Jarrod's head.

Derrick drives his left knee in the direction of Jarrod's feet and rolls forcefully onto his own left hip.

Look at Derrick's legs and feet and how they are controlling Jarrod's body as Derrick sits on his left hip forcing Jarrod to roll forward over his head.

The momentum and explosiveness of Derrick's actions force Jarrod to roll over his head.

As Jarrod rolls over, Derrick swings his left leg over Jarrod's head to control it and keep it on the mat preventing Jarrod from sitting up.

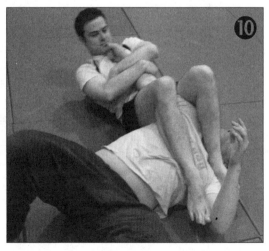

Derrick finishes the armlock and gets the tap out.

HEAD ROLL JUJI GATAME WITH A LEG HOOK OR GRAB

Bill is doing a variation of the head roll Juji Gatame by grabbing or hooking Eric's near leg as Bill posts on his head. Grabbing or hooking with your arm helps scoop your opponent's leg and control his body better to roll him over onto his back.

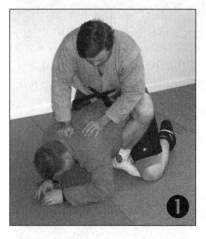

Bill sets up his head roll in the same way Derrick did in setting up his head roll.

Bill continues his head roll attack.

TECHNICAL TIP: The head roll into Juji Gatame is one of the most widely used techniques in judo, jujitsu and sambo. This set up is especially useful for grapplers who are middleweights or lower in weight, but is also used by larger athletes as well. This is an important set up for Juji Gatame and I recommend you drill on it on a regular basis. It really works!

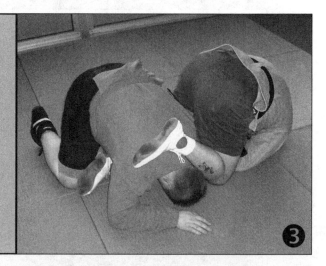

As Bill posts on the top of his head, he uses his left hand to hook Eric's left upper leg. You'll see how he does it in the next few photos.

HEAD ROLL JUJI GATAME WITH A LEG HOOK OR GRAB

Bill is using his right arm and hand to hook Eric's left arm and using his left hand and arm to hook Eric's left upper leg.

You can see how Bill has grabbed Eric's leg to assist in rolling him over his head.

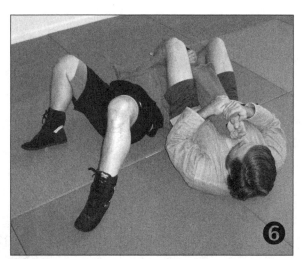

Bill rolls Eric over his head and you can see how he has used his left hand and arm to hook Eric's left leg to assist in rolling him over.

Bill finishes the armlock.

TAP OUT TEXTBOOK

HIP ROLL JUJI GATAME

Bill has a standing ride on Steve.

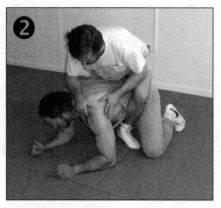

Bill starts the move by using his left foot to hook under Steve's left side. Bill could have started this move from a rodeo ride as well.

Bill jams his left foot in deep at Steve's midsection and uses his left hand to grab Steve's left wrist.

Bill can use his right arm and hand to post out far for stability.

Bill posts on the top of his head and swings his right leg over.

ALTERNATE VIEW

Here's another view of how Bill posts on his head and starts to move his right leg over Steve's head.

HIP ROLL JUJI GATAME

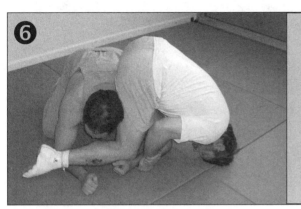

TECHNICAL TIP: Bill posts on the top of his head to provide a better base for the stability of his body. Doing this also gives Bill the option of which way he may want to roll. Be sure to post on the top of your head and don't post on your head and shoulder as this is a weak position and limits your movement. Like my old coach Rene Pommerelle used to say; "That's using your head son!"

Bill uses his right leg to hook under Steve's head and neck as Bill scoops Steve's arms in tight to his chest.

Bill rolls in the direction of Steve's hip (this is why is called the hip roll), which, in this case is over Bill's left shoulder.

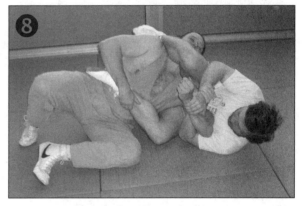

Bill continues to roll and uses his right leg to hook hard on Steve's head for maximum control of Steve's upper body in the roll.

Bill rolls Steve over onto his back.

TECHNICAL TIP: Rolling an opponent allows you to gain momentum and get the armlock quicker.

From here, Bill can roll back and get the armlock on Steve.

HEAD ROLL JUJI GATAME FROM THE GUARD

Bill has Josh in his guard and moves his body away from Josh to gain working room. Notice how Bill uses his left hand to cinch Josh's right arm in tight to his chest.

Bill scoots back pretty far as he rolls over onto his right hip. Look at how Bill is controlling Josh's right arm how Bill is using his right foot to anchor and control Josh's left hip and upper leg.

Bill swings his left leg over Josh and is rolling over.

Bill jams his left shin across the back of Josh's head as shown.

Bill's rolling action causes Josh to roll and Bill makes sure of it by grabbing Josh's right pant leg (or ankle if no gi is being worn) to help drag Josh over.

Bill has rolled Josh over onto his back and can quickly apply the Juji Gatame.

STRAIGHT ARMLOCK FROM THE GUARD

Mike has Derrick in his guard and uses both of his hands and arms to trap Derrick's left arm to his chest.

Derrick may move to his right in an attempt to Get past Mike's guard. Mike rolls to his right side and places his right leg against Derrick's left ribcage. Mike uses his left leg to hook over Derrick's head.

Mike traps Derrick's extended left arm with both of his hands and pulls in with them causing the elbow lock on Derrick's left arm. Mike uses his left leg to hook hard over Derrick's head forcing it downward and uses his right leg to trap Derrick's body. Mike has used his right shoulder and the right side of his head to trap Derrick's left wrist as well. This causes an unexpected and quick straight armlock and can get the tap out.

HUNGARIAN ROLL TO JUJI GATAME

This is an explosive move and really works. I first saw a Hungarian guy do this at some tournament in Europe and that's how this move got its name.

Derrick is doing a standing ride on Jarrod and starts to move his left leg over Jarrod's hip as shown.

Derrick is sideways to Jarrod, with his left foot down across Jarrod's body and on the mat. Derrick is scooping Jarrod's left arm with his right hand and his left upper leg with his left arm.

Derrick does a forward head roll in the "hole" or opening created between Jarrod's leg and arm. As he does this, Derrick continues to scoop and hook with both of his hands as shown.

Derrick rolls forward, pulling Jarrod with him. Derrick is in a compact ball at this point.

Derrick continues his roll, while grabbing Jarrod's leg and arm. Derrick's left leg is under Jarrod and across his torso. Derrick's right leg is swinging over, adding momentum to this roll.

HUNGARIAN ROLL TO JUJI GATAME

TECHNICAL TIP: While this looks like a flashy move (and is, really), this set up works well and usually surprises your opponent.

Derrick rolls Jarrod over and ends up in this modified leg press position. The Hungarian roll is an explosive movement, much like a throwing technique.

Derrick rolls back and secures the Juji Gatame.

NO ROLL JUJI FROM THE GUARD

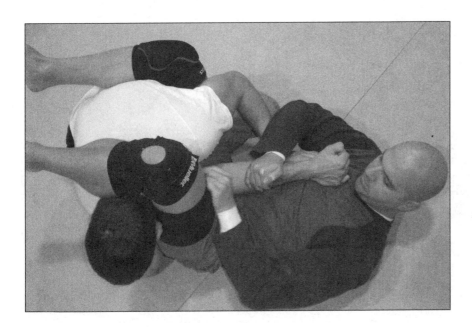

BENT ARM KICKOVER FROM TOP RIDE

This is an old technique from the early days of judo and has seen some success in MMA matches. There are several versions of this move, but this is pretty much the standard way of doing it.

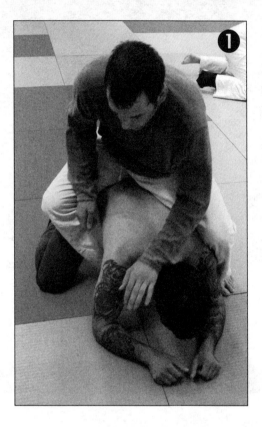

1. Josh has a rodeo ride on Nikolay.

2, Josh moves to his right and drives his right leg under and across Nikolay's torso. As Josh does this he uses his right hand to hook Nikolay's right arm and starts to roll over his right shoulder.

Josh uses his right hand to grab his left leg above the knee and his right leg to hook under Nikolay's head.

Josh rolls to his right hip and side.

BENT ARM KICKOVER FROM TOP RIDE

Josh sits in and hooks his right leg over Nikolay's right shoulder. Josh pulls up on Nikolay's right arm with both of his arms.

Josh sits up and traps Nikolay's right arm.

Josh leans into Nikolay continuing to add pressure to the move.

Josh sits up and traps Nikolay's bent arm as shown causing pain in the shoulder and elbow.

BENT ARM TRIANGLE FROM UNDER HOOK

Bret uses both arms to hook under Scott's right arm and secures it with a square lock with his hands.

Bret lifts up on Scott's right arm as he uses his left leg to hook over Scott's lower arm that's trapped on his back.

Bret rolls back and starts to form a triangle with his legs.

Bret forms the leg triangle and pulls on Scott's bent right arm. The triangle and arm trap causes pain in Scott's shoulder and elbow.

HAMMERLOCK FROM BELT AND NELSON

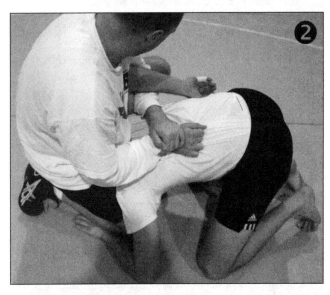

Bret is at Scott's head and uses his left hand to scoop under Scott's right arm and shoulder. Bret places his right hand flat on Scott's back as shown. Look at how Bret uses his left hand to grab his right wrist. This is the "belt and nelson" set up.

Bret uses his left knee to drive Scott's right arm in close to his body as shown. This weakens Scott's right arm and sets him up for the hammerlock.

Bret turns his body into Scott and he uses his left hand to grab Scott's right wrist. Bret uses his right hand to grab his left forearm forming a figure 4 hold. As he does this, Bret drives his right knee down hard on Scott's head to make him think about that more than the hammerlock he's putting on him. Bret cranks hard on Scott's bent right arm and uses his right hand to pull Scott's right wrist toward his head. This is a nasty lock and was popular in the old days of legitimate pro wrestling.

GLAHN SPECIAL TO JUJI GATAME

The Glahn Special was named after Olympic medallist Klaus Glahn and is a great lapel and trap choke.

Kyle starts the choke, but gets Josh in an armlock. Kyle uses his left hand to grab Josh's left lapel

TECHNICAL TIP: Kyle drives his right elbow straight down and into Josh and doesn't drive it sideways against Josh's neck.

Kyle uses his right hand to grab Josh's right shoulder or collar and makes sure to drive his right elbow straight down and in toward Josh's legs.

ALTERNATE VIEW

You can see how Kyle has hooked his left arm under Josh's right arm.

Kyle uses his left foot to prop against Josh's right knee.

Kyle rolls Josh to Kyle's left and Josh's right.

GLAHN SPECIAL TO JUJI GATAME

Kyle rolls over on top of Josh.

Kyle is on top of Josh in a tripod position and can apply the choke.

To continue to the armlock, Kyle moves his left leg out and moves up and away from Josh a bit.

Kyle moves up and away from Josh in this photo.

Kyle swings his body over and uses his right arm to pull Josh's right arm in tight to his body as he keeps his left arm in Josh's lapel.

Kyle swings all the way over Josh and rolls back to apply the Juji Gatame.

HECKADON JUJI GATAME FROM LEG GRAB

Eric is grabbing Steve's ankle, possibly having tried an ankle pick that didn't work.

Steve uses his right leg to step over Eric's body.

Steve squats on Eric as he uses both arms to hook Eric's arms in tight to his chest.

Steve squats on Eric's back as he rolls backward, pulling Eric's right arm with him.

Steve rolls onto his back with his right leg across Eric's torso and his left leg hooking Eric's let arm and shoulder.

World Sambo Champion Chris Heckadon favored this set up to Juji Gatame during his career.

Steve rolls back and applies the Juji Gatame.

LEG TRAP AND KICK BACK TO STRAIGHT ARMLOCK

Steve might have shot in for a single leg takedown or another move or may be grabbing Bill's right leg to control it for a go behind or other move.

Bill backs his body back away from Steve a bit as he hooks Steve's right arm with his right leg.

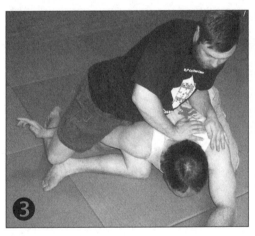

Bill starts his kick back with his right leg and foot as he drives his left knee forward.

Bill kicks back with his right leg as he shoots his left leg forward in a sit through. Bill places his left elbow on the mat above Steve's right shoulder to isolate it.

Bill raises his right leg a bit to cause more pain in Steve's right shoulder and to stretch Steve's right arm out more. This puts the pressure on both Steve's shoulder and entire arm to get the tap out.

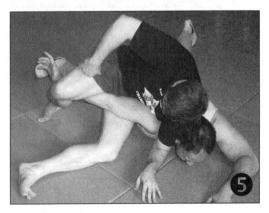

LEG TRAP AND KICK BACK TO BENT ARM CRANK

STRAIGHT ARM TRIANGLE FROM A LEG GRAB OR SINGLE LEG TAKEDOWN ATTEMPT

Josh has grabbed Derrick's left leg as shown. This situation may have come about from a single leg takedown attempt by Josh where Derrick sprawls back or could take place in any situation where the bottom man grabs your leg.

Derrick moves his body to his right (toward Josh's hips and legs) and forms a triangle with his legs. As he does this, Derrick sprawls out and drives his hips forward into Josh's outstretched arm. This causes as much (or more) pain in Josh's shoulder as it does his elbow.

FIGURE 4 STRAIGHT ARMLOCK

"So old-fashioned, it's cool" could be a good description of this armlock. This variation of the straight armlock has been around for along time and used in every kind of grappling known to mankind. There are many ways to get into it, and you can do this armlock instead of some of the others shown in this book. This is a classic "armbar" where you place your arm or other body part behind your opponent's elbow to "bar" or lever it against the fulcrum. Bill makes sure to use his left forearm as the fulcrum against Steve's elbow and trap Steve's upper arm and wrist into Bill's armpit in this photo.

JUJI GATAME COUNTER TO NEAR LEG RIDE LEGLOCK (THE FOBES ROLL)

Chad uses a near leg ride on Jarrod to set him up for a leglock.

Chad turns to Jarrod's back side to apply the bent leglock.

Chad uses his hands to grab Jarrod's right foot.

As Chad sits back on his buttocks to apply the leglock, Jarrod starts to roll over his right shoulder.

JUJI GATAME COUNTER TO NEAR LEG RIDE LEGLOCK (THE FOBES ROLL)

By rolling, Jarrod eases the pressure on the bent knee that Chad want to lock. Jarrod completes his shoulder roll and uses both hands to grab Chad's right arm.

Jarrod rolls onto his back holding Chad's arm and stretching it.

Jarrod arches his hips and applies Juji Gatame to get the tap out.

ALTERNATE VIEW

Here's another view of how Jarrod applies Juji Gatame form this situation. Notice that Jarrod has placed his left foot and leg over Chad's head for more control.

UPPER BODY (NORTH SOUTH) PIN TO JUJI GATAME

Bill has Eric in an upper body hold (north south pin).

Bill moves to his right and over Eric's right shoulder as shown.

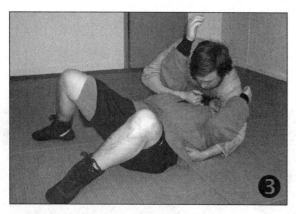

Bill uses his right arm to hook under Eric's right arm.

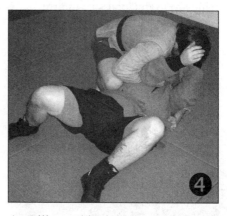

As Bill uses his right arm to scoop in Eric's right arm, Bill jams his right knee on Eric's right ribcage.

Bill squats up on his left leg as shown and pulls Eric's right arm in close to his chest and upper body.

Bill rolls back and applies Juji Gatame for the tap out.

JUJI GATAME FROM SIDE LEG SCISSORS OR HALF GUARD

Steve is on top with Bill using his legs to scissor Steve's right leg in this half guard situation.

Steve makes some space between his body and Bill's body by pulling back a bit.

This is a good armlock from the half guard. Nobody expects you to pull this one off!

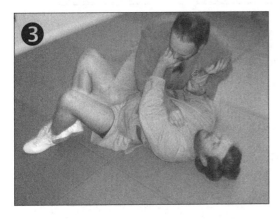

Steve backs away from Bill and uses his left arm to scoop Bill's right arm in to Steve's chest.

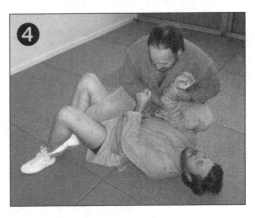

Steve uses both hands to grab Bill's right arm as he squats.

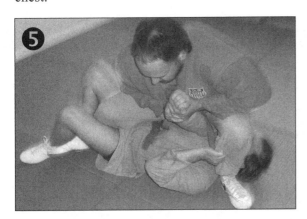

As soon as Steve squats up, he kicks his left leg over Bill's head and sits on Bill's right shoulder. Steve keeps pulling on Bill's right arm with both of his hands.

Steve rolls back quickly and applies the Juji Gatame.

TAP OUT TEXTBOOK

BENT ARMLOCK USING LEG FROM HEAD AND ARM HOLD (SCARF HOLD)

Bill has Steve in a scarf hold or head and arm pin. Bill uses his left hand to push down on Steve's right arm.

TECHNICAL TIP: Applying an armlock on an opponent you are holding to the mat is a good way to finish him off. A lot of moves doing this come from sambo, where the rules of that sport encourage grapplers to apply armlocks from this position.

Bill traps Steve's bent right arm with his left leg and foot as shown.

TECHNICAL TIP: Bill makes sure to drive downward (to the mat) with his right foot to add pressure to Steve's right and elbow.

BENT ARMLOCK WITH ELBOW PUSH FROM HEAD AND ARM PIN

Bret traps Scott's right arm with the bent armlock and adds more pressure by pushing up and forward on his right arm as shown.

LEG PUSH BENT ARMLOCK FROM THE SCARF HOLD

Derrick has Josh in the scarf hold and uses his left hand and arm to push Josh's right arm under Derrick's right leg.

Derrick pushes Josh's right wrist and forearm under his bent right leg as shown. Derrick uses his left hand to grab his right ankle and push down on it causing more pain in Josh's arm. Notice that Derrick is using his left elbow and forearm to trap Josh's bent right arm and lean forward. Doing this makes Josh's right elbow bend up more and adds more pressure to the lock.

KNEE PUSH STRAIGHT ARMLOCK FROM THE SCARF HOLD

Derrick traps Josh's right arm in a straight armlock from the head and arm pin and uses his left knee to drive down toward the mat. Josh's right arm is trapped by Derrick's right leg on the mat and by pushing downward with his knee, Derrick adds more pain to the armlock. Notice that Derrick keeps his left foot on the mat to act as a hinge when pushing down with his knee and leg.

BENT ARMLOCK FROM THE GRAPEVINE

Jorge has secured control over Brian's legs and lower body with his grapevine. This keeps Brian from escaping or neutralizing the situation. Once Jorge controls Brian with his legs in the grapevine, he works in his figure 4 grip on Brian's right arm and secures the bent armlock.

By splitting Brian's legs wide in the grapevine, Jorge gives himself a good base. Jorge moves his upper body to his left side a bit, keeping good weight distribution on Brian to ride him. He jams his right elbow in the right side of Brian's head and neck on the mat, posting for stability and allowing him to get a better figure 4 grip to get the armlock. The grapevine gives Jorge more time to work his armlock in and get the tap out.

BENT ARMLOCK FROM SCARF HOLD WITH LEG TRIANGLE

BENT ARMLOCK FROM HEAD AND ARM PIN WITH ELBOW CATCH

Bret uses his left arm to scoop or catch Scott's bent right arm to add more pressure to the bent armlock from this position.

Brian is using the bent armlock from the head and arm pin and as he pushes up on Drew's bent left arm, Brian forms a triangle with his legs and drives his hips forward and into the pressure of the bent armlock. Using a triangle in this way makes sure Drew's arm doesn't get away.

BENT ARMLOCK FROM HEAD AND ARM HOLD

Steve has Nick in a scarf hold or head and arm pin.

Steve uses his left arm to trap Nick's right arm to his body as he uses his right arm to move under Nick's right arm.

Steve places his right elbow in the right side of Nick's head and neck and uses his right hand to grab Nick's right wrist. Steve is about to form his figure four with his left hand.

Steve forms a figure 4 lock with his arms and cranks on Nick's right elbow. Steve uses his left forearm to lever up and forward on Nick's right arm as he anchors Nick's right wrist with his right hand.

STRAIGHT ARMLOCK FROM HEAD AND ARM HOLD WITH HEAD LIFT

Bret uses his right hand and arm to hook under Scott's left armpit. Bret uses both hands to lift up on Scott's head to add to the pressure of the arm and shoulder lock.

STRAIGHT ARMLOCK FROM HEAD AND ARM HOLD

Steve has Jon in a scarf hold or head and arm pin.

Jon starts to pull his right arm free and as he does this, Steve uses his left hand to grab it and push it down toward the mat.

Steve traps Jon's right arm with his left knee and leg as shown and drives downward with his left knee to cause pain in Jon's right shoulder and elbow.

STRAIGHT ARMLOCK WITH FOOT PUSH FROM HEAD AND ARM HOLD

Steve can use his left foot to push down on Jon's outstretched right arm to cause pain. Steve's right thigh is the fulcrum and is under Jon's right elbow.

STRAIGHT ARMLOCK FROM HEAD AND ARM HOLD W/HAND PUSH ON NEAR SHOULDER

Bret has Scott in a straight armlock from the head and arm pin and is adding pressure by using his left hand to push on Scott's right shoulder. This keeps Scott from rolling his right shoulder to start an escape and adds more shoulder pressure to the armlock.

FIGURE 4 STRAIGHT ARMLOCK FROM THE SCARF HOLD

Mike applies a figure 4 straight armlock on Tyler from a scarf hold or head and arm pin.

FIGURE 4 STRAIGHT ARMLOCK FROM A SEATED TRIPOD POSITION

Sometimes, as your opponent scoots away to get space to start his escape, you can apply the straight armlock. Tyler moves away from Mike and he does this, Mike leans back into Tyler in a tripod position on the mat with Mike's buttocks and his two feet as supports.

ARMPIT LOCK FROM THE SCARF HOLD OR MODIFIED SIDE POSITION

Alan has Caleb in a modified scarf hold or side position as shown.

As Caleb starts to turn into Alan to start his escape, Alan uses his left hand to grab Caleb's right wrist.

Alan uses both hands to pull Caleb over onto his side.

Alan continues to pull with his hands and rolls Caleb over onto his right front side and applies the armpit lock.

STRAIGHT ARM KICKOVER FROM HEAD AND ARM PIN

Alan has Caleb in a head and arm pin.

Alan kicks his left leg over Caleb's head as Alan leans back away from Caleb. As he does this, Alan uses his left arm to hook under Caleb's right arm.

Alan finishes the move by jamming his left foot on the left side of Caleb's head and leaning back to straighten Caleb's right arm as shown.

TAP OUT TEXTBOOK

WRESTLER'S SWITCH TO ARMPIT LOCK

Steve is on his knees and Chris is grabbing Steve's left leg with his arms.

Steve posts out to the side with his right leg for stability. He then uses his right hand to grab Chris's left elbow to anchor it to the mat. Steve starts to drive his left knee forward, pushing Chris's arm back a bit. Steve uses his left hand to grab inside Chris's left leg as shown.

Steve sits through with his left leg as he uses his left hand to pull on Chris's left leg. Doing this forces Chris's left arm to straighten out as shown.

Steve uses his right hand (palm up) to scoop up on Chris's left extended arm as he continues to pull on Chris's left leg with his left hand. This creates pain in Chris's left shoulder and arm.

SIT-THROUGH ARM TRAP TO STRAIGHT ARMLOCK

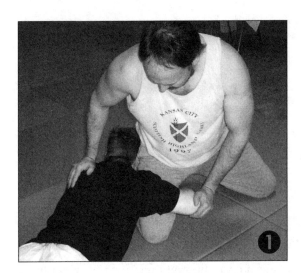

Bill is grabbing Steve's right leg as shown. Steve quickly uses his right hip to "hip out" and moves his right knee and leg forward and to the left to start to extend Bill's right arm and shoulder.

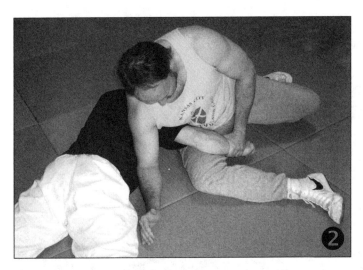

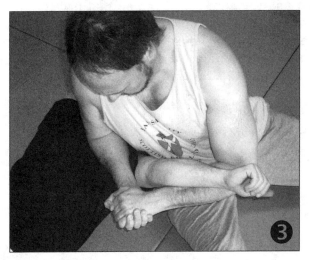

Steve sits through using his right leg and hip to drive forward and extend Bill's right arm. Steve uses his left hand to grab Bill's right wrist for control as he does this.

Steve uses his left forearm to scoop up and under Bill's right wrist and forearm to straighten it. Steve uses his right forearm and elbow to drive directly down on Bill's right triceps. Steve grabs his hands in a square lock to reinforce his arm position. This hurts the shoulder quite a bit and doesn't do anything good for the elbow either!

JUJI GATAME FROM AN INSIDE LEG GRAB

Erik is on his front and has grabbed Mike's right leg as shown.

Mike moves around to his right and uses his right hand to grab Erik's right elbow and his left hand to post on the mat for stability. Mike drives his left leg in the "hole" of Erik's body as shown.

If your opponent shoots in for a front take-down and you snap him down so that his head is on the inside of your legs, or if your opponent is in this position for any reason, this rolling Juji Gatame works well.

Mike leans forward and posts on the top of his head as shown.

Mike rolls over his left shoulder (the one closest to Erik's left hip) as he uses his right leg to hook Erik's head. Look at how Mike is using both hands to scoop Erik's left arm in tight to his chest.

Mike rolls Erik over and stretches his arm for the tap out.

SPIN AND STRETCH TO JUJI GATAME

Steve steps across Bill and puts his right heel on the side of Bill's right knee. As he does this, Steve spins Bill to the mat.

Bill has been knocked on his knees and Steve is standing above him. Steve is using his right hand to grip between Bill's shoulder blades on the jacket and is using his left hand to hold Bill's right elbow at the jacket sleeve.

Steve finishes the spin as shown and jams his right shin into the back and side of Bill.

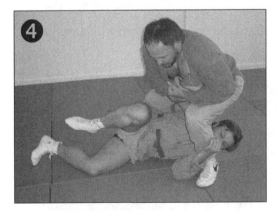

Steve steps over Bill's head with his left foot and squats on Bill's right shoulder. Steve uses both hands to scoop Bill's right arm to his chest and body.

Steve rolls back and stretches Bill's arm out for the tap out.

SAMBO (OR JUDO) STACK TO JUJI GATAME

Eric is in the "chicken position" flat on his face. Steve squats to the side of Eric and uses his left hand to grab Eric's sleeve at the triceps and his right hand to grab Eric's jacket or pants at the hip.

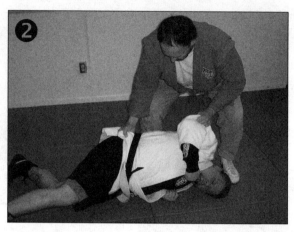

Steve explodes back and pulls Eric back on onto his left side.

Steve squats on Eric's shoulder and starts to hook Eric's right arm with both of his arms as shown.

Steve rolls back and pulls Eric's arm with him.

Steve finishes the armlock by stretching the arm out.

STRAIGHT ARMLOCK FROM OPPONENT'S HIGH GRIP

Roman is using his right hand to grab Yuri's collar.

Yuri uses his left hand to hook over Roman's right arm.

Yuri uses his left hand in a knife edge type of move to drive down hard on Roman's right elbow. Yuri wants to have his left hand come down directly on Roman's elbow joint.

As Yuri drives down hard with his left hand, he uses his right and to grab Roman's right forearm and trap it immediately under his neck as shown.

Yuri drives Roman down to the mat and gets the straight armlock as shown.

STRAIGHT ARMLOCK ON KNEELING OPPONENT

Steve has been knocked to both knees or is on his knees but still has a head and arm grip on Bill, who is standing.

Bill traps Steve's right forearm and wrist into the side of his neck and uses both hands to trap Steve's right arm as shown.

ALTERNATE VIEW

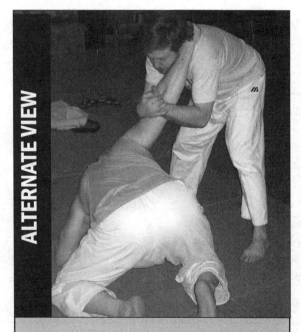

TECHNICAL TIP: Here's another view of how to trap the extended arm. Notice that Bill isn't lacing his fingers, but instead is cupping his hands on Steve's elbow to trap it and create pressure on the elbow. Lacing your fingers isn't a strong grip.

Bill drags Steve down to the mat by quickly backing up a step of two. Doing this forces Steve to be extended as shown and adds more pressure on the shoulder as well as elbow.

ARMPIT LOCK FROM A STANDING RIDE

Chris has Bob in a standing hip ride and places his left foot in front of Bob's right leg. Notice how Chris is using his left hand to hook and control Bob's left hip.

Chris trips Bob forward and drives him to the mat all the while continuing his ride with his left hand hooking Bob's left hip.

Chris drives Bob to the mat and uses both hands to scoop and pull Bob's right arm out and straight for the armpit lock.

TAP OUT TEXTBOOK

ARMPIT LOCK FROM STANDING POSITION

Yuri uses his right hand to grab Roman's right wrist as shown and pulls it. As he does this, Yuri uses his left hand to drive down on Roman's extended right elbow.

Yuri continues to pull on Roman's right arm and uses his left leg and foot to step in front of Roman. As he does this, Yuri keeps pulling on Roman's arm, driving him to the mat. He can finish the armlock from this position or continue on.

Yuri extends his left leg as shown and sits through, driving Roman to the mat forward.

Yuri sits through, using both arms to scoop Roman's right arm in tight. This puts pressure on both the shoulder and entire arm and elbow.

Yuri finishes the move with Roman's arm fully extended and hand pointing up in the air. This one really hurts and is illegal in most grappling sports because it doesn't give your opponent a chance to tap out before you injure his arm, but is a good self-defense move.

STRAIGHT ARMLOCK WHEN OPPONENT ATTEMPTS TO STAND

Bjorn has his right hand on Kirk's sleeve as Kirk attempts to get up off the mat.

Bjorn uses his left hand to grab Kirk's left hand and uses his right hand to grab the left elbow, while moving slightly to his right. At the same time, Bjorn uses his right hand to push on Kirk's left elbow driving him forward onto his front.

Bjorn drives Kirk onto his front trapping Kirk's left hand and wrist with his left hand as shown. Bjorn uses his right hand to push hard on the back of Kirk's left elbow.

To add more pressure, Bjorn drives his right knee down onto Kirk's back. As he does this, Bjorn uses his right hand to wedge in behind Kirk's left shoulder. Bjorn pulls up on Kirk's left wrist and hand. This hurts Kirk's left shoulder and elbow and even can be a wristlock as well.

KC ROLLOVER FROM THROW

Nick has taken Kirt to the mat with a throw or takedown and will follow up with this move.

Nick uses his left hand to grab Kirt's right wrist, while using his right arm to hook under Kirt's right bent arm.

Nick forms a figure 4 with his arms and hand. Nick's right hand is holding his left wrist. Nick pulls Kirt's right elbow in close to his chest.

Larry and Chris Lein teach the moves on page 149 in their CLAMP© law enforcement defensive tactics program. They're effective techniques for police work, self-defense and grappling on the mat.

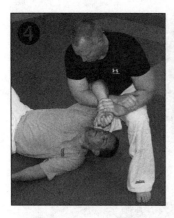

Nick moves to his left around to the top of Kirt's head still with the figure 4 hold on Kirt's right arm.

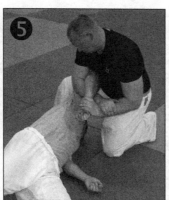

Nick moves all the way over to Kirt's front side with the bent armlock still in place.

The movement of Nick going around the top of Kirt forces Kirt to roll over onto his front side.

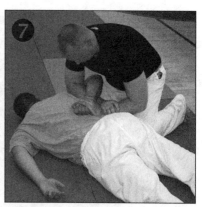

Nick applies a hammerlock variation of the bent armlock on Kirt to get the tap out. Nick is also in a good position to apply the handcuffs in a law enforcement situation.

STANDING CLAMP BENT ARMLOCK

Mike uses his left hand to grab Eric's right wrist and his right hand to grab onto the back of Eric's right shoulder and pull it forward to make the move work more smoothly.

Mike grabs his hands together as shown to form a figure 4 lock. Mike makes sure to use his right elbow to drive directly down on Eric's right shoulder and pull Eric's shoulder and upper arm in close and tight to Mike's chest.

Mike swings his right leg backward and drives Eric to the ground or mat.

Mike drives Eric to the mat and keeps the CLAMP bent armlock on firmly.

STANDING BENT ARM WRAP

TECHNICAL TIP: Be careful when doing armlocks that start from a standing or kneeling position. Sometimes, standing or kneeling armlocks are put on so fast, your opponent may not have time to submit, so be careful and give him time to tap out.

ALTERNATE VIEW

Yuri uses his right hand to grab and control Roman's right hand.

The view is from the other side.

Yuri steps forward with his left foot as he swings his right arm over Roman's right shoulder to start to wrap it in tight.

Yuri wraps his right arm up and over Roman's right shoulder and arm. Yuri places his right hand on Roman's right pectoral area.

Yuri traps Roman's right arm as shown and uses his left hand to push on the right side of Roman's head for more pressure.

Here's the finish to this move. Roman's right shoulder and elbow are really cranked. This technique is not an easy one to master and requires a lot of practice time to get comfortable with it.

STEP OVER JUJI GATAME

Bret has Scott in a head and arm tie up.

Bret drives Scott down and forward by pushing on his head with his right hand and using his left arm to bar down on Scott's right arm.

Bret swings his left leg over Scott's extended right arm and shoulder as shown. Bret uses his left arm to pull on Scott's right arm for control.

Bret completes the step over and uses his left arm to continue to pull in tight on Scott's right arm.

Bret does a shoulder roll over his left shoulder and forces Scott to roll with him.

Bret rolls Scott over onto his back and completes the Juji Gatame.

TAP OUT TEXTBOOK

FOOT PUSH TO BELLY DOWN JUJI GATAME

Drew puts his right foot on Mike's left upper thigh or hip.

Drew uses his right foot to push back on Mike's left hip or thigh area. Drew goes to the mat landing on his right leg and hip.

Drew takes Mike to the mat and swings his left leg over Mike's head, while using both hands to pull on Mike's extended right arm.

Drew rolls over and hooks his left leg under Mike's head and neck. Drew pulls on Mike's arm and arches his hips to make the arm-lock work.

FOOT IN HIP AND SPIN INTO JUJI GATAME

Drew places his right foot on Mike's hip.

Drew quickly swings to his right and under Mike with his right foot still wedged in Mike's hip area.

Drew swings his left leg over Mike's head.

Drew hooks his left leg over Mike's head and rolls Mike onto his back as shown. Drew finishes with a Juji Gatame.

FLYING JUJI GATAME

TECHNICAL TIP: Flying or jumping armlocks are risky, so if you intend on using them, spend a lot of hours on the mat practicing the move. However, don't be surprised if you catch even an experienced grappler who isn't expecting you to do something so gutsy! When these moves work, they are spectacular successes, but when they don't work, they are spectacular failures.

Bill places his right leg on Josh's right hip as shown and as he does this, Bill starts to point his right hip toward Josh's stomach so Bill's body turns slightly to his right.

Bill jumps up on Josh jamming his right knee in Josh's right hip. Bill kicks his left leg over Josh's head as Bill pulls Josh down to the mat with him.

Bill pulls Josh down to the mat with him. Bill makes sure that his head is near Josh's left leg so Bill stays round and rolls more easily.

Bill rolls Josh over Josh's right shoulder.

Bill completes the flying Juji Gatame by rolling Josh onto the mat and applies the armlock.

LEG WEDGE TO JUJI GATAME

Mike wedges his right lower leg across Drew's hips and midsection.

Mike keeps his right shin jammed across Drew's front midsection as he rolls onto the mat pulling Drew down with him.

Mike swings his left leg over Drew's head and bends his right knee a bit more and jams his right shin in Drew's midsection. Mike pulls on Drew's right arm.

TECHNICAL TIP: This variation of Juji Gatame is really more of a "pull down" than a jump. Instead of jumping up on his opponent, Mike will wedge his leg in Drew's midsection and pull him down to the mat with him.

Mike rolls Drew over his right shoulder and onto his back to the leg press.

Mike rolls back and finishes the Juji Gatame.

JUMPIN' JUJI

Scott has Bret in a head and arm tie-up and quickly jumps up on Bret. Scott makes sure to shoot his right leg and foot across and past Bret's left hip as shown. This is a high-risk move, so Scott better have a lot of practice time on the mat doing this before he tries it in a real match.

As Scott jumps, he rolls over to his right shoulder and side so he will land in this position. Scott's right leg and foot is jammed in the left side of Bret's body. Scott uses his left hand to pull Bret's right arm in tight to his body. Notice that Scott is using his right hand to pull Bret's head down as he goes to the mat. Scott is swinging his left leg up and it will go over Bret's head.

As Scott rolls to the mat, he will be in this position. Notice how Scott's left leg in hooked over Bret's head at this point.

Scott hooks his left leg hard over Bret's head as he pulls on Bret's arm. This jumping action and fast roll will force Bret to roll over his right shoulder and onto his back. Scott can finish by rolling back and securing the Juji Gatame.

KNEE ON SHOULDER ARM STRETCH

Eric has shot in for a single leg or ankle pick and ends up in this position on his hands and knees.

Steve drives his right knee down hard on Eric's right shoulder and uses his right hand to hook under Eric's right elbow. Steve uses his left hand to pull up on Eric's right forearm.

Steve pulls Eric's right arm up as shown as he drives with his right knee on Eric's right shoulder to help persuade Eric to give his arm up.

Steve uses both hands to grab Eric's right forearm and wrist, pulling it out and extending it. Steve pulls up on Eric's arm and drives into Eric's shoulder to create the shoulder and arm pressure and get the tap out.

BOTTOM SIT OUT TO ARMPIT LOCK

This is a good way for the bottom man to get out of trouble. Steve is on all fours with Chris riding him from the top.

Steve uses his right hand to grab Chris's left wrist as he pops his head up and out to his right and to Chris's left hip.

Steve uses his left leg to shoot out and sits out onto his left buttocks. Steve uses his right hand to keep Chris's left arm as shown.

Steve rolls across his buttocks and over to his right and settles on his right hip as shown. Steve uses both hands to grab Chris's left arm and stretch it out with an armpit lock.

FALL DOWN ARMPIT LOCK

Steve has thrown Chris and Chris turns onto his front side before Steve can follow up with a groundfighting move. Steve controls Chris with both of his arms holding onto Chris's left arm.

Steve moves his left leg and hip over Chris's head as shown and sits on his left hip. As he does this, Steve pulls in on Chris's left arm.

Steve uses both arms to pull on Chris's left arm as he leans into Chris's left shoulder. Steve's right hip is wedged in tightly next to the left side of Chris's head for added pressure.

SIT UP BENT ARMLOCK FROM THE GUARD

Derrick has Sean's left arm wrapped up with the bent arm-lock from the guard position. Notice Derrick is using the belt line defense with his right knee and shin jammed in against Sean's midsection. Derrick has his left leg hooked over Sean's head. If, for some reason the armlock may not work at this point, go on to the following steps.

Derrick hooks down on Sean's head as he rolls Sean onto his left side as shown. Rolling Sean onto his side can give Derrick more power in applying the bent armlock to get the tap out.

If Sean still doesn't tap out, Derrick rolls over Sean and jams his right knee on Sean's torso as shown as he applies the pressure to the bent armlock. Derrick may even post on the top of his head for more stability if necessary.

HEAD ROLL BENT ARMLOCK FROM THE GUARD

Derrick is using the belt line defense with his right shin jammed in Mike's hips and midsection. Derrick is applying the bent armlock from this position but Mike is resisting. Derrick uses his left leg to hook over Mike's head as shown.

Derrick hooks down hard on Mike's head and uses his right knee, shin and leg to jam in Mike's midsection and roll Mike forward.

Derrick rolls Mike over his head as shown. Derrick still has control with the bent armlock on Mike's left arm.

Derrick rolls Mike onto his back and is on top of Mike with his right knee jammed in Mike's stomach and torso. Derrick still has his left leg hooked over Mike's head.

To add pressure to the armlock, Derrick posts onto the top of his head and rolls to his right bending Mike's left arm in the process. This adds a great deal of pressure on Mike's shoulder as well. Look at how Derrick's left leg is hooked over Mike's head and neck for maximum control.

TAP OUT TEXTBOOK

BENT ARMLOCK ELEVATOR FROM THE GUARD

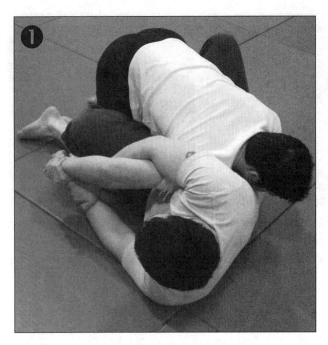

Jarrod has Derrick in the bent armlock from the bottom guard position. Derrick is resisting and Jarrod wants to roll Derrick over to get momentum to make the armlock work better. Jarrod jams his right leg under Derrick's left leg to start the elevator to roll him over.

Jarrod rolls back over his left shoulder (the side he's using to lock Derrick's right arm with). You can see how Jarrod is using his right leg to lift Derrick over in the elevator.

Jarrod rolls Derrick over and lands on top of him and applies the bent armlock.

HIP ROLL JUJI GATAME USING YOUR KNEE

The hip roll into Juji Gatame is one of the best ways to roll an opponent over and get him to give up. Sometimes, your opponent may be balled up so tight it's hard to get your leg jammed under his body.

In this case, you can get the hip roll by driving only your knee (and not your whole foot and leg) across and under your opponent's body. Derrick is standing above Jarrod.

Derrick uses his right knee to slide over Jarrod's back. Derrick uses his left hand to hook under Jarrod's right arm and shoulder. Derrick will launch himself over Jarrod and post on the top of his head for stability.

Derrick jams his right knee down and across Jarrod's right side as shown. Look at how Derrick's right foot is on top of Jarrod. Derrick posts on the top of his head for stability as he hooks his left arm under Jarrod's right and hooks his left leg under Derrick's head.

Derrick rolls over his right shoulder. Look at how Derrick's right knee is bent and hooked across Jarrod's right shoulder and under his right armpit. Derrick's left leg is hooking Jarrod's head. Derrick is pulling Jarrod's right arm in close to his chest as he stays round and rolls over his right shoulder. This forces Jarrod to roll over and onto his back.

Derrick rolls Jarrod over and applies the Juji Gatame for the tap out.

ROLLING BENT ARM LOCK THROW

This is an old one used in judo, sambo and jujitsu. Basically, you get your opponent locked up with a bent armlock then roll back over your shoulder and roll on top of him.

Jarrod has Derrick in a figure 4 bent armlock and steps in with his left foot to close the distance, in preparation to swing his right foot up into Derrick's left hip area.

Jarrod jams his right shin into Derrick's left inner thigh and hip. Jarrod rolls back and pulls Derrick down with him with the bent armlock still in place.

TECHNICAL TIP: Jarrod wants to stay as round as possible through this sequence. This is a rolling throw with the added benefit of getting your opponent in a bent armlock. The rounder you are when you roll, the better. Often, rolling your opponent adds momentum to a lock, which this is the case here.

Jarrod rolls back onto his left shoulder bringing Derrick over with him.

Jarrod rolls over on top of Derrick and finishes the bent armlock.

LOCK AND ROLL TO BENT ARMLOCK

Derrick has Jarrod in a body lock. He uses his left hand to grab Derrick's right wrist and his right hand to grab his own left wrist to form a figure 4 hold.

Jarrod turns slightly to his right and into Derrick, jamming his right knee and foot into Derrick's right upper leg, while starting to lean away from him toward the mat and flex (bend) his left leg.

Jarrod curls up and rolls to his left shoulder as he uses his right leg to hoist Derrick over with him. Look at how compact and round Jarrod is so he can roll Derrick more easily. Jarrod continues to have the figure 4 bent armlock in place.

Here's another rolling armlock that is a gutsy move not for the faint of heart.

Jarrod rolls over his left shoulder bringing Derrick with him as he rolls. Look at Jarrod's right leg and shin jammed in Derrick's right hip and upper leg and how it elevates Derrick over.

Jarrod completes his shoulder roll backward rolling Derrick over onto his back and into the bent armlock as shown. This is a gutsy, but unexpected move and may work on a good opponent.

PEEL AND BEND

Here's another situation where your opponent has you from behind in a body lock as Derrick is doing to Jarrod. The "peel" of this move is how Jarrod uses the figure 4 hold to peel or strip Derrick's hold off.

TECHNICAL TIP: If an opponent gets behind you and does a body lock, look out. He's probably setting you up for a backward throw and will soon launch you if you don't get away quick. An old wrestling move is to "peel" your opponent's hands off of you to escape his grip.

Jarrod moves to his right and keeps the figure 4 bent armlock in place.

Jarrod keeps moving to his right making a complete turn and starts to bend Derrick over from the pressure on his shoulder and elbow with the bent armlock. This is the "bend" of the peel and bend move.

Jarrod keeps moving to his right and finishes with a bent armlock similar to the CLAMP used earlier in this book. Jarrod can take Derrick to the mat from this position or get the tap out from here.

GERMAN PIN AND BENT ARMLOCK

TECHNICAL TIP: You can end the armlock here, but if an opponent is flexible or hard to armlock from this position, keep going with the German pin and armlock.

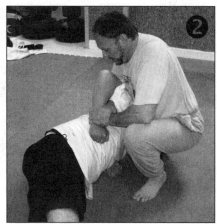

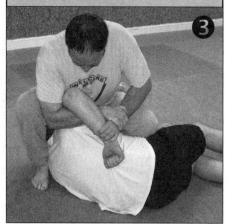

Steve has Greg in a figure 4 bent armlock from the top position. Often when an opponent doesn't know what to do or is tired, he lies flat on his front in the chicken position. This is fairly common .Take advantage of the situation!

Steve moves to his left toward the front side of Greg keeping the figure 4 bent armlock in tight. Steve pulls Greg's right elbow up and to his chest.

Steve steps over Greg's head and shoulders with his right leg and uses his left knee to jam in Greg's torso. He literally sits on Greg's right shoulder and chest.

I first saw this move in Europe used by a German judo athlete with great success, so we named it the German Pin. This should have been included earlier in the section, but better late than never.

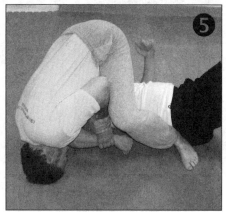

Steve rolls over and posts on the top of his head, while using his right leg to hook under Greg's neck and his left foot to push on Greg's right hip. This keeps Steve from falling too hard on the top of his head and is a good stabilizing position. Steve keeps the figure 4 bent armlock in place.

Steve posts on the top of his head for stability as he slides his left foot under Greg's right hip and lower back as shown.

Steve jams his left leg under Greg's back and rests on his knees while posting on the top of his head. This is a strong stable position and you can hold your opponent on his back with this move if you wish. Steve cranks on the bent armlock for the tap out.

JUJI SLIDE FROM THE SIDE

It's always a good day when you can get a Juji Gatame on an opponent. Here's another way to get Juji Gatame, this time starting from the side position. Bret has Scott is the side position as shown.

Bret moves to the top of Scott's head and quickly pops up into a squat. As he does this, Bret uses his right foot to hook over Scott's head and uses his right arm to scoop both of Scott's arms to his chest. Bret makes sure to be really close to Scott and squatting on Scott's left shoulder.

Bret uses both hands to scoop Scott's right arm into him. Doing this pulls both of Scott's arms into Bret's chest. Ultimately, Bret wants to lock Scott's left arm, but Bret will pull both arms in to his chest for maximum control.

Bret continues to scoop Scott's arms into his chest as he rolls back and applies the Juji Gatame. This move looks like Bret is locking both of Scott's arms, but in reality, Bret is locking Scott's left arm with the Juji.

JUMPIN' JUJI COUNTER TO STANDING STRAIGHT ARMLOCK

As in all jumping or "flying" armlocks or chokes, this is a gutsy move, but if you practice it enough, you can pull it off. Bret is attempting a straight armlock on Scott's right arm.

As he senses Bret is pulling him down, Scott uses his right hand to hook onto the back of Bret's neck and jumps, swinging his right leg and foot up and onto the left hip and side of Bret's body. As he is jumping, Scott starts to swing his left leg up and will go over Bret's head. When Scott jumps, his aim is to get the right side of his head as close as possible to Bret's left foot.

Scott lands and immediately starts to hook his right leg across Bret's body and his left leg up over his head. Scott's head is really close to Bret's left foot to help him roll Bret over. Scott is using his left hand to pull Bret's right arm to his body, while his right hand is still on the back of his neck, helping bend him over and pull him down to the mat.

Scott is in tight and in the process of rolling Bret into the Juji Gatame.

Scott rolls Bret into the Juji Gatame for the tap out.

KICKOVER BENT ARMLOCK IF OPPONENT TAKES YOU DOWN

If your opponent takes you to the mat by either a throw or takedown, the fight isn't over. If you get taken down, keep your cool and deal with the situation at hand. Dave shoots in for a single leg takedown and will take Alan to the mat.

Dave takes Alan to the mat. Alan rolls to the hip closest to Dave (in this case, his left hip) and uses his right hand to grab Dave's left elbow and uses his right hand to grab Dave's left shoulder, scooping them forward as he does.

Alan rolls onto his left side as shown after pulling Dave forward from the momentum of the takedown. Alan moves his right foot out and away to give him room to move.

Alan swings his right foot and leg over Dave's upper arm.

Alan swings his right leg over Dave's left arm, trapping it. Alan sits up as shown.

Alan sits up and applies the kickover bent armlock. Look at how Alan has his right leg over Dave's upper arm, pushing it down onto the mat. Alan uses his left hand to grab Dave's wrist and crank it forward.

Alan helps push Dave's left wrist forward by using his body to push forward. Alan's right bent knee traps Dave's arm and makes the arm crank more effective.

SIT OUT TO KICKOVER BENT ARMLOCK

Dave is riding Alan from the side in a classic wrestler's ride. Alan uses his left leg to sit out. As he does this, Alan uses his right arm to hook immediately above Dave's right arm.

Alan sits out and rolls across his lower back and buttocks into Dave, while using his left hand to grab Dave's right wrist and his left leg to start to kick over Dave's' right arm.

Alan continues to swing his body around and uses his left leg to kick over Dave's right arm. This is a fast movement and takes some practice to be able to do with skill.

Alan swings completely around and drives his left leg downward capturing Dave in the omo plata, ude garami or kickover bent armlock.

A final word or two as this section of the book closes. There are many ways to stretch, bend or crank your opponent's arm. Certainly, not every armlock known to mankind is on the pages of this book. Keep learning from every source you can. Experiment with a variety of moves, and then make a serious effort to see what works best for you. Talk with your coaches and teammates and get their advice. But, the main thing you have to do is practice hard and practice smart. Drill and work on your techniques until they are instinctive behavior and take your time to learn the fundamentals before moving on to more advanced applications of any submission technique. Keep training and now, let's turn our attention to chokes and strangles.

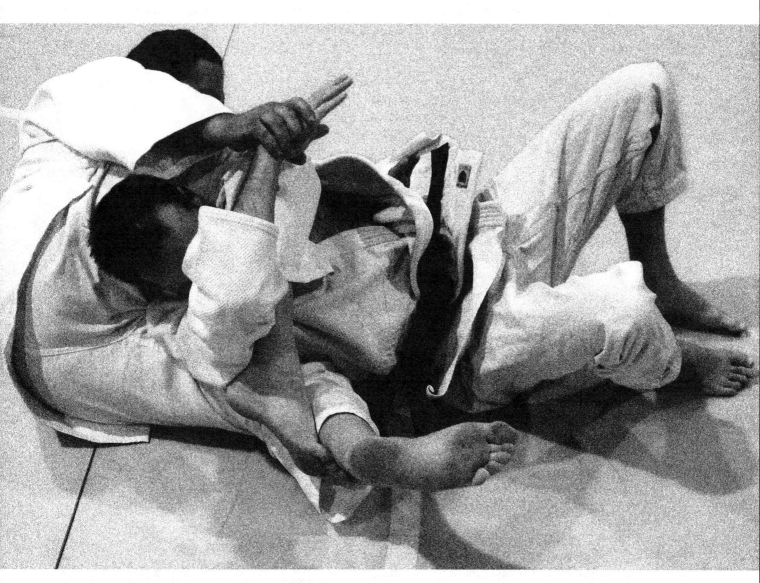

SECTION TWO: CHOKES & STRANGLES
THE GREAT EQUALIZER

Strangles and chokes are often thought of as "the great equalizer." Anyone of any size or strength level can win a fight if a strangle is applied effectively. Forcing an opponent to submit to a choke is proving dominance over him in a personal way. It's one thing to tap out from a joint lock, but it always seems more personal when somebody has to tap out from being strangled or choked. No matter what happens in another match on another day, if you've choked an opponent out, he'll never forget you and never forgive you. I don't recommend anyone strangling anyone else into unconsciousness or being choked unconscious yourself. It's dangerous and too risky to your health, but my point is that the act of being strangled is a very personal one, more so that even having a joint injured from an armlock or leglock.

There are a lot of strangles and chokes in this section, and certainly not every choke or strangle ever invented will appear on these pages. For a further serious, in-depth examination of the technical and theoretical aspects of strangles and chokes, I recommend you read my book GRAPPLER'S GUIDE TO STRANGLES AND CHOKES. However, the study of strangles is infinitely interesting and I hope you will take what's shown in this section (or in the entire book for that matter), work on it, add to it, and then make it work for you.

THE DIFFERENCE BETWEEN A STRANGLE AND A CHOKE

It's common to use the words "strangle" and "choke" interchangeably and this book is no different. Specifically, a "strangle" is the word that describes all the techniques that attack the neck and/or throat. A "choke" is more specific and refers to the action that obstructs or blocks the windpipe. Often, we refer to any strangle aimed against the side of the neck and the carotid arteries as just that, a strangle. Any strangle that closes, blocks or obstructs the front of the neck at the throat is often referred to as a choke. A choke makes an opponent gag and sputter and is often more painful than when you cut off the blood supply to his brain pressing against his carotid arteries. But really, we all use the words "choke" and 'strangle" to mean either action, so it really doesn't matter if you call it a "strangle" or call it a "choke;" we all know what is meant.

SAFETY FIRST: WHEN IN DOUBT, TAP OUT

It may be macho to make claims like "I won't tap, I'll take a nap!" or other statements, but the cold, hard facts are that strangles and chokes are dangerous. I (and many others) speak from experience when I say this. Like many other young men, and before people with common sense warned me, I would refuse to submit to a choke and was choked out cold more often than I care to admit. That was stupid. Take care of yourself and your training partners and opponents. Submit by tapping out, using a verbal signal or any pre-arranged form of signal of surrender. Live to fight not only another day, but in another match on the same day.

TECHNICAL TIP: Don't take shortcuts in learning the basics. Learning the basic application of the rear naked choke from the position shown on page 177 helps you learn how to do it right. You will quickly learn a variety of ways to get your opponent in this choke, but learn to do it this way from the start so you will have the technically correct (and most efficient) way to do this choke memorized. It's also important to point out that the figure 4 naked strangle attacks primarily (although not exclusively) the carotid arteries on the sides of your opponent's neck. This cuts off the blood supply and makes him pass out fairly quickly and this is why it's been called the "sleeper hold" for a long time. The second variation of the naked choke, the square lock naked choke, attacks primarily (although, again, not exclusively) your opponent's windpipe. The square lock naked choke hurts more and often makes your opponent gag. This form of the naked choke will also make your opponent pass out in fairly quick order, but it hurts him more when it does and, in my opinion, gives you the psychological advantage over him the next time you fight him.

REAR NAKED CHOKE FIGURE 4 VERSION

ALSO CALLED SLEEPER HOLD, NAKED STRANGLE OR HADAKA JIME

BASIC POSITION TO LEARN THIS CHOKE: Normally, you have to control your opponent's lower body and legs to get the best possible position on him for the choke to be effective. However, when first learning this strangle, do it the way Alan is doing here. Kneeling behind a partner when initially learning the rear naked choke puts Alan's body up and a bit higher than Chuck's seated body and gives him a better chance to learn the correct (and very important) arm and hand placement. Later you will see a variety of ways to control your opponent's body before applying a choke, but learn the fundamentally correct hand placement for your chokes from the start and they will serve you well.

Alan is kneeling on his right knee, with his left foot on the mat. He uses his right arm to reach around Chuck's neck.

Alan wraps his right arm tight around Chuck's neck and places his right hand on his left biceps. Alan moves his left hand up and over Chuck's head, wrapping around the back of the head and starting to force it forward and into his right arm.

The look on Chuck's face is the natural reaction to having a strong choke applied. When you apply a choke, apply it tight and with the intent of choking him quickly and effectively. Don't apply the choke loosely and then plan on tightening it. Apply it tightly and unrelentingly from the very start of your choke.

Alan places his left hand on the back of Chuck's head (palm on the back of the head) and closes the figure 4 grip. This basic variation places Alan's right upper arm on Chuck's right carotid and Alan's left lower arm on Chuck's left carotid in a classic 'sleeper hold" position.

BASIC FIGURE 4 NAKED CHOKE ARM AND HAND POSITION

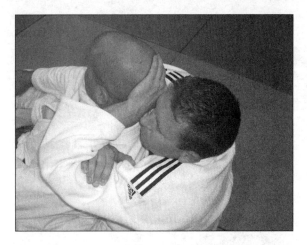

You can see how Chance's left palm is pushing on the back of Erik's head adding pressure into the choke. Chance's right hand is palm down and grabbing his left biceps. This is the basic figure 4 grip for the naked choke, but there are any number of variations that can (and will) work.

FIGURE 4 NAKED STRANGLE PUSHING WITH THE BACK OF YOUR HAND ON HIS HEAD

Josh is placing the back of his left hand against the back of Derrick's head in this variation of the naked strangle. Doing this "slices" against your opponent's head and helps drive his head down further into your choking arm.

TECHNICAL TIP: The figure 4 variation of the rear naked choke is one of the oldest strangles devised. Japanese jujutsu, and later judo, has taught this as one of the most fundamental and basic submission techniques for many years. This version of the naked strangle took a back seat to the newer version using a square lock (shown later in this section) for many years, but gained popularity again with its use in MMA events. This choke was popular in the legitimate professional wrestling of the early part of the 20th century, and is the classic "sleeper hold" seen for many years in pro wrestling. It's a basic skill, but a very important one. Don't take it for granted!

FIGURE 4 NAKED CHOKE AGAINST THE WINDPIPE

Sean is using his right forearm to press against the front of Mike's throat in this variation of the rear naked choke. This puts pressure on the front of neck at the throat on the windpipe rather than the side of the neck and the carotids. If your arms are long enough, you might favor this way of doing the figure 4 naked choke.

NAKED STRANGLE USING THE SQUARE LOCK GRIP

This choke is really a choke in the true sense of the word; it obstructs or blocks the airway or windpipe and is the kind of choke that makes an opponent gag. I believe this is a superior choke to the figure 4 variation because it hurts more, often makes your opponent gag and sputter and works quicker. Again, learn the basic form of the choke in this way so you can concentrate on learning and developing good control with your hands. You'll quickly learn to get your hooks in and control your opponent with your legs.

Josh shows the basic learning position for the rear naked choke or strangle using the square lock grip. Notice how Josh has grasped his hands together and locks the fingers and thumbs over the other hand forming a square. Josh has his right forearm near his wrist (using the bony protrusion just above the wrist) jammed in Derrick's throat immediately below his Adam's apple. Josh's choking hand (his right) is palm down and he makes sure not to bend his wrist so the choke will be more effective. Josh is using his left hand (palm up) to form the square lock and pull his right hand in tighter. He's also placed the right side of his head on the left side of Derrick's head, locking Derrick's head in tight between his arms, right shoulder and head.

TECHNICAL TIP: Remember to get "ear to ear" with your opponent. Use your head to trap your opponent's head and neck in place so you can choke him more effectively. Josh is jamming the right side of his head so the he's "ear to ear" with Derrick. Josh's right shoulder and arm are forming the other parts of the trap that keeps Derrick's head (and throat) from escaping or working loose. Trapping your opponent's head to get the choke in is important.

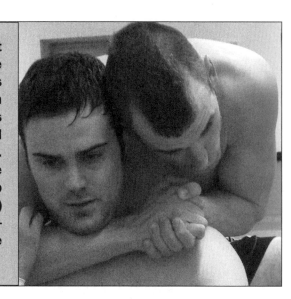

One of the big reasons the figure 4 grip is so popular in MMA is because a lot of fighters have trouble grabbing their hands when wearing gloves. Possibly, a reason they have trouble grabbing the gloves is because they don't practice the square grip for the naked choke as much as the figure 4 grip. This is because the figure 4 grip is the one most MMA fighters learn and work on most of the time. However, you can get a good grip using the square lock in MMA gloves with some practice and a desire to get a nastier, more effective choke on your opponent.

NAKED CHOKE USING MMA GLOVES

Josh is using the square grip wearing some Huck-Face MMA gloves. Use the square grip with MMA gloves and get your opponent to gag.

NAKED CHOKE USING MMA GLOVES WITH PALM UP PULLING HAND

If the MMA gloves are thick, you can grab the edges near your fingers to get a firm grip. I prefer the palm up grip for the left hand (the pulling hand on the hand that's choking your opponent) because you can get a better pull with the hand palm up. In the same way you can curl more weight on a barbell or dumb-bell, the palm up grip helps you pull your hand in tighter for the choke.

NAKED CHOKE USING MMA GLOVES WITH PALM DOWN PULLING HAND

You can get a good grip using your left hand (in this photo) with the palm down when gripping your choking hand. In a real fight, you may not have the opportunity to get your right hand palm up, so if that's the case, grab hold of your choking hand and work the choke in. the important thing to remember is to make sure your choking hand (in this case, the right hand) is palm down.

TECHNICAL TIP: The reason the naked choke is called "naked" is because you're not using any part of your opponent's jacket or clothing to choke or strangle him. This strangle was originally named "hadaka jime" in jujutsu and later (after 1882) judo. The Japanese word "hadaka" means "naked or bare." Any type of choke or strangle that did not use any part of an opponent's (or one's own) clothing was, and continues to be, called hadaka jime, or naked choke. The naked choke or strangle, whether it's in the form of a figure 4, using a square lock or what has come to be called the guillotine is pretty much the same type of choke. As long as you choke or strangle your opponent and don't use any clothing, it's a "naked" choke. A further definition is that any time you use a naked choke but trap your opponent's shoulder in the process of choking him, it's called a "kata gatame" or "kata jime." I refer to this choke as the neck triangle in this book. Kata gatame means, "shoulder lock" and kata jime means "shoulder choke." Actually, the word "jime" or "shime" means to tighten, press, squeeze, shut or close. The original concept or idea of a strangle or choke was to shut off the blood or oxygen to the brain, thus causing an opponent to go unconscious. In the combat-oriented approach to jujutsu, the whole point in strangling an opponent or enemy was to make him pass out or kill him. A little bit of history and understanding the original Japanese terminology goes a long way in understanding how, and why, chokes and strangles are what they are and why they work.

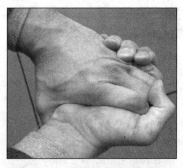

SQUARE GRIP (THUMBS LOCKED, BASIC GRIP)

The "square" grip or lock will be referred to often in this book. This is the basic square grip where you grasp your hands together with each thumb locking over the fingers. This is a secure, strong grip and one I recommend using when doing the rear naked choke or anytime you need to grab your hands together and not let your opponent get away or pry them apart. It's a tried and true grip that's useful in a variety of techniques, positions and situations, not only chokes and strangles.

SQUARE GRIP (THUMBS NOT LOCKED)

Often, you may use this variation of the square grip where you don't lock your thumbs over your fingers. This is a quicker way to get the grip and is also a good one.

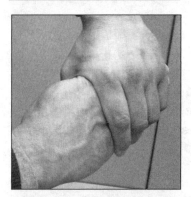

FINGERS GRIP OR KNIFE GRIP (PULLING HAND PALM DOWN)

If for some reason, the square grip doesn't work for you, grabbing your hands at the fingers and knuckles can work. The top hand (the left hand in this photo) pulls the choking hand (the right hand in this photo) into the throat or neck.

KNIFE GRIP (PULLING HAND PALM UP)

The right hand in this photo is the hand that actually presses against the neck or throat and is palm down. The left hand is the pulling hand and is palm up and grabbing the fingers of the right hand. This is a useful grip and really pulls the hand in to choke your opponent.

KNIFE GRIP (GRABBING EDGE OF HAND)

This is similar to the knife grip but instead of grabbing the fingers on your right hand, you grab the outside edge of your right hand with your left hand and pull your arm into his throat or neck.

HEAD GRAB FIGURE 4 REAR NAKED CHOKE

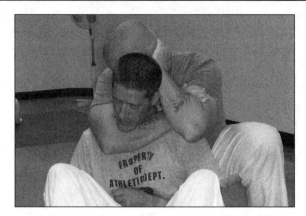

Eric places his left hand on the back or side of his head to add leverage to the figure 4 naked strangle on Travis.

SIDE NAKED CHOKE

While the rear naked choke is better known, the side version of this choke works pretty well also. Derrick is riding Mike from the side and jams his right knee across the left hip and side of Mike for support and stability. Derrick uses his left arm to reach around Mike's neck and apply the naked choke form the side. Look at how Derrick is jamming his head on the back of Mike's head and how Derrick's left elbow is directly under Mike's chin. This places the pressure on the side of Mike's neck and is a classic "sleeper hold" where you cut the blood supply off to the brain.

REAR NAKED CHOKE (SQUARE LOCK) AGAINST THE CAROTIDS

This is what many in law enforcement call a "neck restraint." It's still a strangle because Eric is using his right upper arm and forearm to squeeze the sides of Travis's neck. Eric's right elbow is directly under Travis's chin in this version of the naked choke.

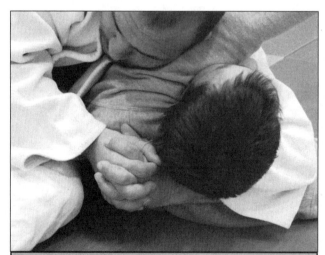

LACING YOUR FINGERS: Grasping your hands together by lacing your fingers isn't usually a strong grip. Your opponent can pry or pull your hands and grip apart too easily. Also, your hands aren't in a good position to change to another grip or grab your opponent in another way quickly. Having your fingers laced together is an awkward and not very strong of a grip. Not only that, trying to apply a choke with this grip often isn't successful, so it's recommend that you avoid using a grip where you lace your fingers together.

REAR NAKED CHOKE FROM THE RODEO RIDE

Derrick is on all fours and Josh applies the naked choke after controlling Derrick with the rodeo ride.

TECHNICAL TIP: One way of working out of and possibly escaping a rear naked choke is to arch or bridge out and quickly whip over to face your opponent. This can be countered by good use of leg wrestling or leg control. Here, Jeff is locking Roy and preventing him from getting away using a body triangle. Look how Roy is bridging to try to escape, but Jeff has good control with the body triangle and can concentrate on working his hands in for his choke or strangle.

Rolling your opponent creates momentum and helps you apply the choke with more control and force. Josh rolls Derrick over with the rodeo ride with the naked choke getting tighter as he rolls.

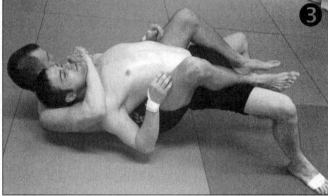

Sometimes you may roll your opponent over and he keeps rolling trying to escape. In this case, keep the choke on and make sure to keep your legs hooked in as shown. You may also keep him under control with a body triangle or other way of controlling him with your feet and legs. A good way of applying more pressure in the choke is for Josh to arch his back and drive his hips into the back of his opponent. This makes your opponent arch upward as shown and gives Josh more control in the choke.

ROLLING REAR NAKED CHOKE (FIGURE 4)

Josh controls Derrick with a near wrist ride using his left hand to control Derrick's left wrist and forearm.

Josh uses his left hand to pull Derrick's left hand and arm back as shown.

Josh uses his right leg to hook Derrick's left arm and his right hand to reach around Derrick's neck as shown.

TECHNICAL TIP: EVERYTHING'S A HANDLE
This move illustrates how every part of your opponent's body, your body or any part of his (or your) jujitsu uniform is a handle for you to grab, control and use to control him better.

Josh starts to form the figure 4 naked choke as he rolls over his right shoulder, forcing Derrick to roll with him.

Josh rolls Derrick over and uses his legs to scissor or triangle Derrick's left arm. Josh sinks the naked choke in to get the tap out.

FIGURE 4 REAR NAKED CHOKE WITH OPPONENT FLAT

Steve has Bill in a flat rodeo ride and uses his right hand to reach around Bill's neck.

Steve uses his left hand to form the figure 4 for the naked choke.

Steve forms the figure 4 and applies the choke. It's important for Steve to drive forward into Bill and force Bill's legs and hips to come off the mat. This "rocking" action forward produces more pressure in the choke.

BULLDOG HIM INTO THE NAKED CHOKE (SIDE NAKED CHOKE TO THE REAR NAKED CHOKE)

Mike is working the naked choke from the side on Chris. Mike may actually try to choke Chris from this position or he can use this to set Chris up. Either way, this is a good starting position for Mike. Mike is using his left hand and arm to reach under Chris's neck and Mike is using his right hand to grab his left hand in a square grip.

Mike keeps a solid hold with his hands around Chris's neck as he quickly jumps onto Chris's back and drives him forward to flatten him out. Mike uses both of his feet to push on Chris's hips and drives with his feet as he stretches Chris out for the "hanging" naked choke.

TECHNICAL TIP: CONTROL HIS LEGS AND LOWER BODY SO YOU CAN CONTROL HIS NECK
You usually have to control your opponent's lower body before you can apply an effective choke or strangle. It may sound crazy to some people, but the fact remains that you must control his lower body before controlling his upper body, principally his neck and throat. Don't rush in and try to get your hands around his throat until you control him so he won't get away or counter your attack. When you flatten your opponent on his front from the rodeo ride, make sure you dig your legs in, and drive him forward onto his face. Eric is rocking John's legs up in the air for maximum leg control. There are quite a few effective ways to break your opponent down so you can dig your choke in and I recommend you refer to my books published by Turtle Press **GRAPPLER'S BOOK OF STRANGLES AND CHOKES** or **GROUNDFIGHTING PINS AND BREAKDOWNS** for some detailed information on breakdowns.

RODEO RIDE TO REAR NAKED CHOKE

When you get your opponent's back and get your hooks in (your "hooks" are your legs), you have a better chance of controlling your opponent's lower body and legs with what many people call leg wrestling or leg control. Having good leg control is vital to setting your opponent up for a choke, especially from the rear. This photo shows Brian with his hooks in and rolling Tyler over to apply the rear naked choke.

DOUBLE TROUBLE-BODY TRIANGLE AND FIGURE 4 REAR NAKED CHOKE

Scott has Bret in a body triangle and a neck triangle using the figure 4 rear naked strangle.

BODY TRIANGLE FROM A RODEO RIDE

Scott adds additional pressure on Bret's torso by applying a body triangle from the rodeo ride. Not everybody has long enough legs or even if you do have long enough legs, sinking in a body triangle isn't always possible, but if you can lock your opponent up in this way, he's pretty well stuck there for a while. Experiment with this ride and see if you like it.

"HANG HIM HADAKA" NAKED CHOKE - SQUARE LOCK W/ FEET PUSHING ON FLAT OPPONENT'S HIPS

Here's an old photo of the author choking an opponent and using his feet to push on his hips to "hang" him with the naked choke.

TECHNICAL TIP: Pushing on your opponent's hips with your feet may not be for everybody, but if you can't sink your hooks in (get your leg in for control), this is a good way to get more pressure into your choke.

This is a useful way of getting the naked choke if you can't get your hooks in after getting your opponent's back. Josh is using his feet to push on Derrick's hips as he applies the rear naked choke. By pushing with your feet, you are stretching both your opponent out and literally hanging him with your choke. You can use the figure 4 grip but I prefer the square lock when using this control method with the feet on the hips.

HANG HIM HADAKA REAR NAKED CHOKE FROM A SEATED RODEO RIDE

HANG HIM HADAKA REAR NAKED CHOKE IF OPPONENT ARCHES TO ESCAPE

Jeff is arching to try to escape from Jarrod's choke and Jarrod uses both feet to push downward on Jeff's hips to hang him with the rear naked choke.

Jarrod is using the rear naked choke on Jeff and using both feet to push downward onto Jeff's hips. Look at how Jeff's head is trapped by Jarrod's arms and upper body. The action of trapping the head and pulling up and in on the throat along with the action of pushing on the hips with his feet enables Jarrod to "hang" Jeff.

REAR NAKED FIGURE 4 CHOKE WHEN YOUR OPPONENT TRIES TO ESCAPE YOUR BODY TRIANGLE

Sean has Mike in a body triangle and Mike is reaching to grab Sean's right foot to try to pry his legs apart and escape. Sean hasn't committed himself to trying a choke or armlock from either the left or right side waiting to see what Mike will do. The body triangle is a great "ride" and way to control your opponent.

Since Mike used his right hand to reach down to pull Sean's right foot away, Sean will take advantage of the situation and use his right hand to reach around Mike's neck to start the choke. Mike committed his right hand and arm to free him from the body triangle and this gave Sean the opening he needs to start the choke from that side.

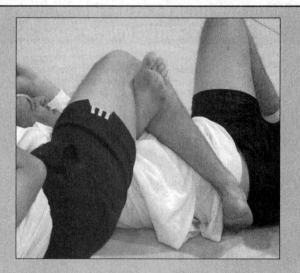

Sean works the figure 4 naked choke in on Mike using his body triangle to maintain firm control of Mike with a neck triangle and a body triangle. This type of situation gives you total control of your opponent's body and he knows it.

TECHNICAL TIP: When you form the triangle, place your extended foot (right foot in this photo) under your opponent's body as shown to add more control. Your extended foot can also be placed under your opponent's leg as well depending on where you form the triangle. Anchoring your foot like this will give you much better control over your opponent and add more pressure to your triangle.

BODY TRIANGLE ROLL FROM GUARD INTO FRONT FIGURE 4 NAKED CHOKE

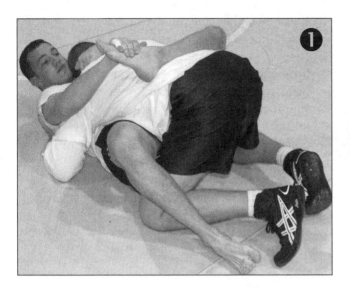

Scott has Bret in his guard and uses his left hand to help pull his left foot up and around Bret's waist.

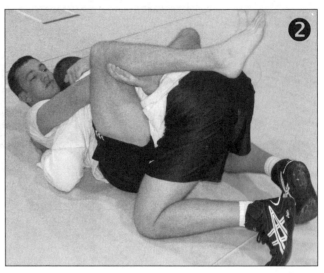

Scott forms the triangle with his legs on Bret's waist.

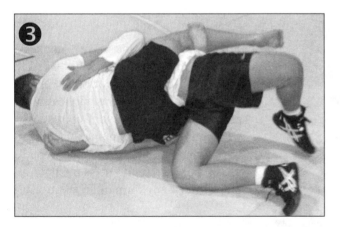

Scott squeezes hard on Bret's torso, taking as much steam out of Bret as possible. Scott rolls Bret over to Scot's left. As Scott rolls, he starts to form a front naked figure 4 choke on Bret's neck.

Scott rolls Bret over with both the figure 4 naked choke and the body triangle in place.

BODY TRIANGLE HOLDS HIM THERE TO APPLY A CHOKE FROM THE FRONT

You can apply about any type of choke or strangle (using his jacket or not using his jacket) from the front of your opponent if you control him with a body triangle. This is a good way of keeping him there to give you time to work your choke in. Make sure to apply a lot of pressure on your opponent's midsection when you put on the body triangle. Squeeze him and suck as much air out of him as possible. The body triangle is a good way to take a lot of fight out of your opponent so you can more easily apply a submission technique or break him down further.

FRONT NAKED CHOKE WITH LEG SCISSORS FROM THE GUARD

Jeff is applying the naked choke on Chris from the front. The naked choke can be applied from most any direction or angle and this application proves it. Controlling your opponent with your legs is vital in making your choke more effective, whether you use a body triangle, scissors hold, grapevine or any form of leg control.

TECHNICAL TIP: Not everybody can get his or her legs formed into a body triangle. Your legs may not be long enough or you may not have the flexibility necessary. In this case, one way you can control him is to trap your opponent with a body scissors as shown in this photo.

TURN AND CHOKE

This is a useful application of the naked strangle in self-defense, law enforcement or bar bouncer situations. Steve confronts Larry.

Larry uses his left hand to pull on Steve's right elbow and uses his right hand to quickly push on Steve's left shoulder. This turns Steve slightly. As he does this, Larry moves to his left and behind Steve immediately.

ALTERNATE VIEW

The angle has changed so you can get a front view of the action.

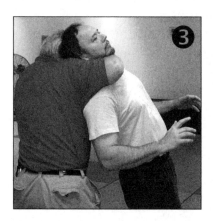

As soon as Larry turns Steve, Larry moves behind him and applies the rear naked choke. For maximum gag effect, Larry is using the square lock method of the choke.

Larry walks Steve backward to tighten the choke and to move Steve out the door or to the floor.

BOUNCER'S REAR NAKED CHOKE
Larry has turned Bill around and applied a naked strangle, placing his choking hand on the back of his head. Larry has his other arm free to ward off other attackers or clear the way to get a rowdy customer out of the bar.

TAP OUT TEXTBOOK

FIGURE 4 NECK AND SHOULDER CRANK FROM THE GUARD

Scott has Bret in his guard and pulls Bret's head to Scott's left side. Scott uses his left hand to hook under Bret's right arm and shoulder.

Doing this traps Bret's head under Scott's left armpit as shown here. Scott uses his left hand to grab onto his right biceps to start to form the figure 4.

Scott forms his figure 4 with his hands and uses his right hand to hook over Bret's right shoulder as shown. This drives Bret's head forward in a neck crank and gets the tap out.

PANCAKE OR SPRAWL TO FRONT FIGURE 4 NAKED STRANGLE

If your opponent grabs your leg to set up a go-behind to get your back, this move is useful.

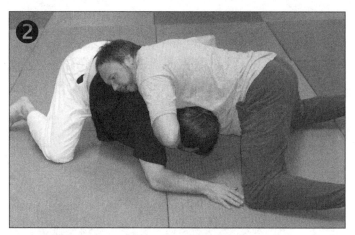

Steve shoots or sprawls back and uses his left hand to reach around Bill's neck.

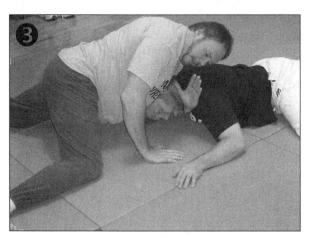

Steve's left forearm is across Bill's throat.

Steve forms the figure 4 grip with his arms.

Steve sinks in the choke and rolls a bit to his left to add pressure to the choke. Steve makes it a point to use his left hand, which is placed palm down on Bill's back, to press hard as he rolls. This makes for a tighter choke.

> **One of the best counters against an opponent who shoots in for a leg grab or takedown is a choke from a sprawl.**

FIGURE 4 NAKED CHOKE POLISH WHIZZER VARIATION

Alan locks onto Dave with a front headlock trapping Dave's left arm. Alan pulls Dave forward onto his chest to control him better.

Alan forms a figure 4 arm position for his naked choke as shown.

Alan rolls to his left hard and whips Dave over with him.

Alan squeezes hard with his figure 4 naked choke and rolls back into Dave as shown to add more pressure to the choke and get the tap out.

SIT THROUGH FIGURE 4 NAKED CHOKE FROM WRESTLER'S RIDE

Derrick is at the side of Kirk and uses his right arm to reach around Kirk's neck as shown.

Derrick forms a figure 4 naked choke from this side ride and posts his left leg out wide to his left for stability.

Derrick uses his right leg to sit through and applies the naked choke. This sit through forces Kirk forward and into the direction of the choke.

ROLLING FIGURE 4 NAKED CHOKE FROM THE TOP

Jeff uses his right hand to reach around and under Chris's neck to start the choke.

Jeff forms the figure 4 naked choke from the top.

Here's another view of how Jeff has the top position and choke in place.

Jeff starts to roll to his left with the figure 4 naked choke in place.

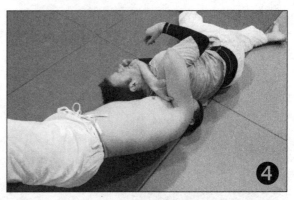

Jeff rolls over his left side hard and fast and whips Chris over with him. Jeff keeps the choke in and gets the tap out.

HEAD PULL TO NAKED CHOKE

Steve has Bill flattened out and uses his left hand to pull up on Bill's forehead to open him up for the choke.

Steve quickly moves his right arm in and around Bill's neck to get the naked choke.

CROSS FACE TO NAKED CHOKE USING A HAND

Steve has Bill flattened out in a rodeo ride and uses his right hand to cross face Bill. Steve uses the cross face to lift Bill's head up.

As Steve cross faces Bill with his right hand, he uses his left hand to sink in the choke.

Steve grabs his hands together in a square lock and finishes the choke for the tap out.

WRESTLER'S RIDE TO THE NAKED CHOKE (FLATTEN HIM OUT AND CHOKE HIM)

Drew is riding Brad and uses his right leg to trap Brad's left lower leg and foot as shown. Drew is also using his left hand to grab inside Brad's right thigh for control of Brad's body during the ride. Drew's left hand (not shown) reaches under Brad's left arm and grabs Brad's left wrist for a near wrist ride.

Drew uses his left hand to pull in on Brad's left wrist that he has grabbed to flatten Brad out. To help flatten Brad onto his front, Drew uses his right hand to pull Brad's knee out and drives Brad forward onto his chest. This flattens Brad onto his front as shown.

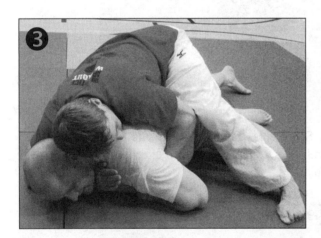

Drew uses his right hand to reach around Brad's neck as he drives Brad forward. Look at how Drew is starting to get onto Brad's back.

Drew grabs his hands in a square lock (or a figure 4 grip if he wishes) and secures the naked choke. Look at how Drew is using his feet to push on Brad's hips. Drew does this because he can't get his feet in quick enough for the rodeo ride, so he is using his feet to push on Brad's hips to make the choke tighter.

GUILLOTINE CHOKE (BASIC)

Anytime you apply the naked choke from the front, it's referred to as the "guillotine" for pretty obvious reasons. Mike is showing the basic application of the guillotine on Derrick. There are some major points to look at when doing this choke. First, the guillotine works very well when you have your opponent's head tucked tight to your side as Mike has Derrick's head tight on his right side. Derrick's head is tucked up and into Mike's right armpit as well. Try to have your opponent's head on your side and hip as you apply pressure with the choke. This choke works best when your forearm (Mike's right forearm) is pressed tightly up and against the front of the neck at the throat. Mike's goal is to trap Derrick's head on his right hip, reach over and around Derrick's head and slide his right forearm in against Derrick's throat. Mike will grasp his hands together in a square lock (or any firm grip) and apply the choke.

TECHNICAL TIP: This bottom view shows how Mike has used his right forearm to jam against Derrick's throat. Mike uses the square grip, knife grip or any firm hand grip to lock his hands in tight to apply the choke. Sometimes, it might not be possible to get a good square grip with your hands. In these situations, get the best grip possible so that you can drive your forearm into your opponent's throat as strongly as possible. To apply pressure to the choke, Mike can drive his right forearm up and into Derrick's throat. This traps the head and makes the choke happen. The guillotine is also a good neck crank and even if your opponent toughs it out or escapes from it, he's worse the wear for having it put on him.

GUILLOTINE (NAKED CHOKE) AGAINST A DOUBLE LEG ATTACK

TECHNICAL TIP: Derrick is applying his guillotine by wrapping his left arm all the way around Jeff's neck and the pressure will be mainly on the sides of Jeff's neck at the carotid arteries. This illustrates how the guillotine can be done as a choke (with the forearm jammed in against the throat and attacking the windpipe) or as a strangle (with the arm wrapped around the neck and attacking the carotid arteries.

Jeff attacked Derrick with a double leg or single leg takedown and as Derrick sprawled back, he applied the guillotine. This is a pretty common situation.

BASIC GUILLOTINE (NAKED CHOKE) FROM CLOSED GUARD

Bret is using the guillotine on Scott from a closed guard. You can see how Bret has Scott's head at his right side and has his right arm wrapped around Scott's neck. As Bret drives his right forearm into Scott's throat, he uses his legs to keep Scott from getting away and pull Scott's body in tight. Bret rolls back onto the back of his right shoulder as he uses his right arm to pull in tight on Scott's throat and neck to tighten the choke.

GUILLOTINE WITH SHOULDER AND ARM TRAP FROM CLOSED GUARD

Bret has Scott in a tight guillotine using his left arm which is reached around Scott's left shoulder, head and neck. Bret grabs his hands together and lifts Scott up and into him getting the choke.

STANDING GUILLOTINE (FRONT NAKED CHOKE)

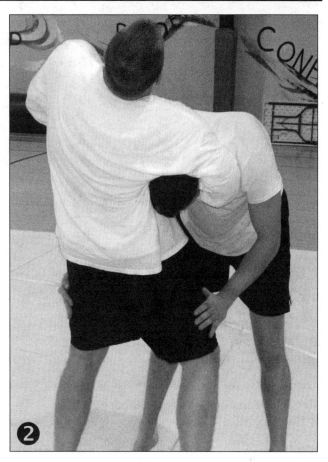

From a standing position, Bret uses his right hand to reach over Scott's head.

Bret drives his hips forward and arches his back as shown. This forces Scott's head forward, cranking the neck as well as choking him. This is popular in MMA where Bret may have Scott backed up into the cage, keeping him from moving away or escaping.

GUILLOTINE PULL TO GUARD

Bret starts the standing guillotine with his right arm hooked over Scott's neck and head.

Bret jumps up and onto Scott and starts to wrap his legs around Scott. Bret still has good control of Scott's head.

TECHNICAL TIP: It's important for Bret to jump into Scott, swinging forward and onto him really hard so Bret can be as round as possible. By doing this, Bret forces Scott to bend over more so the fall to the mat isn't as hard on Bret. This jumping into Scott and forcing him to bend forward rather than merely jumping onto the front of Scott also makes the choke tighter once they go to the mat.

Bret pulls Scott onto the mat and finishes the choke for the tap out. Bret makes sure to close his guard or may even form a body triangle to make the choke tighter and keep Scott from getting away.

STAND-UP GUILLOTINE FROM THE GUARD

Derrick has Mike in the guillotine from the guard position.

Derrick moves his right knee and sits on his left buttock. This puts him in position so that he can get up onto his right knee. Derrick makes sure to uses his right shoulder to drive down on Mike's head as he pulls Mike's head in tighter.

Derrick gets up onto his right knee and uses his right forearm to pull up on Mike's head. Look at how Mike's head is trapped tightly under Derrick's right armpit. Derrick drives his hips forward arching his back. This causes the choke to happen. Derrick can continue and stand up if necessary.

GUILLOTINE TO COWCATCHER

Bret has Scott in a guillotine as shown.

If, for some reason, Bret can't get Scott to submit from the choke or neck crank, Bret uses both of his arms to scoop under Scott's arms. Bret grabs his hands together and pulls up and into him creating a strong shoulder lock and neck crank.

GUILLOTINE (NECK TRIANGLE) WITH BODY TRIANGLE

Bret has a tight shoulder lock and guillotine on Scott and makes is tighter with his body triangle.

GRABBING THE JACKET WHEN DOING GUILLOTINE IN A GI

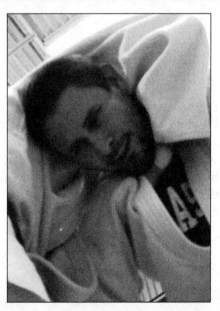

Derrick uses his right arm to reach over the back of Jeff's head and uses his right hand to grab Jeff's right lapel. This traps Jeff's head and forms a tight choke.

GUILLOTINE IN A GI FROM THE BELT LINE DEFENSE

This set up puts an opponent's head in place to get him in the guillotine. Derrick is on his back and rolls to his left side, placing his right knee across Roy's belt line or midsection and jamming his right shin at the belt line.

Derrick's right shin is jammed across Roy's midsection. Derrick uses his right hand to pull Roy down low as shown. Derrick pulls Roy to the right, in the direction of Derrick's right hip.

Derrick uses his right hand and arm to reach over Roy's neck and head, pulling him down and forward and starting to slide his right forearm under Roy's chin on the throat.

TECHNICAL TIP: The guillotine works best if you can get your opponent's head to your hip and under your armpit so you can wrap your arm around his head more deeply and use your hand to grab his lapel. This creates a strong choke, using his lapel like a rope to choke him.

Derrick grabs his hands together to form a square lock (or uses his right hand to grab the inside of Roy's left lapel for a lapel choke) as he rolls Roy to Derrick's right side. Doing this, Derrick moves Roy over by Derrick's right hip and allows his right hand to get deep around Roy's neck and throat for the choke. Roy's head is trapped under Derrick's right armpit. Derrick rolls back onto his back pulling Roy's head in and as he rolls back, Derrick cinches in the choke for the tap out.

POWER HALF AND NECK CRANK FROM GUARD IF GUILLOTINE DOESN'T WORK

Bret is in Scott's guard and has resisted Scott's guillotine. Scott uses his left hand (the one that he used to reach around Bret's head and neck) to let go of the guillotine and scoop up and under Bret's right shoulder.

Scott uses his right hand to grab his left hand and form a square grip, driving his left forearm across the back of Bret's head to secure the power half.

GUILLOTINE WITH HAND SLICE

GUILLOTINE FROM THE TOP POSITION

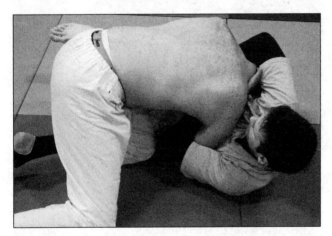

Chris uses his right arm to reach over Jeff's head to start the guillotine. To make the choke work, Chris uses his left hand to reach over Jeff's right upper arm and slides his left hand up on the right side of Jeff's neck as shown. Chris uses his right hand to grab his left wrist to create pressure against Jeff's throat. Chris uses his left hand to slice or drive down on Jeff's head to create pressure.

Chris uses his right arm to reach over Jeff's neck to start the guillotine. To create pressure for the choke, Chris uses his right hand to grab his left hand. Chris uses his head to post on the mat for stability as he applies pressure for the tap out.

COWCATCHER TO GUILLOTINE

This is the reverse of the guillotine to the cowcatcher. Bret has Scott locked up in a cowcatcher.

Bret releases his grip.

Bret uses his right hand to slide under Scott's neck and throat and uses his right forearm (very near his wrist) to jam up and into Scott's trachea. Bret should also grab the inside of his shorts to extra leverage. Bret uses his left arm to wing Scott's right arm as shown. All the while, Bret pulls Scott forward as Bret rolls onto his back and shoulders, adding pressure to the choke.

ODD SIDE GUILLOTINE AGAINST OPPONENT'S DEFENSE OR A GUARD PASS

Usually, the guillotine works best if you apply pressure on his head and neck and put all your effort into the specific side. This set up for the guillotine is an odd one where you apply the choke with your opponent's head more on your side.

TECHNICAL TIP: A common, and effective, way of defending against or stopping and easing the pressure of your opponent's guillotine is to move to the side so that your body is in an "L" position in relation to your opponent. Mike is easing the pressure of Derrick's guillotine in this photo.

While Mike (on top) is in a pretty good defensive position to keep Derrick from applying more pressure with the guillotine, Derrick can still pull it off. To get the choke form the "odd" side, he must curl his body in tightly as possible resembling a shrimp (as shown). Derrick must use his right forearm to forcefully pull up and in on Mike's throat and neck. The pressure is more on the left side of Mike's neck against the carotid artery and not the front of the throat as is often the case in the guillotine. While not the most ideal position to apply the guillotine from, this still can work. Even if it doesn't, Derrick can keep Mike here and keep him from passing his guard or getting past his legs further to start his own offensive series of moves.

ALAN'S PREDICAMENT (GUILLOTINE WITH FOOT ASSIST)

Alan has Dave locked in from the top with a head and arm trap and front guillotine as shown with his hands locked on his right (Dave's left). Alan's right leg is posted out to the side for stability and to start his sit through.

Alan uses his left leg to sit through and moves in close to Dave's body with his left hip. As he does this, Alan places his right foot on Dave's left hip as shown.

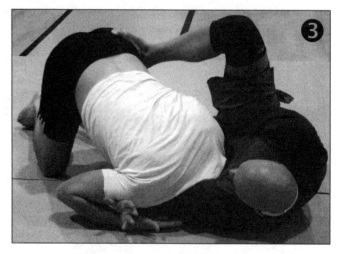

Alan rocks Dave forward (onto Alan's left shoulder) and uses his right foot to push Dave to Alan's left. This forward and leftward movement along with Alan's hard squeeze on the choke gets the tap out.

JUMPING OR PIGGY BACK REAR NAKED CHOKE

Sometimes, it's possible to get behind your opponent, jump on his back and sink in a rear naked choke (or a lapel choke of any type). This photo taken at the Shingitai Jujitsu Open shows a grappler who jumped on his opponent and almost forced him to tap out from a rear naked choke. Notice that the guy on his opponent's back has his feet (hooks) in and is doing a good job controlling the standing man's body (even though he's standing). You can see how the standing athlete still has his arms at his side and hasn't had time to react to his opponent's bold move of jumping on his back and trying to choke him.

PIGGY BACK REAR NAKED CHOKE USING THE SQUARE GRIP

Chuck is applying a piggy back naked choke on Bret using the square grip. After years of training, fighting and coaching on the mat, I've seen a lot of amazing things, but am constantly impressed at the ingenuity of athletes who will stretch the boundaries of what is possible. It's a gutsy move, but it can work. Remember, if you're the man trying the move; keep your hooks in and keep your hands locked tight around his neck. The standing man may throw you down, fall to his knees or any number of things, so be prepared to ride him until he taps out.

JUMPING FIGURE 4 REAR NAKED CHOKE

TECHNICAL TIP: Josh can step up quickly onto Ben or literally jump onto his back, but he must make sure that Ben is turned enough so that he can get past Ben's arm and have a free open "shot" at Ben's back.

Josh and Ben are standing facing each other. A good way for Josh to start his jump onto Ben's back is for Josh to cross-grip or use a Russian tie-up on the side he wants to jump. Josh intends to jump to his right onto the left side of Ben so Josh is using his left hand to pull Ben's left arm to Josh's left hip. Josh is using his right hand to hook Ben's neck in a collar grip as an anchor.

Josh jumps onto Ben's back and immediately forms a figure 4 naked choke. In this situation, Josh's right arm is around Ben's neck. Josh might be able to finish the choke from this position, but in many cases, Ben will fall to the mat or ground.

Often, the force of Josh jumping onto Ben's back and applying the choke will force Ben to fall. Josh tries to make Ben (and himself) fall to the right so he can keep a tighter hold of Ben's neck and throat with his figure 4 grip. Actually, it doesn't matter all that much which direction Ben falls other than directly backward, because if Ben falls directly back, it will be a really hard fall for Josh! Josh's best bet is to try to get Ben to fall forward and in a direction that the choke works.

NAKED CHOKE FROM THE HEAD AND ARM PIN

Jarrod has David in a head and arm hold and switches into front figure 4 naked choke.

Here's a closer view of how Jarrod is using his right arm to wrap around David's head as he places his right hand (palm down) on his left biceps. Jarrod bends his left elbow and raises his left hand toward his head to make the choke work. Jarrod can also place his left hand on the side or back of his head to add more pressure.

TECHNICAL TIP: DON'T LOSE CONTROL-BETTER SAFE THAN SORRY
Whenever you have good control of your opponent, don't let him out unless you have to, or believe you have him held tight enough to move to another technique without losing control. Jarrod has Mike in a solid chest hold or side position (opposite page) and can keep him there for the win in judo or pick up hold-down points in sambo or other forms of grappling. Jarrod can keep Mike in this position for a long time and take a lot of fight out of him by keeping him there and applying pressure. Jarrod wants to not only hold Mike to the mat, but also make it so uncomfortable that he's taken a lot of the fight out of Mike. When you know you can move to a submission technique from here, do it, but not until you know you can move from one stable position to the next without losing control of your opponent and letting him off the hook.

SIDE NECK CRANK AND TRAP CHOKE FROM CHEST HOLD

Jarrod has Mike in a chest hold or side position.

Jarrod uses his left arm to hook under Mike's neck and his left hand to grab the front of Mike's left shoulder. This cranks Mike's head forward as shown.

Jarrod adds pressure by driving his left shoulder forward on the right side of Mike's head. He moves his right hand to start to grab Mike's head.

Jarrod uses his right hand to grab Mike's head and his left shoulder to continue to drive Mike's head forward. This causes a neck crank and often gets the tap out.

To get the choke, Jarrod moves his right hand to the top of Mike's head and grabs his left sleeve, while grabbing Mike's right lapel and pulling it with his left hand.

FOREARM CHOKE FROM SIDE POSITION

Forearm chokes are basically naked chokes, but you don't usually have both arms around your opponent's neck. Bret has Scott is a side hold and wedges his right forearm down and across Scott's throat. Look at how Bret is using his right knee jammed on the left side of Scott's head to trap it and keep it from moving. Bret is using his left arm to scoop up under Scott's right shoulder and pull it in. This action of trapping the head with the knee and trapping the far (right in this case) shoulder keeps him from moving and makes working the forearm choke in better.

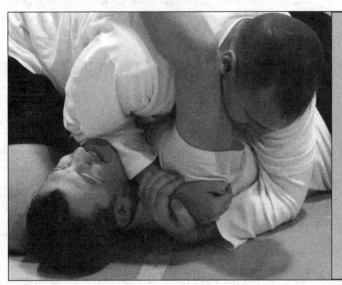

TECHNICAL TIP: Bret's left elbow is resting on the mat and his left forearm is scooping under Scott's right shoulder. His right hand is palm up, forcing Scott's right shoulder to come up off the mat a bit which gives Bret a solid base for the choke. Bret uses his left hand to grab his right wrist as he drives his right forearm across the right side of Scott's neck at the carotid artery, and then flat down across his throat quickly, like slicing bread. As you can see by Scott's face, this really punishes him and even if he's tough enough to avoid the choke, Bret is in a great position to go on to another submission technique or simply hold Scott to the mat.

SHOULDER CHOKE ON TRACHEA FROM THE CHEST HOLD OR SIDE POSITION

Jon is using the point or tip of his shoulder to drive into the front of Steve's throat as he holds him with the chest hold. This blocks the trachea and gets a gag reaction from Steve for the tap out. It may not always work, depending on the thickness of your shoulders and of your opponent's neck, but even if it doesn't choke him, it punishes him and makes think more about his head and neck than being stuck in the hold, which will help keep him held down that much longer.

SHOULDER CHOKE ON CAROTID ARTERY FROM SIDE POSITION

From a more direct side position, Jon can drive the tip of his left shoulder into the side of Steve's neck cutting off the carotid artery.

SHOULDER CHOKE FROM HALF GUARD

Josh is driving his left shoulder into the right side of Nikolay's neck from the half guard. This may not always choke your opponent, but it creates a diversion so you can go on to another move. It's a good way of "parking" him where you want him while you figure out what to do from here or move to your next set up, submission or position.

TRIPOD TO PLANT HIM HIGH ON HIS SHOULDERS AND GIVE SOME NECK AND HEAD PRESSURE

Chris is in Alan's closed guard and drives into Alan's chest so that he is tilted high on his shoulders as shown. Chris is driving into Alan with his feet wide on the mat for a stable base and has his chest and left shoulder jammed into Alan's chest and neck. Chris may be able to jam his left shoulder tighter into Alan's neck or throat from this position, but what this really does is punish Alan and soften him up for another move. This is a good tactical reaction to a guy who is good at fighting from the closed guard.

TECHNICAL TIP: The high tripod is a good way to break open your opponent's closed guard, or at least force him to give you some working room. When you use the tripod, make sure to have a good base and keep your legs wide and feet planted on the mat.

NECK TRIANGLE WITH A TRIPOD BASE AGAINST THE CLOSED GUARD

TECHNICAL TIP: The tripod from a closed guard is a good position to apply the neck triangle from. You can see how much pressure Drew is exerting into Chris's neck and head. This in combination with the tight neck triangle produces a tight choke. Drew's right upper arm is pressed hard against the left side of Chris's neck. Drew's right forearm under Chris's head creates a strong trap that enables Drew to drive hard with his head against Chris's right upper arm. Drew has a strong square grip and squeezes Chris hard to get the tap out.

Here's a good example of how to get a choke when you tripod and plant your opponent high on the back of his shoulders. As Drew tripods up on his feet, he drives his upper body into Chris and works in a neck triangle. The neck triangle is really effective from this position. (More on the neck triangle later in this section.)

SCISSORS CHOKE FROM HEAD AND ARM HOLD

Steve has Bill in a head and arm (scarf) hold.

Steve's right arm is already around Bill's head so Steve uses his left forearm to jam onto the front of Bill's neck on the throat. Steve uses his left hand to grab his right biceps or upper arm. Steve uses his right hand to grab his left forearm as shown. Doing this creates a scissors position with Steve's arms with Bill's head in the middle. Steve squeezes his arms together and gets the tap out.

If your opponent is wearing a jacket as Bill is, you can use your left hand to grab the left lapel of his jacket. Make sure to grab as deeply as possible so you can get your left forearm wedged across his throat better.

Steve's left hand is grabbing Bill's left lapel and his left forearm is driving down on Bill's throat. Steve uses his right hand to grab his left forearm creating a scissors hold and getting the tap out.

REACH OVER CHOKE (FIGURE 4 NAKED CHOKE FROM THE SIDE) FROM THE HALF GUARD

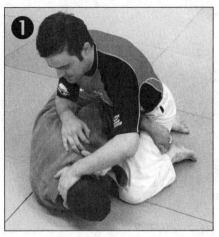

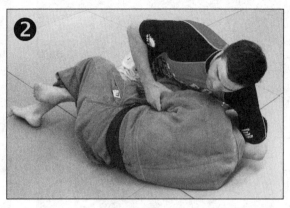

Kirk has shrimped in and worked a half guard on Derrick. Derrick moves his left hand over and around Kirk's head.

Derrick uses his left hand to reach around Kirk's head and neck and uses his right arm to grab Kirk's left arm as shown.

Derrick uses his right hand to push Kirk's left arm forward.

Derrick uses his left hand to reach deep around Kirk's head and will form the figure 4 grip with his hands.

Derrick starts to form the figure 4 grip for the naked choke.

Derrick sinks in the figure 4 grip and uses his left forearm, which is jammed into Kirk's throat, to choke him.

FIGURE 4 NAKED CHOKE (ARM TRIANGLE) FROM HALF GUARD

Josh keeps moving his left hand down and snakes it over Nikolay's left upper arm and under Nikolay's neck.

Josh is on top of Nikolay, but Nikolay has Josh in a half guard or is using his legs to scissor Josh's right leg. Josh has his left hand under Nikolay's head.

Josh uses his right hand to grab Nikolay's left arm and push it down and across Nikolay's body.

ALTERNATE VIEW

Here's another view of how Josh has moved his right hand down and under Nikolay's neck.

ALTERNATE VIEW

This shows how Josh has formed the figure 4 naked choke from this position and applies the choke for the tap out.

Josh uses his left hand to reach over Nikolay's head. Josh uses his right hand to grab his left biceps. This forms a figure 4 naked choke from this position.

FIGURE 4 NAKED CHOKE FROM THE SIDE WITH OPPONENT ON ALL FOURS

Roy is at Chas's right side and uses his left hand to reach under Chas's right armpit. Roy's left hand is palm forward as shown.

Roy uses his left hand to grab his right biceps to form the figure 4 naked choke from this position.

THE NECK TRIANGLE (KATA GATAME, THE SHOULDER LOCK)

Bill is using the neck triangle on Steve in the basic application of this choke.

Alan shows how you can work a neck triangle from different positions. In this situation, Alan is in a north south and to the top of Scott.

NECK TRIANGLE ON KNEE AND POSTING LEG (KATA GATAME)

Derrick is doing kata gatame (the shoulder lock) on Kelly in the time-honored way it's done in judo and jujitsu. This basic way to learn this move is excellent and teaches you a great deal on how to make it work. Derrick has placed his bent right leg along the right side of Kelly's body and jammed his right knee under his right shoulder. Doing this forces Kelly's shoulder up off the mat a bit. Derrick's left leg is extended to his left and posted for stability. This is a strong base and gives him stability and mobility to work the neck triangle in place. In judo, this is taught as a hold-down, but it does double duty as a good choke as well, which is how it has been taught in jujitsu for many years.

You can see how Derrick has his right arm squeezing against the left side of Kelly's neck as he uses his head to drive into Kelly's right arm. Derrick is creating pressure on the left side of Kelly's neck with his right forearm and pressure on the right side of Kelly's neck with Kelly's own right upper arm and shoulder. Not only is this a good choke, it's a good neck crank and hold-down.

TECHNICAL TIP: There are basically two ways to perform the neck triangle. The first is when you wrap your arm around your opponent's neck and grasp your hands together near his shoulder. Bret is driving his head into Scott's right upper arm as he uses his right hand to wrap around Scott's neck. Trapping Scott's right upper arm and shoulder and pinning them to the right side of Scott's head makes his grip around Scott's neck tighter. Scott is being choked by his right shoulder and upper arm. I strongly recommend you form a square lock as Bret is doing for maximum control and strength.

The second basic way to perform the neck triangle is to grasp your hands on the far side of your opponent's head with the square lock formed under his ear. Steve's left forearm and wrist are wedged tightly under Bill's right ear on the side of his neck like a knife and cuts off the blood flow in the carotid artery. Steve is jamming the left side of his head against the left side of Bill's head to help trap Bill's neck and head.

TAP OUT TEXTBOOK

NECK TRIANGLE CHOKE AND PIN STARTING FROM THE SIDE

Bret has Scott in a chest hold and has his head jammed under Scott's armpit and shoulder.

Bret lifts up and uses his left foot to post out to give himself room to move. Bret turns to his left and will move over and across Scott's body.

Bret kicks his right leg over Scott's body as shown and now shifts his hold to Scott's right side.

Bret has shifted his body over to the opposite side and secures the neck triangle from this position.

NECK TRIANGLE CHOKE USING ARM SHUCK FROM HEAD AND ARM HOLD

Bill has Steve in the scarf hold or head and arm pin.

Bill uses his right hand to move (shuck) Steve's left arm over in front of and then behind Bill's head. Bill immediately uses his head to drive down and trap Steve's left arm as shown.

While this set up looks pretty basic and you're probably thinking it might not work, think again. It's amazing how this simple arm shuck gets you in position to work the neck triangle on your opponent.

Bill secures his hands in a square grip and applies pressure on Steve's left upper arm and shoulder getting the choke.

NECK TRIANGLE ROLL

Bill locks up with Steve with his head on the outside of Steve's right shoulder. Bill makes sure to squeeze hard with his hands and arms and uses his head to drive hard into Steve's shoulder for maximum control.

Bill shoots his legs back hard and wide in a tripod forcing Steve forward and down as shown.

Bill moves to his left around to the back of Steve.

Bill uses his left leg to hook around Steve's left hip as shown and drives him to his left.

Bill drives Steve to the mat and locks his ankles together for a body scissors as he applies the neck triangle to get the tap out.

NECK TRIANGLE DRAG DOWN

Steve uses his left hand to shuck Bill's right arm and moves to his left behind Bill.

Steve does the duck under and forms a neck triangle as shown.

Steve moves to his left around Bill and drives Bill down onto the mat. Steve applies pressure to the neck triangle from this position.

NECK TRIANGLE FROM THE TOP USING A LEG TRIANGLE (TRAP HIS LEGS)

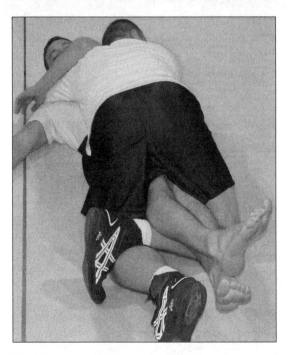

Bret has gained the top position and worked his legs into a triangle to control Scott's legs. Bret keeps solid control with the triangle on Scott's legs to keep him from escaping, and then works in a neck triangle to get the tap out.

CAN OPENER

TECHNICAL TIP: The can opener isn't a choke or strangle but it's definitely a useful neck crank. Any time you pull up or down forward on your opponent's head with one or both hands, it's a can opener. By itself, it can be a good way to get the tap out, but the can opener is often used to assist another technique such as a triangle choke or a leg choke.

Bret is in Chuck's guard and uses both hands to grab onto the back of Chuck's head and pull it forward. Bret places both elbows on Chuck's chest to give himself leverage and add to the pulling effect.

TAP OUT TEXTBOOK

CAN OPENER COUNTER TO TRIANGLE FROM THE GUARD

TECHNICAL TIP: There are several good ways to get the can opener on your opponent and the opportunity to do the can opener often presents itself in many positions and situations. Always have it as an option to get a tap out or make a triangle or other move work better.

Chuck has Bret in his guard and is starting his triangle on him. Bret moves to his left and uses his left hand to reach under Chuck's neck. Bret uses his right hand to reach across Chuck.

Bret grabs his hands together as he pulls up on Chuck's head. Bret drives forward and down onto Chuck as he pulls up on Chuck's head to get the can opener.

CAN OPENER TO ASSIST TRIANGLE CHOKE

CAN OPENER TO ASSIST ANKLE / LEG CHOKE

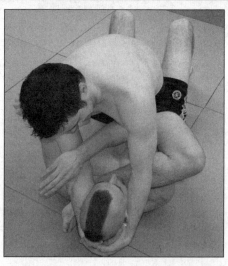

Scott has Bret in a triangle choke and adds pressure by using the can opener to pull Bret's head into the choke, making the choke tighter.

Derrick has jammed his left ankle and lower leg across Josh's throat and is using both of his hands to pull Josh's head into his ankle for a tighter choke.

CAN OPENER (1 HAND) ASSISTING LEG TO CHOKE OPPONENT

Bret has Scott on his back and is working in a triangle from this position. He can get the tap out from this position by using his left hand to pull up on Scott's head. Bret uses his right lower leg to help drive Scott's head upward. Bret is actually pulling Scott's head slightly to his left, jamming it into his right shoulder. This is both a choke and a neck crank. Again, if none of this works, Bret can go on to his triangle or even swing around and go for an armlock with Juji Gatame.

WRAP CHOKE FROM MOUNT

TECHNICAL TIP: While there are many applications to set up this choke, there are a couple of basic ways to use the wrap choke; the first is wrapping your opponent's arm around his head and wedging your arm in as shown here and the second is when you wrap your opponent's arm around his neck and use it to choke him.

Alan is on top of Scott and uses his head to pry against the back of Scott's right upper arm. Alan uses his left hand to reach around and under Scott's head and grabs Scott's right wrist. Alan reaches in with his right hand between Scott's right shoulder and the right side of Scott's neck and grabs his left forearm. Alan uses his right forearm to drive down (slicing) into the side of Scott's neck as he uses his left hand to pull Scott's right arm (wrap it) around his head.

WRAP CHOKE AND TRIPOD FINISH AGAINST OPPONENT'S CLOSED GUARD

Bryan is between Jarrod's legs in his closed guard and leans in onto Jarrod with his chest. Bryan uses his left hand to grab Jarrod's left wrist and pull it across Jarrod's face and head. He uses his right hand to push on Jarrod's left elbow to help force Jarrod's left arm to move.

Bryan uses his left hand to wrap Jarrod's left wrist and arm around Jarrod's head as shown. As he does this, Bryan uses his right hand to reach under Jarrod's head and grab Jarrod's left wrist. Doing this wraps Jarrod's left arm around his head and neck.

Bryan uses his right hand to grab Jarrod's left wrist tight and pulls Jarrod's wrist and arm around Jarrod's head. Look at how Bryan has posted his left foot and leg out wide for balance.

Bryan slides his left hand between the left side of Jarrod's head and neck and Jarrod's left shoulder as shown. As soon as he does this, Bryan uses his left hand to grab his right forearm. This tightens the wrap choke and Jarrod is ready to tap out at this point. Bryan can finish the move from here by leaning forward with his body as he tightens the "warp" around Jarrod's neck.

TRIPOD FINISH TO WRAP CHOKE
To really put the squeeze on Jarrod, Bryan tripods up with his hips high and both of his legs split out wide as shown and leans into Jarrod as he wraps the choke in tight to get the tap out. This wrap choke variation is a nasty one and works in both "gi" and "no gi" situations.

WRAP AND STRETCH FROM THE MOUNT

Jarrod has Bryan on his back and is in the mount position. Jarrod uses his left hand to push Bryan's left hand down as shown. This will start the wrap choke.

Jarrod secures the wrap set up and uses his right hand to reach under Bryan's head and neck and grab Bryan's left wrist. Doing this wraps Bryan's left arm tight around his neck. After he secures the wrap set up, Jarrod moves his left leg back a bit as shown. Jarrod uses his left hand to grab Bryan's right arm and pulls it in tight.

Jarrod turns his body to his left a bit and sits up, making sure to uses his right hand to pull on Bryan's left wrist, wrapping it tightly around Bryan's neck. This is a secure position for Jarrod and he can finish the choke here by using his right hand to pull on Bryan's wrist, wrapping his neck.

Jarrod uses his left hand to reach back and grab Bryan's right leg at the knee. As he does this, Jarrod uses his right hand to pull really hard on Bryan's left wrist, making the wrap extremely tight around Bryan's neck. By using his left hand to grab Bryan's leg as he uses his right hand to control Bryan's wrist, wrapping his arm around his neck, Jarrod stretches Bryan as he applies the wrap choke and pretty much ruins Bryan's day.

WRAP CHOKE FROM THE LEG PRESS TO THE MOUNT POSITION

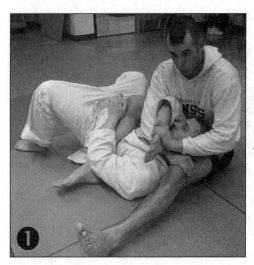

Josh has Ben in the leg press position and is most likely trying for a Juji Gatame. Josh can switch to a wrap choke from here. Josh uses his left hand to grab Ben's right wrist and his right hand to reach under Ben's chin and grab his left thigh. This action starts the wrap choke and keeps Ben in place.

Josh straddles Ben as shown making sure to place his left bent knee close to the right side of Ben's head for stability. Josh's goal is to position himself so he can climb on top of Ben's chest in a mount. Notice that Josh is using his left hand to grab Ben's wrist and Josh's right hand is sliding around the left side of Ben's neck.

Josh quickly turns to his left as he climbs up on top of Ben. Josh has wrapped Ben's right arm around his neck as shown and Josh's right hand is placed under Ben's head as shown.

Josh uses his left hand to pull down on Ben's right wrist. Doing this wraps Ben's arm tighter around his neck. As he does this, Josh uses his right hand to scoop Ben's head up making the choke tighter.

WRAP CHOKE FROM THE LEG PRESS TO THE SIDE POSITION OR CHEST HOLD

Josh has Ben in the leg press position and forms a figure 4 with his hands around Ben's neck as shown. This is a good wrap choke, but Josh will move into another one from here. Josh has Ben in a good choke from this position, but Ben may start to escape.

Josh straddles Ben and uses his left hand to control Ben's right wrist as Josh makes the transition.

Josh may have to place his right hand out and post it on the mat as shown for stability. Josh is now moving to the side position from here.

Josh uses his left hand to wrap Ben's right arm around his neck to form the wrap choke. Josh can apply a strong wrap choke form this position and get the tap out.

NECK TRIANGLE FINISH FROM THE MOUNT

Josh can also finish the move with a neck triangle.

WRAP CHOKE WITH ELBOW PUSH FROM A HIGH MOUNT

Erik has Nick in a high mount and jams his left knee on Nick's right shoulder and upper arm. Erik uses his right hand to grab Nick's left wrist and wraps Nick's left arm around his head and neck tightly. To make the wrap choke tighter, Erik uses his left hand to push on Nick's left elbow and he uses his right hand to pull on Nick's left wrist.

NECK TRIANGLE FROM THE SIDE POSITION OR CHEST HOLD USING A WIDE FLAT BASE

TECHNICAL TIP: When Josh flattens out, he makes it a point to spread his legs wide and dig his toes into the mat. Josh also wants to make sure his hips are flat on the mat. Doing this is a strong distribution of weight for Josh and he can control Ben really well from here. Remember: hips on the mat and create a wide base with your legs for good control from this side position.

Josh flattens out as he uses his right hand to wrap around Ben's neck and throat. Josh uses his right hand to grab his left forearm below his elbow.

WRAP CHOKE WITH ARM FROM SCARF HOLD

Nick has Erik in a scarf hold (head and arm pin) and uses his right hand to reach under Erik's head and neck and grab Erik's left wrist and wrap it around Erik's head as shown. To add pressure to the choke, Nick slides his left hand in between the left side of Erik's neck and Erik's left shoulder and grabs his right forearm.

WRAP CHOKE FROM SCARF HOLD

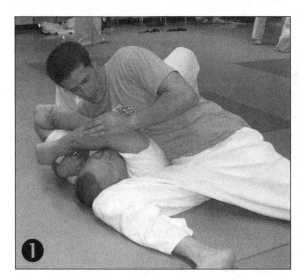

Travis has Eric in the head and arm hold and uses his left hand to move Eric's right arm over his head.

Travis uses his right hand to grab Eric's right wrist as Travis pushes Eric's right elbow with his left hand.

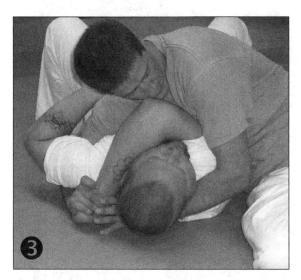

Travis moves Eric's right hand from his left hand to his right and Travis leans down onto Eric to trap his arm.

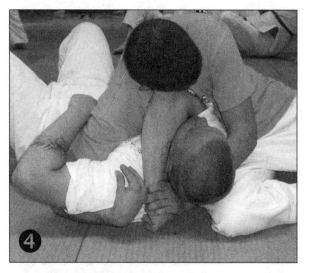

Travis has a firm grip with his left hand on Eric's right wrist and pulls Eric's right forearm into the left side of his neck. Travis uses his head to drive into Eric's right upper arm. This chokes both the left side of Eric's neck (with Eric's right forearm) and the right side of Eric's neck with Eric's right shoulder and upper arm.

HENGES HANGER (WRAP CHOKE FROM THE LEG PRESS POSITION)

Josh has Kelly in the leg press.

Josh has a figure 4 grip on Kelly's left arm. Josh starts to lean to his right.

Josh lifts his right arm while still holding onto Kelly with the figure 4 grip.

Josh starts to pull Kelly's left arm into his body so he can move his right arm over Kelly's head.

Josh loops his right arm over Kelly's head.

Here's a top view of how Josh loops his right hand over Kelly's head to trap it.

ALTERNATE VIEW

HENGES HANGER (WRAP CHOKE FROM THE LEG PRESS POSITION)

Josh loops his right arm around Kelly's head and traps it in this wrap choke grip.

Josh moves his left leg up and will move it over Kelly's body.

Josh places his left leg on Kelly's torso and rolls to his left (toward Kelly's legs and feet). As he does this, Josh uses his right forearm to lift Kelly's head up and into the action of the choke.

Josh rolls to his left side and swings his right leg up and over Kelly's right shoulder.

The leg press position is a strong one and there are a lot of moves using it in this book. Armlocks, chokes, holds and leglocks can be worked from this strong grappling position. This particular technique, the Henges Hanger, is a sneaky and effective way to choke (or even armlock) your opponent from the leg press position.

Josh has rolled onto his left side and forms a triangle with his legs on Kelly's right shoulder and arm to squeeze Kelly in tight and get the tap out.

DRIVE YOUR KNEE INTO BACK OF HIS HEAD TO ADD PRESSURE TO THE HENGES HANGER

Josh has Derrick in the Henges Hanger and adds pressure to the choke by driving his right knee and upper leg into the back of his right forearm and Derrick's head.

NAKED CHOKE USING SQUARE GRIP VARIATION OF THE HENGES HANGER

Josh has Ben in the Henges Hanger and quickly slips a naked choke in using the square lock grip. Ben's head is trapped on all sides and this is a strong choke.

NAKED CHOKE VARIATION OF THE HENGES HANGER

If you choose not to use the square lock grip or for some reason, can't work it in, you can use your right hand to grab your left wrist as Derrick is doing here. Look at Derrick's left hand which is palm up. Having your hand and arm in this position works really well. Try it and you'll see.

NAKED CHOKE GRABBING YOUR LEG VARIATION OF THE HENGES HANGER

Josh uses his right hand to reach around Ben's neck and throat and grabs the top of his left thigh near the knee. This is a good choke and gets the tap out.

CLAMP CHOKE (WRAP CHOKE AFTER TAKING OPPONENT TO THE MAT)

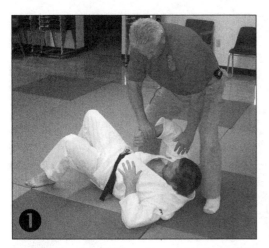

Larry has taken Bill to the mat and uses his right hand to grab Bill's right wrist.

Larry uses his right hand to push Bill's wrist to Bill and Larry uses his left hand to hook under Bill's bent right arm.

Larry uses his left hand to loop Bill's right wrist around Bill's head as shown. Larry uses his left hand to start to grab his right biceps.

Larry completes the wrapping of Bill's right arm around his neck and uses his left hand to firmly grab his right biceps. Larry pulls with his right hand to Bill's right wrist to wrap it tighter as Larry squeezes with his right hand on Bill's neck.

THE WEDGE CHOKE (NECK WEDGIE) BASIC APPLICATION

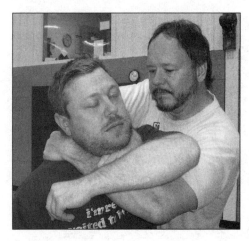

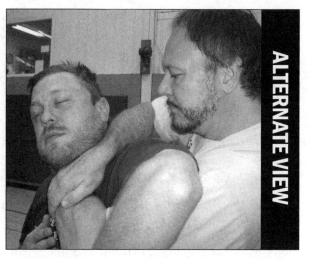

ALTERNATE VIEW

The neck wedge is an old choke, but not often used. Steve uses his left hand to reach under Bill's left armpit. Steve uses his left hand to grab Bill's right trapezius near the neck. Steve uses his right hand to grab his left forearm and jam his right forearm into the left side of Bill's neck. Drew Hills named this move the "Neck Wedgie."

This view shows how Steve uses his right hand to grab his left forearm.

WEDGE CHOKE FROM THE MOUNT

WEDGE CHOKE w/THE JACKET FROM HALF GUARD OR IF OPP. SCISSORS YOUR LEGS

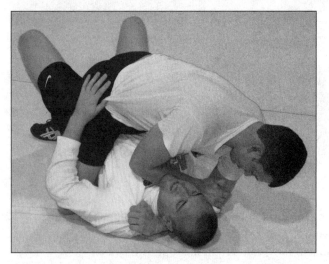

Scott is on top of Bret in the mount and uses the wedge choke from this position. Instead of reaching under Bret's armpit, Scott uses his left hand to reach around the back of Bret's head to control it.

Will is applying the wedge choke by using his right hand to reach under Jake's neck and grab Jake's collar as shown. Will uses his left hand to grab the sleeve of his jacket on the forearm and drives his left forearm down onto Jake's throat. To add pressure, will drives down with his left elbow.

WEDGE CHOKE FROM SEATED RODEO RIDE

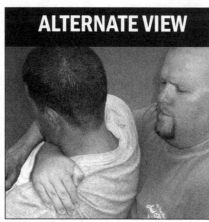

Eric is behind Travis is the seated rodeo ride position. Eric uses his right hand to reach under Travis's right armpit.

Eric uses his right hand to anchor Travis in and control him better.

Eric uses his left hand to grab his right forearm and drives his left forearm into the right side of Travis's neck. This creates a scissors movement, trapping Travis's neck and cutting off his carotid arteries.

TECHNICAL TIP: There are two basic ways of applying the wedge choke. The first is when you reach under your opponent's armpit as Eric is doing in this photo. This traps your opponent's entire shoulder and is useful when you're behind him as in a rodeo ride. The second way of applying the wedge choke is when you don't reach under your opponent's armpit and grab either the back of your opponent's neck or his shoulder as an anchor to control his head, then work in the choke.

WEDGE CHOKE FROM THE GUARD

Mike uses his right hand to grab behind Derrick's head and neck.

Mike uses his left hand to grab his right forearm and drive his left forearm into Derrick's throat for the choke.

WEDGE CHOKE FROM A RIDE WITH OPPONENT ON ALL FOURS

Derrick is riding Mike from the side and uses his left hand to reach under Mike's head to grab Mike's far (right) shoulder.

As he does this, Derrick moves his right knee in the "hole" between Mike's left knee and left elbow resting on the mat. This places Derrick in closer to Mike for better control.

Derrick uses his right hand to get the wedge choke.

WEDGE CHOKE FROM RIDE AGAINST A FLAT OPPONENT

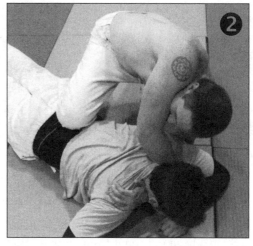

Jeff has broken Chris down onto his front and Chris is flat on the mat. Jeff uses his left hand to reach under Chris's neck and grabs Chris's right shoulder.

Jeff places his right knee on Chris's back as shown while using his right hand to sink in the wedge choke. Jeff's knee keeps Chris in place pretty well and allows him the option of moving over onto Chris's back for more control if he thinks it's necessary.

STANDING WEDGE CHOKE

Mike uses his right hand to hook onto the back of Derrick's head and neck.

Mike uses his left hand to grab his right forearm and drive his left forearm into Derrick's throat. This works best if Derrick is backed up against a wall or in a cage for an MMA match. Even if this choke doesn't work, it catches Derrick off guard and gives Mike the chance to work into another move.

TAP OUT TEXTBOOK

FIST CHOKE FROM MOUNT OR TOP POSITION

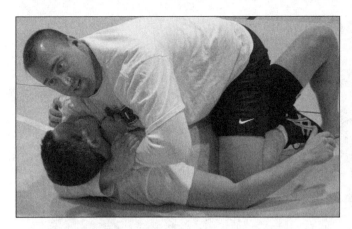

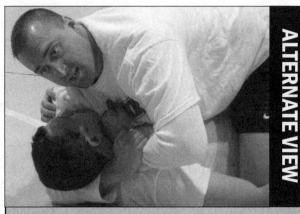

ALTERNATE VIEW

Bret is on top of Scott, wrapping his right hand and arm around Scott's head to keep it from moving. Bret uses his left fist to drive into the side of Scott's neck at the carotid artery. Bret could also drive his left fist more directly down and into the front of Scott's neck at the throat.

TECHNICAL TIP: It's fundamental and basic, but it's also effective; driving your fist in the side or front of your opponent's neck with one hand while you hold his head still with the other chokes him!

FIST CHOKE FROM THE GUARD

TECHNICAL TIP: If Bret wanted to use another form of controlling Scott's lower body, he could grapevine Scott's legs and split him wide, which would force Scott down onto Bret so Bret could apply the fist choke from there.

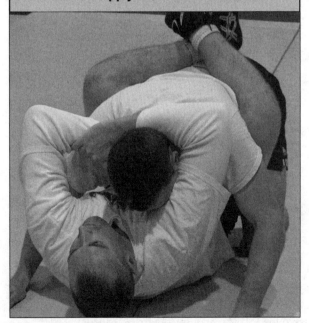

Bret is applying the fist choke on Scott from the bottom (guard) position. It helps Bret to use his legs and feet to pull Scott in tight with a closed guard to keep Scott from getting away or stopping the choke.

FOREARM CHOKE WITH LAPEL PULL (TSUKI JIME OR FOREARM THRUST CHOKE)

Eric is on top of Craig, using his right hand to grab Craig's right lapel high about the level of the collarbone. Eric uses his left hand to grab Craig's left lapel and pulls up on it. Eric drives his right forearm across Craig's throat. This is a simple, but effective choke that can be applied from a variety of positions!

SLEEVE CHOKE OR SCISSOR CHOKE FROM THE TOP

ALTERNATE VIEW

Ben is on top of Bret and uses his right hand to grab the collar behind Bret's neck. As he does this, Ben uses his left hand to grab his right sleeve.

Ben drives his left elbow straight down with his left forearm jamming into Bret's throat. Ben uses his right hand to grab his left sleeve to tighten the choke.

Here's another view of how this choke works.

SCISSORS OR SLEEVE CHOKE (GRAB HIGH ON YOUR ARM TO ADD MORE PRESSURE)

BOTH FISTS CHOKE (BASIC APPLICATION) ON TOP OF OPPONENT

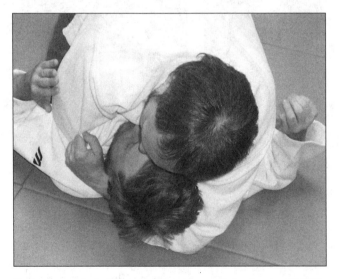 

Steve uses his left arm to wrap around the back of Bill's head and uses his left hand to grab his sleeve on his left upper arm. Steve's right forearm is jammed across Bill's throat. This scissors Bill's head and creates a choke.

Jamming your fists in the side of your opponent's neck is a pretty simple concept, but does indeed work. You can either grab his lapels if he's wearing a jacket or simple jam your fists in each side of his neck.

SCISSORS CHOKE OR SLEEVE CHOKE USING OPPONENT'S LAPEL

Bret is on top of Ben and uses his right hand to grab Ben's left lapel and pull up on it, opening Ben's lapel. Bret quickly uses his left hand to grab deep inside of Ben's left lapel.

Bret drives his left elbow down with his left forearm, jamming it into Ben's throat.

Bret uses his right hand around the back of Ben's head trapping it and grabs his left sleeve creating a strong choke

BOTH FISTS CHOKE FROM THE TOP GRAPEVINE

BOTH FISTS CHOKE ON FLAT OPPONENT

RODEO RIDE TO BOTH FISTS CHOKE

Chris is using the both fists choke on Chas as he keeps Chas from getting away by using a grapevine. As Chris grapevines Chas's legs, he drives in harder with his choke.

If your opponent is flat on his front, you can work him over with the both fists choke. Even if you don't get him to tap, you can distract him or soften him up for another move.

Chas has Chris in a rodeo ride and is using the both fists choke. Chas rocks Chris forward with his legs as he drives forward forcing Chris to be flat on his face. Doing this helps Chas drive in harder for the both fists choke.

THE TRAP CHOKE (ALSO CALLED THE BASEBALL BAT CHOKE-BASIC SET UP)

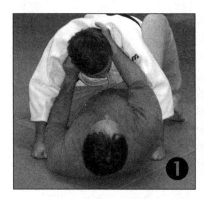

The trap choke is sneaky, nasty to have put on you and has a high ratio of success. In other words, it's one of the best chokes invented! You can do it with or without a gi and from a variety of positions. Here, Bill is between Steve's legs in his guard.

Steve uses his right hand to grab (palm up) deep into Bill's collar. Steve uses his left hand (palm down) to grab on the other side of Bill's neck deep in his collar. Look at how Steve's hands are under Bill's ear in a good deep grip.

Bill passes Steve's guard to Steve's right. Steve can "lure" Bill to do this by relaxing his right leg and allow Bill to pass. Steve rolls a bit to his right side as Bill passes.

ALTERNATE VIEW

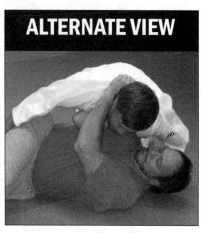

Bill has moved to his left (Steve's right) and Steve drives his right wrist and forearm deep across his neck. Steve's left hand squeezes hard on Bill's neck. The choke has been set in and now Steve only has to squeeze it tighter.

Steve drives his right forearm in and across Bill's throat and neck. Steve pinches his elbows together to "trap" Bill's head and neck in his forearms. Look at how Steve rolls to his left to get more torque to the choke.

This view shows the position of Steve's body and his choking action on Bill. You can see how Bill's head and neck are trapped in Steve's choke. This is a nasty, sneaky and sudden choke; all of the requirements for an effective choke!

TRAP CHOKE FROM THE GUARD BASIC GRIP SET UP POSITION

The trap choke is sneaky and that's why it works so well. Mike has Erik in his guard and has worked his right hand so that it is palm up and grabbing Erik's lapel as shown. Mike's left hand is palm down. The most common way of doing this choke is from the bottom (guard) position. You can tie your opponent up in a closed guard or keep him busy by trying to sweep him or roll him over from the bottom. All the while you're doing this, make it a point to sneak your hands in position to do the trap choke with one palm up and one palm down as shown in this photo.

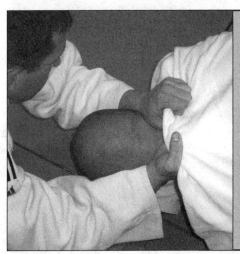

TECHNICAL TIP: When doing the trap choke, the hand that actually chokes your opponent is palm up. Your anchor hand is palm down. However, your anchor hand also serves as a powerful choking hand, but the palm up hand is the main attacking hand in the trap choke. Chance's right hand is palm up and his left hand is palm down. It's also important to grab your opponent's collar with your hands close to each other in much the same way you would grab a baseball bat. (That's why some people call this the ball bat choke.) Always make it a point to move your opponent into the direction of your choking (palm up) hand to make the trap choke work.

TRAP CHOKE HAND POSITION USING THE NO GI GRIP

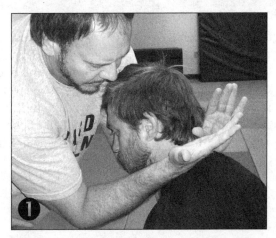

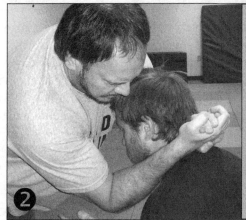

TECHNICAL TIP: It's a good idea for Steve to slide his right forearm down and across the front of Bill's neck at his throat to get a nastier choke.

Where there is no jacket to grab, Steve places his right hand palm up on the left side of Bill's neck and his left hand palm down on the right side.

Steve grasps his hands together with his hands behind Bill's head. Steve pinches his elbows (and forearms) together to create the choke.

TRAP CHOKE NO GI GRIP FROM THE GUARD

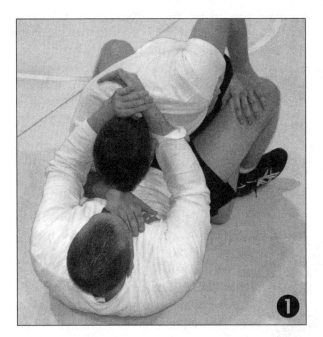

Bret has Scott in his guard and forms his hands in the trap choke grip.

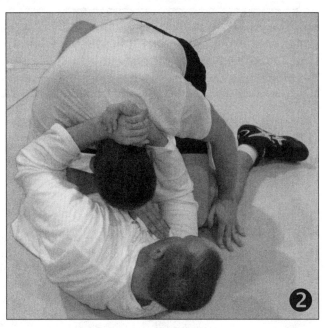

Scott moves to his left passing Bret's guard. Bret starts to sink in the trap choke.

As Scott passes to his left, Bret swings in to apply the trap choke.

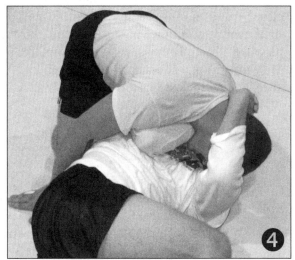

Bret sinks in the trap choke, firmly trapping Scott's neck and head in his arms. Look at how Bret's right forearm is jammed directly into Scott's throat.

TRAP CHOKE FROM THE CLOSED GUARD

TECHNICAL TIP: This truly is a sneaky (and nasty) choke and takes advantage of the fact that your opponent will almost always want to pass your guard and get a side position on you. It's an old choke that I learned as a young athlete and I've seen it used (and used it) very often. It's one of those moves that's "so old fashioned, it's cool." You can choke your opponent out cold very suddenly with this move!

TECHNICAL TIP: The top grappler almost never feels you make this switch to the palm up grip on his collar from this position. Drew, the bottom grappler, "lures" Mike into this grip by keeping Mike's head pulled down to Drew's chest until Drew wants him to move. This is a sneaky little move and one you will get away with time and again.

This is one of the best set ups for the trap choke ever invented! Drew has Mike in his closed guard and is using his right hand to pull down hard on Mike's head. Drew wants Mike to think that he wants to keep him in his closed guard.

Drew moves his right hand and grabs (palm up-very important) into Mike's collar. Drew wants to make sure his right hand is palm up near the middle of the back of Mike's neck and head as shown.

TECHNICAL TIP: Drew's right hand (palm up) is the primary choking hand and will eventually be driven up and under Mike's chin and across his throat. Drew makes sure that he keeps his right wrist straight and gets a good grip with his right hand in the palm up position on Mike's collar.

Drew uses his left hand to grab the back of Mike's collar as shown (palm down). Look at how close Drew's hands are together, much in the same way he would grab a baseball bat.

TRAP CHOKE FROM THE CLOSED GUARD

Drew lures Mike into the trap by rolling to his right side and placing his right leg on the mat as shown. To make it even more realistic, Drew "relaxes" his right leg making it all the more tempting to pass around for Mike. Mike takes the bait and immediately moves to his left (Drew's right) to pass over Drew's right leg. Look at how Drew continues to keep the solid grip on Mike's collar.

As Mike passes Drew's guard over Drew's right leg, Drew immediately (and forcefully) closes the choke in by driving his right forearm under Mike's chin and across his throat.

Drew drives his right forearm across Mike's throat and uses his left forearm to squeeze against the right side of Mike's neck. This is the "trap" in the trap choke and Mike's head and neck are trapped between Drew's forearms. Look at how Drew is driving his right shoulder up and into Mike and Drew has rolled to his left slightly with his right hip upward. Drew's right forearm is jammed directly across the front of Mike's neck on his throat.

TRAP CHOKE FROM BELT LINE DEFENSE

Mike is on his back and uses his right leg to wedge across Erik's midsection as shown in his belt line defense. Mike uses his right hand (palm up) and left hand (palm down) to set Erik up for the trap choke.

Here's another view of the belt line defense with Mike setting up the trap choke.

Erik probably thinks this is an easy guard to pass and he's lured to move past Mike's right knee. As he does, Mike quickly swings in with the trap choke.

Mike keeps rolling in with the trap choke and gets the tap out.

TRAP CHOKE WHEN OPPONENT IS ON ALL FOURS OR KNEES

The trap choke can be used from a lot of positions as this set up shows. Steve is standing above Bill who is on all fours. Steve adjusts his hands to get the trap choke grip (palm up and palm down grip).

Steve drives hard into Bill. Bill's natural reaction is to resist and as he does, he rises up, exposing his upper body. This opens him up for the choke. Look at how Steve's feet are ready to swing into action.

Steve starts to swing his right leg forward and across his body to start the choke.

Steve swings his right leg across the front of his body and sinks his hands and arms in for the choke on Bill.

Steve swings in forcefully with the choke in place and getting the tap out.

TRAP CHOKE WHEN OPPONENT IS FLAT

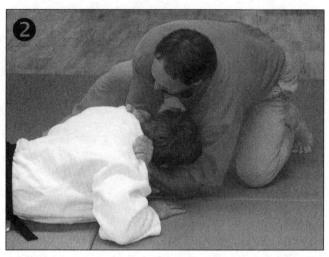

This is similar to when your opponent is on all fours, but this time, he's flat on the mat. Steve is standing above Bill who is flat on his front. Steve grab's Bill's collar with his hands (palm up and palm down) in the trap choke grip.

Steve moves to his right (to Bill's left) and pinches his elbows tight together. This sinks in the choke.

Steve traps Bill's head and neck with his hands as shown. Steve can finish the choke here by applying pressure to the neck with his forearms to get the tap out.

Steve can also drive hard into the direction of the choke as shown. This turns Bill a bit on his right side as Steve continues to drive the choke in for the tap out.

STANDING TRAP CHOKE (THE WATSON ROLL)

TECHNICAL TIP: Your opponent usually won't simply let you grab him and set him up for the trap choke. Be sneaky and work it in out of a head and arm tie-up or a Muay Thai clinch. Set him up and then sneak your right hand palm up and left hand palm down, then grip them together to get the grip, and ultimately, the choke.

Shawn Watson surprised everybody, including his opponent, in the final match of the first Shingitai Nationals when he used this "no gi" version of the trap choke and choked his opponent out cold. Steve and Bill are standing facing each other. Steve uses his hands and arms to get the trap choke grip.

Steve swings his right leg hard across his body as shown as he swings his right arm across with it.

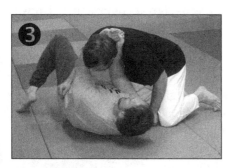

As Steve swings his foot across, he drops to the mat pulling Bill with him as shown.

Immediately upon hitting the mat, Steve sinks the trap choke in on Bill.

TECHNICAL TIP: This is a sneaky, sudden and violent choke. Please be careful when applying this choke.

TRAP CHOKE FROM THE CHEST HOLD, HALF GUARD OR SIDE POSITION

This is a "double palm up" application of the trap choke. Drew is top of Mike in the half guard.

Mike starts his escape and pushes on Drew to open some space. As he does this, Drew uses his left hand to grab Mike's collar palm up.

Drew moves to his left (to Mike's right) and uses his right hand to grab (palm up) Mike's left lapel.

As Drew moves to his left, he moves his right hand across Mike's throat as shown. Look at how Drew's left forearm is behind Mike's head to trap it.

Drew drives his right forearm across Mike's throat by rolling into Mike with his shoulder as shown. Drew uses his left leg to post out so he can turn his hips and shoulders into the choking action. Drew chokes Mike and gets the tap out.

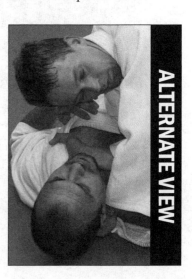

ALTERNATE VIEW

TRAP CHOKE FROM SIDE POSITION AND SIT THROUGH

Mike has Derrick in the trap choke from the side, but for some reason, the choke won't work.

Mike posts out and forward with his left foot for stability and to give himself room to sit through with his right leg. Mike drives his right elbow and forearm into the front of Derrick's neck at the throat. Mike's left forearm is on the back of Derrick's head trapping it. This is a nasty choke and a neck crank as well. Mike can finish the choke here or sit through with his right leg.

Mike shoots his right leg through sitting on his right side as shown. Mike makes sure to keep Derrick's head cradled with his left forearm as Mike drives his right forearm tighter into Derrick's throat. This cranks Derrick's head up and forward and creates the choke.

NO GI TRAP CHOKE FROM SIDE POSITION OR CHEST HOLD

Mike is at Derrick's side in a side position or chest hold. Mike uses his left hand and arm to reach under Derrick's neck and head and his right hand to grab his left hand to form a square lock. As he does this, Mike drives his right forearm across and down onto Derrick's throat. Mike drives down with his right elbow and uses his left forearm to drive up on the back of Derrick's head, driving Derrick's head up forward into his right forearm which is across Derrick's throat to add pressure to the choke.

TRAP CHOKE FROM THE SIDE WITH OPPONENT ON ALL FOURS

Bret is using the trap choke from the side on Scott, who is on all fours. Bret slides his right hand under Scott's left armpit and across Scott's throat and neck as shown. Bret uses his left forearm to jam down against the back of Scott's neck and forms a square grip. Bret squeezes his elbows (and forearms) together and gets the choke and tap out.

TRAP CHOKE FROM SIDE ON FLAT OPPONENT

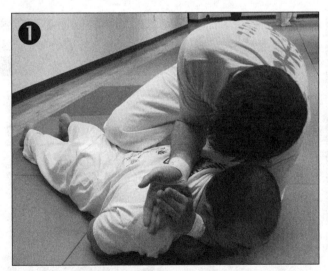

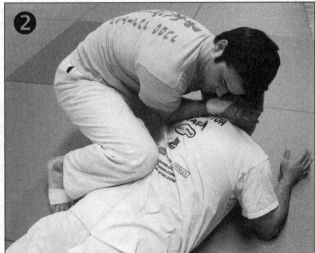

Derrick is at Mike's left side and rides him with his right knee in Mike's back. Derrick's uses his left hand to slide under Mike's chin and uses his right hand to start to grasp his left hand as shown.

Derrick secures his grip and drives his right forearm down against the back of Mike's neck as he drives upward into Mike's throat with his left hand to get the trap choke.

TECHNICAL TIP: Derrick keeps his knee on Mike to add leverage and control.

CROSS CHOKE

Drew is on the bottom and uses his left hand to yank down on Mike's right lapel as shown. Think of the lapel as a rope that you want to make tight to choke him better. As Drew pulls down on Mike's lapel, he uses his right hand to slide into the collar as far as his hand can go. Drew's right hand in way up in Mike's collar so the choke will work better when he puts it on. Drew can use either palm up or palm down placement with his right hand, whichever works better for him.

Drew slides his left hand up and under (not over) his right forearm, which makes for an easier (and more powerful) choke. Drew keeps Mike in place using a closed guard or other method of keeping Mike from moving away.

TECHNICAL TIP: Drew's right hand is his "anchor" hand when doing this choke, meaning he sets his hand in Mike's lapel and controls him with it. Setting this anchor hand is important so Drew can develop and keep control of Mike when he works his other hand in for the actual choke.

Drew slides his left hand in and under his right forearm, grabbing Mike's left lapel as far up and deeply as possible. Drew quickly uses both hands to pull Mike into him. Drew does not want to flair his elbows out wide, but instead keeps his elbows close to Mike's chest. Doing this places more pressure on the sides of Mike's neck at the carotid arteries and gets a quicker, more effective choke.

CROSS CHOKE FROM THE TOP

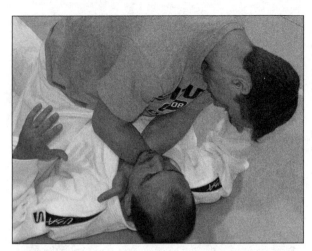

You can apply the cross choke from the top position as well, but I prefer to use it from the bottom. Applying it from the bottom gives you more leverage and mobility.

CROSS CHOKE GRAPEVINE OPPONENT'S LEGS FROM BOTTOM

Eric wrapped his legs around Travis's legs and grapevined them. He straightens both legs to flatten Travis out and fall forward. As he does this, Eric applies the cross choke from the bottom.

CROSS CHOKE HAND POSITIONS

There are 3 basic hand positions you can use to grab your opponent's lapels for the cross choke.

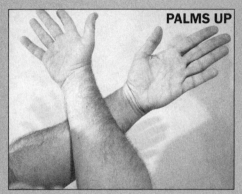

PALMS UP

Having both palms up works well in many situations. Think of how you curl a barbell. You can curl more weight and control it better with your palms up and this is the same when doing a cross choke.

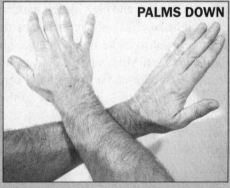

PALMS DOWN

It's a matter of personal choice and what may present itself as the choke develops, but some people prefer doing the cross choke with both palms down.

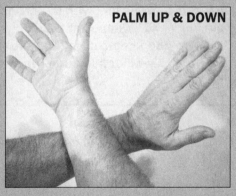

PALM UP & DOWN

Some people prefer to anchor with the palm up (or palm down) and use the other hand to slide in to make the choke work. Again, it's a matter of personal choice and what works best for you.

GRAPEVINE ROLLOVER TO CROSS CHOKE

Mike grapevines Steve's legs from the bottom as shown. As he does this, Mike works his hands in for the cross choke.

Mike rolls Steve over with the grapevine.

Mike rolls over on top of Steve and applies the choke getting the tap out. The momentum of rolling your opponent over helps make this choke work very well. Even if the choke doesn't work, Mike is on top of Steve and can continue on to another move from here.

MONKEY ROLL CROSS CHOKE

Mike has both feet placed on Erik's hips as he works in the cross choke. If Erik stands up to escape, Mike will use the monkey roll.

Mike rolls in between Erik's legs as Erik stands. Mike also pulls Erik forward a bit to make him roll.

Mike rolls Erik over with the cross choke still in place.

Mike rolls over on top of Erik and finishes the choke from this position.

LEG PUSH CROSS CHOKE

Steve pushes Bill back with his feet and sinks the choke in.

Steve sinks in the cross choke and places a foot on each of Bill's knees as shown. Steve's feet are at Bill's knees close to the mat.

JUMPING CROSS CHOKE (PULL OPPONENT TO YOUR GUARD)

A gutsy move, but it works. Chuck has the cross choke in on Bret from a standing position.

Chuck swings in and jumps up on Bret and pulls him down to the mat.

Chuck pulls Bret to the mat applying the cross choke.

LOOP CHOKE FROM THE GUARD

Steve is on his buttocks with Bill in his guard as shown. Steve uses his left hand to grab the inside of Bill's left lapel and his right hand to grab outside of Bill's left lapel as shown.

Steve uses his right hand to loop over the top of Bill's head and he uses his left hand to pull Bill down with the lapel.

TECHNICAL TIP: Steve drives his right elbow down onto Bill's chest and drives his elbow forward pretending he wants to drive his elbow to Bill's belt, rather than using his right forearm to push against and away on the left side of Bill's neck.

Steve completes the loop and tightens the choke by using his right forearm to jam across the right side of Bill's neck.

LOOP CHOKE WITH FOOT PROP WHEN OPPONENT IS FLAT

The loop choke can often be applied when your opponent is flat on his front. Steve is kneeling at the top of Bill who is flat. Steve secures the grip for the loop choke.

Steve moves to his left and loops the lapel around Bill's neck.

Steve extends his left leg and uses his left foot to prop onto Bill's left hip. Doing this will help roll Bill over to Steve's left.

Steve rolls Bill over to Steve's left and rolls over on top of him.

Steve rolls onto Bill and applies the choke from this tripod position.

LOOP CHOKE AGAINST A FLAT OPPONENT

If you choose not to roll your opponent with the loop choke, you can use this version of the choke. Bret is standing above Ben who is on all fours. Bret sinks in the loop choke grip on Ben's right lapel.

Bret quickly moves to his right (to Ben's left side) and loops the choke in place as shown.

Bret drives Ben forward and flat onto his front as shown. Doing this moves Ben into the action of the choke and Bret can finish the choke here if he chooses.

If Ben resists a lot, Bret can finish the choke by driving forward to Ben's right shoulder to sink in the choke and get the tap out.

LOOP CHOKE FROM THE GUARD

Travis had Tom in his guard and uses his left hand to grab Tom's right lapel (palm down) and his right hand (palm up) to grab Tom's right lapel. Look at how Travis is grabbing on Tom's lapel directly under Tom's right ear. This is a deep grip.

Travis loops his right hand and arm over Tom's head.

Travis completes the loop, trapping Tom's head between his forearms.

Travis rolls to his left side and moves away from Tom a bit as he applies the choke to get the tap out.

GLAHN SPECIAL

Named for Olympic medal winner Klaus Glahn who made this choke famous, this is a sneaky, effective choke that has been used for many years with successful results.

Kyle uses his left hand to grab under Josh's right arm and grabs Josh's left lapel. Kyle is to his left and to Josh's right side to start this move.

Kyle uses his right elbow to drive forward (and not sideways against Josh's neck).

Kyle extends his left leg and uses his left foot to prop the side of Josh's right knee. Kyle starts to roll Josh to Kyle's left (Josh's right).

ALTERNATE VIEW

TECHNICAL TIP: Steve uses his left foot to wrap around his opponent's right knee and uses his left foot to prop the knee as shown.

GLAHN SPECIAL

Kyle rolls Josh over with the choke in place.

Kyle uses the momentum of the rolling action to roll over on top of Josh.

Kyle lands in a tripod position on top of Josh and sinks in the choke for the tap out.

GLAHN SPECIAL FROM THE GUARD

Steve is on his buttocks with Bill in his guard. Steve uses his left hand to reach under Bill's right arm to grab his left lapel deep and high under Bill's left ear.

Steve uses his right hand to grab Bill's jacket on Bill's right shoulder near the collar.

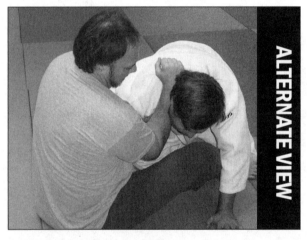

ALTERNATE VIEW

This shows how Steve uses his right hand to grab Bill's right shoulder and collar.

Steve drives his right hand in directly down and onto Bill's chest as he uses his feet to push Bill forward and down into the choke.

Steve flattens Bill out forward applying the choke.

HEAD LEVER CHOKE (PITCHFORK CHOKE)

Trevor is facing Drew who is on all fours.

Trevor reaches over Drew with his right arm and hand and grabs Drew's right lapel as deeply as possible.

Trevor has grabs Drew's right lapel with his right hand and moves to his left (Drew's right). Trevor uses his left hand to grab Drew's right leg as shown.

Trevor makes the choke work by pulling on Drew's lapel with his right hand and pulling on Drew's right leg with his left hand and driving his head into Drew's right side.

SUPER CHOKE WITH BELT PULL

The super choke is a tight choke that looks like a "show off" move but really isn't. Basically, you place your leg over your opponent's head and force him to roll forward into the choke. Steve is at Mike's right side.

Steve uses his right hand to grab Mike's left lapel and has his right wrist and forearm tight under Mike's chin on the throat.

Steve drives his right leg over the back of Mike's head forcing it down and choking Mike. Steve leans to his right, forcing Mike forward. As he does this, Steve uses his left hand to pull up on Mike's belt, lifting Mike forward. This makes the choke tighter.

SUPER CHOKE LEG PULL (THE BRINK SPECIAL)

Steve has moved into position for the super choke as shown here. Steve uses his left hand to reach around behind Mike's right buttocks and grab Mike's left ankle or foot.

Steve uses his left hand to lift Mike's left foot and ankle as shown as Steve rolls to his right forcing Mike to roll forward and over his head.

SUPER CHOKE WITH CROTCH OR JACKET GRAB (WATSON'S ASS JACK)

Mike places his left leg over the back of Steve's head and neck and uses his right hand to lift up whatever he has grabbed forcing Steve forward and into the choke.

Mike is at Steve's side and uses his left hand to grab Steve's right lapel and uses his right hand to grab deep between Steve's legs. Mike can grab Steve's belt, the apron of his jacket or Steve's leg.

SUPER CHOKE WHEN OPPONENT IS FLAT

Steve is flat on his front in the "chicken" position. After Mike says a silent "thank you" for having his opponent in this position, he goes to work on him.

Mike slips his right hand under Steve's neck and grabs Steve's left lapel. Mike uses his left hand to grab Steve's belt.

Mike places his right leg over onto the back of Steve's head as shown. Mike uses his left hand to pull Steve forward into the direction of the choke.

TECHNICAL TIP: In the super choke, always try to roll your opponent into the direction of your knee. Look at Mike's right knee in this photo and you will see how he is pulling and rolling Steve in the same direction as where his knee points. Mike's right leg is bent and hooked over Steve's head and neck.

SUPER CHOKE FROM THE GUARD

Mike has Steve in his guard and uses his left hand to pull Steve's lapel open.

Mike uses his right hand to grab deep and high into Steve's right lapel.

Mike rolls to his right.

Mike lifts his left leg and hooks it over Steve's head trapping Steve's head in Mike's bent knee as shown.

ALTERNATE VIEW

Here's another view of the set up for this choke. Mike drives his left leg forward as he uses his right hand to pull on Steve's lapel choking him.

SUPER CHOKE WHEN YOU'RE STANDING ABOVE YOUR OPPONENT (THE HECKADON WRAP)

World Sambo Champion and AAU Judo Grand Champion Chris Heckadon used this set up often during his judo career. Steve is standing above Mike and uses his right hand to grab Mike's left lapel as shown.

Steve moves to his left (to Mike's right), looping his right hand around and under Mike's chin and neck. Steve uses his left hand to grab Mike's belt as shown.

Steve wraps his right hand around Mike's neck with the lapel in tight against Mike's neck and throat.

Steve places his right leg over the top of Mike's head and drives down hard with it. This drives Mike's head forward into the choke. Make sure you use the part of your upper leg that is immediately above your knee to drive down on his head.

CHOKE FROM THE GUARD WITH BOTH LEGS OVER (THE KELLY CURL)

Kelly has Derrick in his guard, sitting on his buttocks. Kelly uses his left hand to grab Derrick's right lapel and open it up. Kelly uses his right hand to grab deep inside Derrick's right lapel.

TECHNICAL TIP: Kelly uses his left hand to open Derrick's right lapel and his right hand to grab the lapel inside, under the right ear. This helps Kelly work his right wrist and forearm under Derrick's throat.

Kelly sinks in the lapel choke with his right hand under Derrick's neck on his throat, using his left hand to pull down on his right jacket shoulder.

Kelly scoots out and away from Derrick enough to get room to maneuver. Kelly places his left leg over the top of (and on the back of) Derrick's head. Kelly rocks to his left forcing Derrick forward.

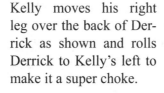

Kelly moves his right leg over the back of Derrick as shown and rolls Derrick to Kelly's left to make it a super choke.

TAP OUT TEXTBOOK

278

ROLL OPPONENT FORWARD IF THE LEG PRESSURE DOESN'T MAKE HIM TAP

If, for some reason, the combination of tightening the choke on his lapel with your right hand and driving his head down into it with your right leg doesn't make him tap out, finish with the super choke roll by using your left hand to pull up on his belt and lift him off the mat as shown. As in the other super chokes, this drives his head forward and into the direction of the choke. A good tip is to really drive down hard with your right leg on the back of his neck. This forces his head forward more and tightens the choke.

FAR HIP SIT THROUGH CHOKE (ALSO KNOWN AS KOSHI JIME, THE HIP CHOKE)

Steve is riding Bill from the side and uses his left hand to slip under Bill's chin to grab Bill's right lapel high and deep.

Steve uses his right arm to grab over Bill's lower back and hook Bill's right upper leg and hip as shown.

Steve uses his right leg to sit through, driving Bill forward into the direction of the choke. Steve helps flatten Bill out by using his right hand to push out on Bill's right leg.

HIP CHOKE OR SIT THROUGH CHOKE WITH WRIST CONTROL

Steve is riding Bill on his back as shown and uses his left hand to reach under Bill's chin and secure a grip on Bill's right lapel. As he does this, Steve uses his right hand to grab Bill's right wrist and traps it.

Steve quickly and forcefully jumps over to his right, sitting through with his left leg as shown. Steve's momentum and the tightening of the lapel choke get the tap out.

HIP CHOKE OR SIT THROUGH CHOKE WITH ARM SPLIT

Steve is at Bill's right side and slides his right hand under Bill's chin to grab Bill's left lapel. Steve uses his left hand to reach over Bill's back and under Bill's left arm to start to control Bill's left wrist or forearm.

Steve uses his left hand to chop out on Bill's left arm and straighten it out as he sits through with his left leg to get the choke and tap out.

HIP CHOKE WITH ARM SLICE

Bill is at Steve's left side and has his left hand in under Steve's chin grabbing Steve's right lapel deep and tight. Bill is on his toes for mobility.

Bill uses his left hand to pull up on Steve's lapel and uses his right forearm to drive down and hard against the left and back sides of Steve's neck. Bill is up on his left foot as shown.

Bill sits through with his right leg, driving his right arm into the left side of Steve's neck and pulling his left hand to pull on Steve's lapel.

KASHI JIME (THE KASHI STRANGLE) WITH FOOT ON KNEE OR LEG

Named for World Judo and Sambo Champion Katsuhiko Kashiwazaki who made this famous, this choke is a good one to use from the guard.

Derrick is on his buttocks as shown and has his right foot on Kelly's left knee. Derrick is using his left hand to grab deep and high into Kelly's left lapel.

Derrick reaches with his right hand over Kelly's head and grabs Kelly's belt.

Derrick uses his right arm to drive Kelly down and forward and applies the choke.

KASHI JIME USING FOOT ON OPPONENT'S HIP

This is a similar set up to the other Kashi Jime, but this time Derrick uses his right foot to jam in Kelly's left hip for control.

Derrick uses his right hand to reach over Kelly's head and grab Kelly's belt. Derrick starts to pull Kelly forward as shown.

Derrick applies the choke, rolling Kelly forward.

KATA HA JIME (THE SINGLE WING CHOKE)

I believe the kata ha jime is one of the most effective "gi" chokes ever invented. This photo shows what it looks like. The "wing" describes the action of placing your hand behind your opponent's arm to extend it and trap the arm, shoulder and head. There are numerous ways to set this choke up and this choke can be done from just about any angle or position. We often refer to this choke simply as "kata ha."

BACK OF THE HAND ON THE BACK OF HIS HEAD FOR MORE PRESSURE

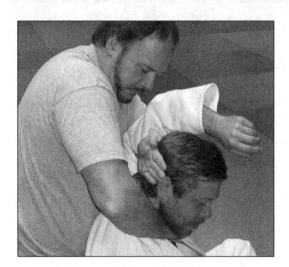

Steve places the back of his left hand against the back of Bill's head. Doing this drives Bill's head into the action of the choke better than placing your palm against the back of his head.

KATA HA "CLOSED GRIP"

Steve uses his left hand to grab his right forearm to "close" the grip. You may prefer this variation.

ROLLING KATA HA JIME (ROLLING SINGLE WING CHOKE)

My wife Becky Scott used this on a lot of opponents during the judo part of her athletic career. This is an effective and nasty choke that can choke your opponent out midway through the roll. Rolling your opponent creates momentum and makes the choke tighter and more effective.

Steve is standing above Bill in a standing ride as shown to start the move.

Steve uses his left hand to pull down on Bill's left lapel, opening it up so Steve can grab it easer to apply the choke.

Steve uses his right hand to reach around Bill's neck and grab Bill's left lapel.

Steve uses his left hand to catch Bill's left forearm near his hand. Doing this extended "wing" give Steve room to move his left hand in better behind Bill's head.

Steve places the back of his left hand on the back of Bill's head as he rolls to his left, in the direction of Bill's winged arm.

Steve's left foot is pointing as shown here. Doing this allows Steve to roll easier, faster and with more control, thus creating more pressure in the choking action. Look at how Steve's right hand is gripping Bill's left lapel. Rolling to his left and in the same direction he has winged Bill's arm created a tighter hold around Bill's neck with the lapel. It literally "hangs" your opponent and the better you hang him when you roll him, the quicker he will either tap out or pass out.

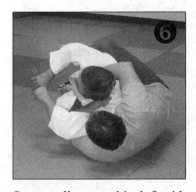

Steve rolls over his left side and shoulder and the momentum of the roll brings Bill with him, creating momentum.

Steve rolls Bill over with complete control of the action.

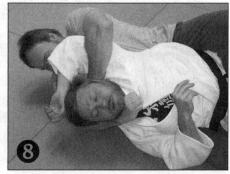

Steve finishes the choke by rolling Bill completely over to his left side.

SIT BACK KATA HA JIME

Ken is in a standing ride above Eric and reaches in to secure Eric's lapel.

Ken uses his left hand to wing Eric's left arm as shown and starts to lean back a bit pulling Eric up.

Ken gets both of his legs hooked in for a rodeo ride as he uses his right hand on Eric's lapel to tighten the choke and uses his left hand to wing Eric's left arm and shoulder. Ken continues to lean to his left rear as he does this. This continues to force Eric up.

Ken sits backward toward his left rear side. Doing this pulls Eric back toward his left rear side as well. This movement helps tighten the strangle Ken has on Eric's lapel with his right hand and helps sink in Ken's left hand and arm deeper for the winging action on Eric's left arm. To add pressure, Ken can remain on his back and buttocks as shown here and squeeze with his right hand on Eric's lapel as Ken uses the back of his left hand to push on the back of Eric's head.

KATA HA JIME FROM THE GUARD

Not many people think to use the single wing choke from the guard, but it's a good, sneaky choke. When it comes to chokes, sneaky is a good thing!

Derrick uses his right hand to loop over Kelly's head as shown.

Derrick uses his left hand to wing Kelly's right arm and places the back of his left hand on the back of Kelly's head as shown.

Derrick has his hands in correctly and then makes the choke happen by driving his hips in forward toward Kelly as Derrick rolls back. This 'arching' action really puts the pressure on Kelly's neck and head and gets a quick tap out.

EXTEND YOUR OPPONENT'S ARM

Roy is rolling Drew into the kata ha jime. Look at how Roy has extended Drew's left arm, which makes it much easier for Roy to wing Drew's left arm and make the choke tighter.

TECHNICAL TIP: Sometimes, you don't have to place your hand on the back of your opponent's head and can extend your opponent's arm out straight like this. You can see by Drew's facial expression that this choke works.

KATA HA ROLL CHOKE FROM THE GUARD

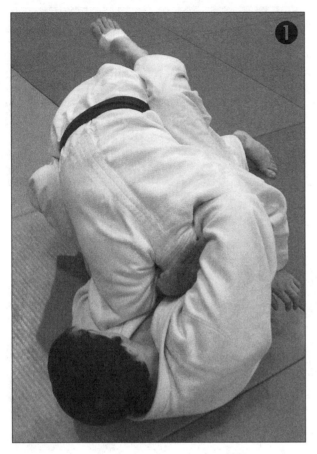

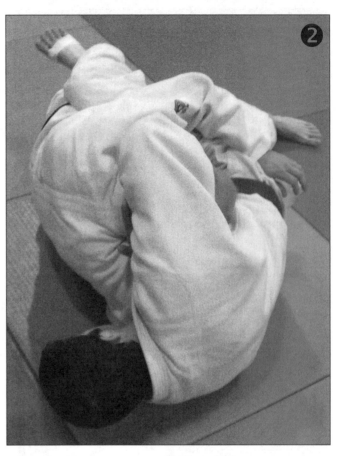

If Derrick chooses, he can roll Kelly into a single wing choke from this position. Derrick rolls Kelly to Derrick's left (toward the wing).

Derrick rolls Kelly to Derrick's left. This momentum creates more pressure in the choking action.

Derrick rolls over on top of Kelly. This rolling action really helps apply the pressure. Look at how Derrick finishes the choke in the tripod position, posting on the top of his head and with both of his feet wide and toes driving onto the mat for stability.

THE POLISH WHIZZER CHOKE (ALSO KNOWN AS THE OKANO ROLL OR KATA HA JIME)

This looks like a show-off move, but it really works if you're gutsy enough to try it.

Josh uses his left hand to wing under Derrick's right arm to secure the single wing choke.

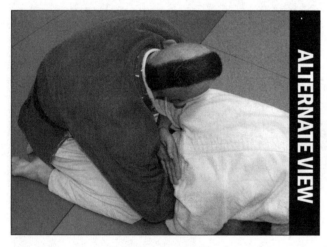

ALTERNATE VIEW

Here's a top view of how Josh places the back of his hand on the back of Derrick's neck.

Josh drives his head through the "hole" between Derrick's right armpit and hips and knees. Josh really drives his head hard and through. Josh doesn't want Derrick's body rolling over his head but rather Josh's head shoots into the hole to whip Derrick over.

Josh completes the roll, comes up on his front as shown for better leverage and gets the tap out.

KATA HA WHEN OPPONENT IS FLAT

Kelly is above Derrick in this position and uses his left hand to slide in under Derrick's right shoulder. Kelly uses his right hand to reach around the left side of Derrick's neck and grab Derrick's right lapel. This forms the kata ha choke.

KATA HA JIME WITH CLOSED GRIP (FOREARM GRAB) ON FLAT OPPONENT

Brian is using his right hand to place or grab his left forearm when applying this choke. If you prefer not to "slice" the back of your hand on the back of his head, this is a good way to choke your opponent.

Kelly is angled over Derrick's right shoulder and not in a north south position. Kelly places his left hand on the back of Derrick's head.

Kelly kicks back with his right foot and leg and sinks in the choke.

KATA HA NEAR LEG ROLL

This is a good set up for the single wing choke and one not often used (but it should be). Josh has Ben in a near leg ride as shown.

Josh uses his right hand to reach around the right side of Ben's neck and grabs Ben's left lapel.

Josh slides his left hand in with the back of his hand against the back of Ben's head and starts to roll to the left.

Josh rolls Ben over and tightens the choke as he rolls.

Josh finishes the roll with the choke in tight and gets the tap out.

TECHNICAL TIP: The "wing" in the single wing choke along with sliding the back of your hand along the back-side of your opponent's head slices and squeezes your opponent's neck in a scissoring action when you roll him. As mentioned before, rolling your opponent gives you the momentum to make the choke tighter and this is what actually "hangs" him. The fingers on Steve's left hand want to reach almost to Bill's ear to create a "slicing" action and Steve's right hand grabbing Bill's left lapel should be gripping deep and high near Bill's left ear. This "ear to ear" control makes the choke tight and gives you the ability to make it tighter if there's any slack in the lapel as you roll or finish your roll on your opponent.

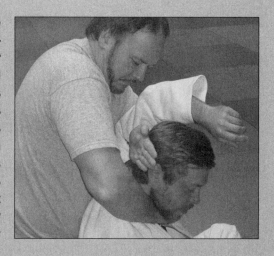

ROLLING LAPEL CHOKE (SANDI SLIDE)

Josh is at the side of Derrick and uses his right hand to slip under Derrick's chin and grab his left lapel.

Josh starts his roll and drives his head into the "hole" between Derrick's left arm and left hip.

Josh rolls over his head and left shoulder and brings Derrick with him as he rolls.

Josh rolls Derrick over and completes the choke as shown.

SLIDING LAPEL CHOKE (BASIC) ALSO KNOWN AS OKURI ERI JIME

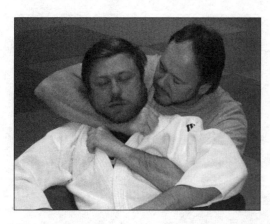

Steve's left hand reaches under Bill's left armpit and grabs Bill's right lapel. Steve uses his left hand to pull down (important: pull down) on Bill's right lapel. This makes Bill's right lapel into a "rope" and creates a stronger choke. Steve's right hand and arm reaches around Bill's neck and Steve uses his right hand to grab Bill's left lapel. Bill's head is trapped in against Steve's shoulder and right arm. Steve uses his right hand to pull the lapel in as he uses his left hand to pull down on Bill's other lapel creating a strong, effective lapel choke.

SLIDING LAPEL CHOKE FROM A RODEO RIDE WITH LEG CONTROL OF OPPONENT'S ARM

1. Drew is behind Roy in a seated rodeo ride and is applying the sliding lapel choke.

2. To get more momentum and create a stronger choke, Drew rolls to his left rear and pulls Roy with him as he swings his right leg over Roy's right shoulder.

OPTIONAL

3. Drew hooks his right leg over Roy's right arm to control it and rolls to his rear left side as he applies the choke.

OPTIONAL: You can lean back rather than roll to the side to apply pressure to the choking action. Steve is rolling directly back and applying the sliding lapel choke on Bill.

NEAR WRIST LAPEL CHOKE FROM A SEATED RODEO RIDE

This is a variation of the sliding lapel choke and is useful if you are unable to reach your hand in and pull on his lapel or simply prefer to control his wrist.

Drew controls Chris with a seated rodeo ride. Drew uses his left hand to grab Chris's left wrist and pull it in tight to his body to trap it. Drew uses his right hand to secure the lapel choke to get the tap out. Drew can keep Chris in this position or roll him.

Drew rolls Chris to Drew's right side so Drew can use his right hand to pull Chris's left lapel tighter as he rolls. Drew continues to use his left hand to trap Chris's left wrist to his body for control. Drew can arch back a bit as he rolls to his right to make the lapel choke work better.

NEAR WRIST SLIDING LAPEL CHOKE AGAINST A FLAT OPPONENT

Erik is riding Chance who is flat on his front. Erik uses his left hand to grab Chance's left wrist and pull it in tight to Chance's left chest area to trap it.

Once Erik has trapped Chance's left hand, he uses his right hand to reach around Chance's neck and grab Chance's left lapel. Erik pulls on the lapel to get the choke and tap out.

ROLLING SLIDING LAPEL CHOKE (OKURI ERI JIME)

This is a standard, tried and true, move. Josh has Ben in a rodeo ride. Josh uses his left hand to pull open Ben's left lapel and uses his right hand to reach around Ben's neck. Josh will use his right hand to grab Ben's left lapel.

Josh uses his left hand to grab Ben's left lapel and uses his right hand to grab Ben's right lapel.

Josh rolls to his left so that the lapel choke with the right hand will work better.

Josh rolls Ben over, keeping control with his legs and applies the choke.

ARM HOOK ROLLING LAPEL CHOKE

Drew uses his right leg to hook over Roy's right arm. Also, Roy might have used his right hand to grab Drew's right leg. Drew uses his right hand to grab Roy's left lapel.

Drew rolls over his left shoulder.

As Drew rolls, his right leg, which is hooking Roy's right arm, pulls Roy over as well.

Drew completes his roll and rolls over onto his back with Roy on top of him. Drew still has the lapel choke in place. Drew uses his left hand to hook under Roy's left arm.

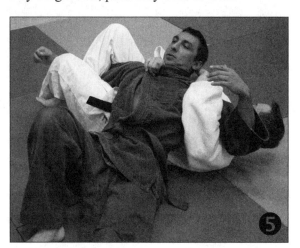

Drew traps Roy's right arm with both of his legs and uses his left hand to trap Roy's left arm while Drew slides in the lapel choke.

HELL STRANGLE (LEG KICKOVER LAPEL CHOKE)

Trevor has Chris in a rear lapel strangle, but Chris resists. Trevor swings his left leg over Chris's left shoulder as shown.

Trevor's left leg is placed behind Chris's head as shown. Trevor drives his left leg against Chris's head and pulls with his right hand on Chris's left lapel to get the choke.

LAPEL CHOKE USING KEYLOCK GRIP

LAPEL CHOKE USING HEAD PUSH

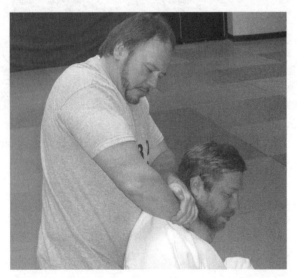

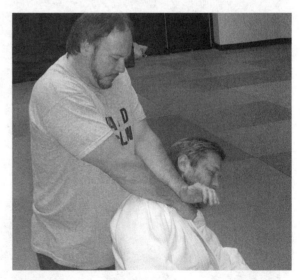

As Steve uses his right hand to pull on Bill's left lapel, he uses his left hand to grab his right wrist or forearm. Steve's left forearm is jammed behind Bill's neck and head, trapping it.

As Steve pulls with his right hand on Bill's left lapel, he uses his left hand and forearm to jam across the right side of Bill's neck. This makes the lapel choke tighter.

KNEE AND LAPEL STRANGLE TO ESCAPE THE HEAD AND ARM HOLD

Bill has Steve in a scarf hold or head and arm pin.

Steve turns in toward Bill and uses his left hand to reach under Bill's chin and grab Bill's left lapel.

Steve rolls to his left side and props himself up on his left shoulder as he moves his left leg up as shown.

Steve jams his left shin behind Bill's head as he uses his left hand to pull on Bill's left lapel to get the tap out. A weird choke, but if you're stuck in a hold or pin, it may be the thing that gets you out of the pin, even if the choke doesn't work.

TRIANGLE FROM THE SIDE IN THE GUARD POSITION (BASIC POSITION)

TRIANGLE, LEG AND ANKLE CHOKES
Choking or strangling your opponent with your legs is a powerful way to get the tap out. Your legs are stronger than your hands and arms and using your legs to squeeze against his carotid arteries or windpipe gives you an edge. Let's take a close look at triangle, leg, ankle and foot chokes.

Scott is using the triangle choke on Bret and is turned sideways to Bret. Doing this gives Scott "more leg" to choke Bret with. In other words, by moving to your side when doing the triangle from this angle, you can reach further with your legs and form a better triangle with them. This is useful for anyone, but especially useful for people who have shorter legs. This is my preference for doing the triangle off the back or guard position and you might want to practice this method of the triangle choke. The straight on method is the older version and is useful as well, but this sideway application really works and works with a high ratio of success.

TECHNICAL TIP: This technique is called the triangle because of its origin in Japanese jujitsu and judo. A popular move in sport judo as well as BJJ, submission grappling and MMA, this move has been called "sankaku" for many years. What does sankaku mean? It simply means "three angles" or "triangle." For many years in both professional and amateur wrestling, positioning your legs in this way has been called a "figure 4" and while this name is still used, the name "triangle" has come to mean any choke, armlock or hold where you form your legs in this position. Another point is that triangles can be done as chokes, armlocks, pins or leglocks and in many cases, you can get your opponent in "double trouble" or "triple trouble" with a combination of two or more different types of submissions all coming from the triangle you put him in.

TRIANGLE STRAIGHT ON FROM THE GUARD (BASIC POSITION)

Derrick is applying the triangle on Trevor from the basic position where he is straight in front of his opponent. This is the older form of the triangle and requires good flexibility.

PULL AND CONTROL YOUR OPPONENT'S ARM WHEN DOING THE TRIANGLE (FROM GUARD POSITION): Look at how Derrick has pulled Trevor's left arm across and to Derrick's left hip. Doing this helps Derrick reach his legs tighter around Trevor's shoulder and neck to form the triangle with his legs. It also cinches the choke in much tighter than if Trevor's shoulders were square.

TECHNICAL TIP: Controlling your opponent's arm is important in getting a stronger triangle on him. It not only helps draw or pull him in tighter when you're setting up the move, but it also helps cinch the triangle in tighter once you have him.

TRIANGLE FROM THE SIDE WITH ARM PULL AND CONTROL (BASIC POSITION)

Scott is applying the triangle from the side or supine position and look at how he is using his right hand to pull on Bret's right arm. Doing this pulls Bret's arm in tight and helps cinch the choke in tighter.

TRIANGLE FROM THE BOTTOM WITH ARM PULL AND CONTROL (BASIC POSITION)

Mike is doing the triangle choke from the bottom and uses his left hand to pull on Drew's arm to cinch the choke in tighter. Pulling on your opponent's arm really helps tighten the effect of your leg triangle no matter what position you are in when you try the move!

TRIANGLE WITHOUT ARM CONTROL

Applying the triangle on your opponent from any angle or position can be done without pulling in and trapping his arm. In this case, Bill is forming a triangle on Steve's neck and head and using it as more of a neck crank, although he can use it as a choke as well. I recommend pulling and trapping your opponent's arm when doing the triangle as it controls your opponent's head, neck and shoulders better than not trapping his arm. However, there are times when the triangle can be done without using his arm. I have several ways in my book GRAPPLER'S BOOK OF STRANGLES AND CHOKES.

TRIANGLE WITH PRESSURE TO THE SIDE OF THE NECK WITH YOUR UPPER LEG OR THIGH

Bret is using his right upper leg to reach across the left side of Chuck's neck to get the pressure against the side of the neck at the carotid artery. The upper leg is thick and muscular and can apply a lot of pressure on your opponent's neck in a triangle.

TRIANGLE WITH PRESSURE TO FRONT OR SIDE OF THE NECK WITH YOUR LOWER LEG

Josh's right lower leg and ankle are jammed against Derrick's throat and neck. A lot of pressure can be applied against your opponent's neck and throat using your lower leg!

TECHNICAL TIP: Most triangle chokes attack the carotid arteries at the side or sides of your opponent's neck, but you can also attack the front of his neck at the throat and windpipe. In any case, you're locking your opponent's head and shoulders and making the whole situation a lousy place to be for him!

ANKLE CHOKE (WEDGING YOUR ANKLE, LOWER LEG OR FOOT INTO YOUR OPPONENT'S NECK TO CREATE PRESSURE)

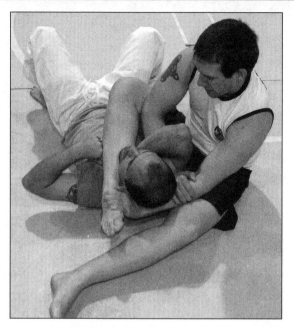

Jarrod is pulling with his left hand on his right ankle to jam his right ankle into Mike's neck creating the choke.

ANKLE CHOKE (PULLING YOUR OPPONENT'S HEAD INTO YOUR ANKLE, LOWER LEG OR FOOT TO CREATE PRESSURE)

Derrick is using his right hand to pull up on Josh's head and pull it into the left ankle. He is pulling Josh into the ankle and not pulling his ankle into Josh.

THE TRIANGLE AS A PIN OR HOLD-DOWN

The triangle position is extremely versatile and can be used for chokes, armlocks and pins. World Sambo Champion Jan Trussell is using "sankaku gatame" (the triangle pin) on her opponent in an international judo event.

TIGHTEN THE TRIANGLE USING ONE HAND ON YOUR LEG

Derrick is using his right hand to grab his lower leg to pull his left leg in tighter against the back of Trevor's head. Derrick is placing the top of his left foot on the inside of his right knee to form the triangle. Sometimes, you need a little assistance, so grab your leg or foot to cinch the triangle in tighter.

TIGHTEN THE TRIANGLE USING BOTH HANDS ON YOUR LEG

Sometimes, one hand isn't enough; so don't hesitate to use both hands to grab your leg or foot to move it in to tighten the triangle.

TIGHTEN THE TRIANGLE BY ADJUSTING YOUR BODY POSITION OR HIPS

Sometimes you have to adjust your hips or your body position to make the triangle work better. Derrick is turning his hips to make the triangle tighter on Kirt.

TIGHTEN THE TRIANGLE BY ADJUSTING YOUR FOOT INTO THE BACK OF YOUR KNEE

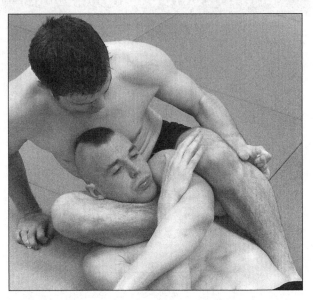

Derrick is using his left hand to grab his right foot so he can adjust it tighter in behind his left knee, making the triangle choke more effective.

TIGHTEN THE TRIANGLE BY PULLING OPPONENT'S ARM IN WITH YOUR LEG

Sometimes, when you roll your opponent into the triangle from this side position, his far arm won't be close enough to grab so you can pull it to cinch the triangle in tighter. In this case, use your leg and foot to hook his arm for control. Scott is using his right foot and leg to draw Bret's right upper arm in tighter.Scott will use his right hand to grab Bret's right arm to pull it in tighter to cinch the triangle in tighter. Using your leg in this way really controls your opponent's upper body, shoulder and arms.

TRIANGLE FROM THE GUARD (IN A GI) APPLIED SIDEWAYS

This is a very effective way of getting the triangle choke from the guard position and I prefer it to the straight on (and older) method.

Steve has Chance in his guard and Chance uses his left hand to hook under Steve's right leg to pass.

As Chance moves to his left with his left arm hooked under Steve's right leg, Steve rolls to his right.

Steve uses his right hand to grab or hook under Chance's left leg and knee. Steve uses this to pull himself in to his right. Steve is sideways to Chance. Steve places his right leg against the left side of Chance's neck as shown. Notice how Steve is pulling Chance's right arm across his body for more control and a tighter triangle.

Steve forms the triangle by placing the top of his right foot on the back of his left knee and applies pressure.

TECHNICAL TIP: Another reason I favor the sideways approach to setting up the triangle from the guard position is that you can pull your opponent's arm farther across your body. This results in a tighter choke and a quicker tap out.

TRIANGLE FROM THE GUARD (NO GI) APPLIED SIDEWAYS

Bret has Chuck in the guard and Chuck tries to pass by using his left hand to scoop under Bret's right leg. Bret jams his right leg against the left side of Chuck's neck.

Bret uses his right hand to hook under Chuck's left knee and leg and pulls his head to Chuck's left knee as shown. Look at how Bret is angled sideways to Chuck and has a lot of room to use his legs to form a triangle. Bret uses his left hand to pull Chuck's right arm. Doing this makes Bret's triangle stronger.

Bret forms the triangle with his legs as he uses his right hand to lift and roll Chuck over to Chuck's right. Bret can roll Chuck to his side and apply the triangle choke or add an armlock for double trouble (opposite page).

NORTH SOUTH TRIANGLE (OR DEEP SIDE) ROLL

Chris is applying a sideway triangle from the guard and Brad attempts to stand up.

Chris uses his right hand to pull hard so that he actually moves his head very close to or under Brad's left leg. As he does this, Chris uses his right hand to scoop up and uses his legs (still in a tight triangle) to roll Brad over.

TECHNICAL TIP: Sometimes, to escape your triangle, your opponent may attempt to stand up. If he does, try this technique.

Doing this rolls Brad back down on his right side and Chris is in a better position and gets the tap out.

DOUBLE TROUBLE USING THE TRIANGLE AND FIGURE 4 STRAIGHT ARMLOCK

Bret finishes the move on the previous page with this optional move, by applying a figure 4 straight armlock with the triangle choke.

TRIANGLE FROM THE GUARD (STRAIGHT ON POSITION)

Applying the triangle from the guard directly in front or straight on your opponent is the oldest way of using this choke. From the early days of Kodokan Judo, this choke has been applied from this position. While my preference is for the sideways version, it's very popular and useful. It requires good flexibility.

Derrick has Trevor in his guard and uses his left leg to swing over Trevor's right shoulder.

Derrick uses his right hand to pull his left leg over and behind Trevor's neck.

Derrick swings his right leg up and over his left foot, so the top of his left foot is behind and under his right knee. Derrick is using his left hand to move his foot in deeper under his knee. Notice that Derrick is using his left hand to pull Trevor's left arm across Derrick's body, helping move his legs in place better to make the triangle tighter.

Derrick has formed the triangle and is cinching it in tight. Look at how he is using his left hand to pull Trevor's left arm across his body.

To add pressure to the triangle, Derrick drives downward with his right foot. Doing this pulls Trevor in tighter and adds pressure to the triangle. As I said before, this is an old one, but a good one!

ADAMS TRIANGLE CHOKE FROM LEG PRESS SITTING BACK

World Judo Champion Neil Adams made wedging a leg across your opponent's body and getting a triangle choke and armlock famous. That's why the following moves are named for him.

Scott has Bret in the leg press position.

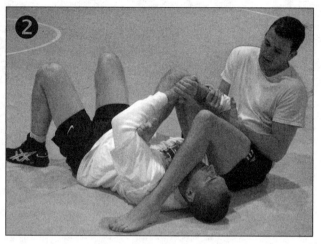

Scott uses his right leg to slip through Bret's arms as shown.

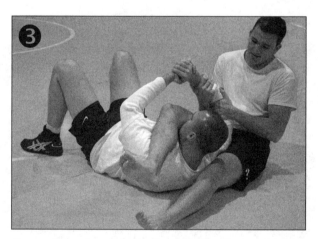

Scott places his right leg across the front of Bret's neck at the throat as shown. A lot of pressure will be directly on Bret's throat and windpipe when Scott forms the triangle.

Scott rolls back a bit to his left hip and cinches in the triangle for the tap out.

ADAMS TRIANGLE CHOKE ROLL (ROLL TO SIDE)

Bill has Steve in the leg press position.

Bill slips his right foot between Steve's arms. Bill uses is left leg to control Steve's head on the mat.

Bill drives his right leg across Steve's left shoulder and left side of his neck.

> **TECHNICAL TIP: ANKLE CHOKE FINISH (IF YOU WANT)** Bill can finish the move with an ankle choke shown in step 5 below. This is a powerful strangle against Steve's left carotid and is a good neck crank as well. But if Bill doesn't want to finish here or thinks it's not tight enough, he can finish with a triangle choke.

Bill pulls his right leg in tight across Steve's neck and will use his left hand to grab his right ankle or foot to pull it in tight.

Bill uses his left hand to grab his right ankle, trapping Steve's head.

Bill gets the tap out by rolling to his right rear. This forces Steve to rise up as shown and allows Bill to sink his triangle in tighter as he rolls back. The pressure is on the side(s) of Steve's neck.

ANKLE CHOKE AND BENT ARMLOCK FROM LEG PRESS

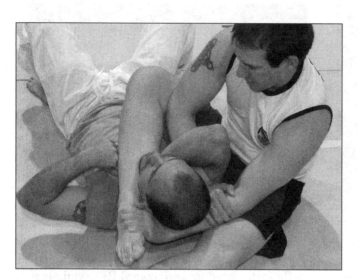

Here's a good ankle choke and armlock combination. Jarrod has a tight ankle choke on Mike and uses his right lower leg to trap Mike's right wrist and forearm. Sometimes, the grappler on the bottom (as Mike is) will use his right hand to try to pull Jarrod's choking leg (in this case his right) off his neck. In this case, Jarrod can use his lower right leg to trap Mike's right arm. Jarrod slides his right forearm between Mike's right forearm and upper arm and uses his right hand to grab his left forearm. The action of squeezing Mike's neck with his right leg and using his right hand to pull his right ankle in tighter creates the "double trouble" effect of a choke and a bent armlock. This may look complicated, but think of it as tying a knot. It takes some practice, but after a while, you do it without thinking and tie the knot tighter each time.

ROLL BACK TO TRIANGLE CHOKE IF ANKLE CHOKE DOESN'T WORK

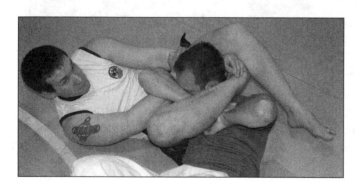

Jarrod adds pressure to the ankle choke by hooking his left leg over his right foot and using the triangle choke. Jarrod rolls onto his back to add pressure.

WEST PRETZLE (TRIANGLE CHOKE FROM LEG PRESS PULLNG ON HIS HEAD AND ROLLING BACK)

The major difference in this set up from the others is how much you pull up on the bottom man's head to apply the choke. This is Bill West's variation of the Adams Triangle that Bill used with great success in his judo career. Bill has Josh in the leg press.

Here's the big difference. Bill really pulls up hard on Josh's head with his left hand as shown. Bill pulls Josh's head up and toward Bill, while jamming his right leg through Josh's arms and over Josh's left shoulder. Bill uses his right arm to continue to hook Josh's right arm to Bill's body.

Bill rolls to his right rear side and continues to use his left hand to pull hard on Josh's head. This forces Josh up as shown. Bill slides his right leg deeper in across Josh's neck.

Bill applies the triangle choke with his legs and can roll back to stretch Josh's arm for a Juji Gatame. This is what double trouble is all about.

ADAMS TRIANGLE CHOKE ROLLING TO SIDE

Bill has Steve in the leg press position.

Bill slides his left foot (the one near Steve's head) over and under Steve's left arm as shown.

Bill rolls to his right and places his right foot on Steve's near (right) hip.

Bill rolls to his right side and shoots his right leg out straight under Steve's head forming a "pillow" that is placed under Steve's head. Bill uses his left leg to hook under Steve's left armpit as shown.

Bill drives his left leg under Steve's armpit to start the triangle.

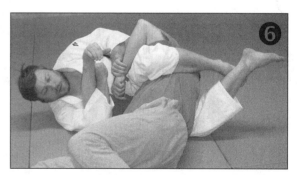

Bill forms the triangle to get the tap out and does a little double trouble on Steve by pushing on Steve's left forearm to get the bent armlock.

TRIANGLE CHOKE TO JUJI GATAME

This probably should have gone in the first section on armlocks, but this is a good set up from a triangle choke to an armlock so it was put here. Brad has Chris in a triangle choke, but Chris is starting to work out of it.

As Chris pulls his head out of Brad's triangle, or if Brad senses he is losing too much control, he uses his left leg to kick over Chris's head. This traps Chris's right arm in a Juji Gatame.

Brad stretches Chris's arm and rolls him to the mat to get the tap out.

BENT ARMLOCK AND TRIANGLE CHOKE DOUBLE TROUBLE

Ken is applying the triangle choke and using his right hand to push on Bjorn's right wrist and forearm creating a bent armlock. If your opponent is tough and won't tap out soon enough from the choke, you can use this armlock to get the job done.

ANKLE CHOKE FROM MOUNT POSITION

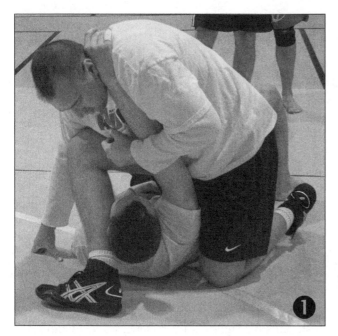

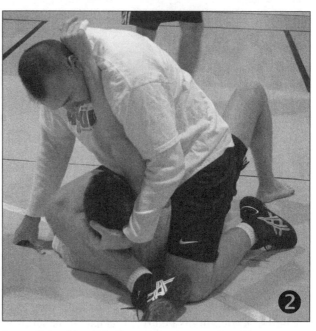

Bret has Scott in a high mount position and uses his right leg to stat to drive under Scott's head as shown. Bret uses his left arm to trap Scott's right arm.

Bret slides his right leg under Scott's head, tightening the hold.

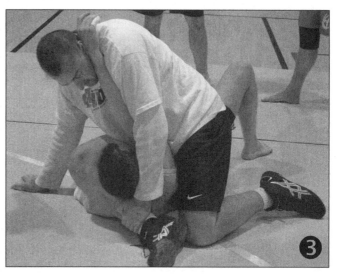

Bret uses his left hand to pull up on his right ankle, creating a powerful leg and ankle choke and neck crank.

ANKLE CHOKE FROM THE GUARD

Josh has Derrick in his guard and is using his hands to pull his right leg over Derrick's left side.

Josh pulls his right leg over Derrick's head and starts to jam it under Derrick's chin.

Using the ankles or lower leg to choke an opponent takes a lot of flexibility. Also, these types of chokes are often applied one step at a time and not applied in a hurry. That's not to say you don't need to be quick and use your time efficiently, but the key word is "efficient." Move from one step to the next, wasting no movement and continually increasing both the control and pressure much in the same way a snake tightens its hold on its prey.

Josh jams his right ankle under Derrick's chin, keeps it in place with his left hand (not shown) and then uses his right hand to grab it and pull it into Derrick's throat. This gets the tap out.

ANKLE CHOKE FROM THE MOUNT OR STRADDLE PIN

Derrick is sitting on top of Josh in a mount or straddle position. Derrick rolls slightly to his right so he can slide his left leg under Josh, and then across, Josh's right shoulder.

As Derrick sits onto Josh, he wings his left foot over Josh's head and jams it across the front of Josh's neck at the throat. As he does this, Derrick uses his right hand to pull up on Josh's head to start the pressure for the choke.

Derrick uses both hands to pull up on Josh's head, pulling it into Derrick's left ankle and lower leg. This is a popular choke in MMA and BJJ among the athletes who are very flexible.

ANKLE CHOKE AND TRIANGLE AGAINST A LOW ANKLE PICK OR SINGLE LEG TAKEDOWN

Bill is standing above Steve as shown. Steve may have tried a low ankle pick or leg grab.

Bill swings around and places his left leg over and behind Steve. Doing this puts Bill's right leg over Steve's shoulder as shown.

Bill uses his left hand to reach around the left side of Steve's neck and grab his right ankle.

ANKLE CHOKE FINISH (IF YOU WANT)

Bill rolls to his right using his left hand to pull his right leg in tighter around Steve's neck. This creates a good ankle choke from this position.

Bill can continue on to a "no arm" triangle. This is a good choke and neck crank as well.

ANKLE CHOKE AGAINST A FLAT OPPONENT

Bill is flat on his front with Steve at his side.

Steve uses his right leg to step over Bill's head.

Steve uses his right hand to grab his right ankle and works in an ankle choke.

This is one of those moves that can take an opponent by surprise. It may not always work, but the time it does, people will remember it.

ROLLING TRIANGLE CHOKE AGAINST A FLAT OPPONENT

1. Steve can continue on to a triangle choke from here by using his right hand to grab under Bill's right shoulder.

2. Steve rolls over his left shoulder using his right hand to help pull Bill over with him.

3. Steve rolls Bill over and starts to form the triangle with his legs.

4. Steve forms the triangle, tightens it up and gets the tap out.

TRIANGLE SIDE ROLL AGAINST OPPONENT ON ALL FOURS

Josh is controlling Nikolay from a top ride position.

Josh leans forward over Nikolay's left shoulder.

Josh rolls to his left and is stabilized on his head and left shoulder. Josh slips his left leg over Nikolay's left shoulder.

Josh uses his right hand to pull his left ankle and foot up.

Josh uses his right hand to pull his left ankle and foot up and under his right knee to form the triangle.

Josh drives his right foot back, bending his right leg and tightening the triangle to get the tap out.

TRIANGLE FROM A BENT ARM SET UP OUT OF THE GUARD

Josh uses his right hand to pull Kyle's right arm across his body. Josh uses his left hand to grab his right ankle to start to form the triangle.

Josh has Kyle in his guard and has already placed his right leg over Kyle's left shoulder. Look at how Josh has trapped Kyle's right arm by using his left hand to trap the right forearm on his chest. Josh is using his left hand to grab Kyle's right forearm to help trap it.

Josh tightens the triangle by using his left hand to pull his right foot in tighter on the back of Kyle's head and neck to form the triangle. Josh uses his right hand to pull Kyle's right arm across Josh's body. This helps tighten the triangle as well.

HEAD AND ARM HOLD ESCAPE USING THE TRIANGLE CHOKE

Bill has Steve in a head and arm hold.

Steve uses his right hand to push on Bill's chin.

Steve swings his left leg over Bill's right shoulder and neck

Steve forms the leg triangle and applies the choke for the tap out. This is a "no arm" triangle where Steve has not trapped Bill's arm but still has the triangle choke.

TRIANGLE CHOKE ESCAPE FROM THE SIDE HOLD OR POSITION

Drew has Mike in a side hold.

Mike creates space by using his left hand to push on the side of Drew's head.

As he does this, Mike swings his left leg over Drew's head. Mike uses his left hand to grab Drew's right wrist or forearm.

Mike forms a triangle with his legs and uses his left hand to pull on Drew's right arm to tighten the choke and get the tap out.

TAP OUT TEXTBOOK

TRIANGLE AND LAPEL CHOKE ESCAPE FROM SIDE HOLD OR POSITION

Bill has Steve in a side hold. Steve uses his left hand to grab Bill's right lapel as shown.

Steve shrimps into Bill and swings his left forearm under Bill's neck across the throat.

Steve lifts his left leg up and hooks it over Bill's head. Steve can push with his left leg against Bill's head as he continues to pull on Bill's right lapel with his left hand. You can see by the expression on Bill's face that this is a good choke and Steve can finish the move here if Bill taps out.

To really cinch in the choke, Steve forms a triangle with his legs and has Bill in double trouble with a lapel choke and a triangle choke.

DOUBLE TROUBLE TRIANGLE CHOKE AND JUJI GATAME FROM SEATED RODEO RIDE

Drew is behind Mike in a seated rodeo ride.

Drew scoots back to his left, away from Mike a bit. This give Drew more room to maneuver.

Drew rolls to his left side and swings his right leg over Mike's right shoulder. Look at how Drew is using his left leg across Mike's left hip for control.

Drew uses his left hand to grab his right ankle and foot to pull across the right side of Mike's neck.

Drew forms the triangle as shown.

Drew finishes with a double trouble situation of a triangle choke and a Juji Gatame.

TAP OUT TEXTBOOK

REAR TRIANGLE FROM A SEATED RODEO RIDE

Bill has Steve in a seated rodeo ride.

Bill scoots his body out to his right rear side and away from Steve and uses his left hand to hook under Steve's right shoulder.

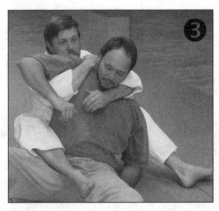

As Bill scoots out and away from Steve, he moves his left hand over Steve's left shoulder.

Bill rolls to his right, pulling Steve to his right. while using his left hand to reach over Steve's left shoulder and move his right foot up.

ANKLE CHOKE FINISH (IF YOU WANT)

Bill uses his left hand to pull his right foot and ankle in across Steve's throat, creating a good ankle choke to get the tap out. Bill can also pull his right foot under his left knee to form a triangle.

Bill forms the triangle and gets the tap out.

TRIANGLE CHOKE WHEN YOU TRY JUJI GATAME AND YOUR OPPONENT STANDS UP

Josh is trying to do a Juji Gatame, but Nikolay stands up and may try to pull Josh up off the mat to stop the armlock. Josh has pulled himself to his right as close as possible to Nikolay's left foot. This angle is important.

Josh moves his right leg from across Nikolay's left side and will swing it over Nikolay's left shoulder to start the triangle.

Josh has initially pulled himself in as close as possible to Nikolay's left foot as he uses both hands to pull Nikolay's right arm across his body to his own right shoulder. Josh starts to use his legs to form the triangle.

Josh uses his left hand to grab his right ankle to help for the triangle tighter.

TECHNICAL TIP: ARM CONTROL Controlling your opponent's arm helps form a tighter, more secure triangle with your legs. Josh is pulling Nikolay's right arm across his body so he can wedge his right leg tighter onto the left side of Nikolay's neck. Josh's right leg is farther across the back of Nikolay's head and neck, allowing his left leg to hook over tighter onto his right foot. **This sequence started with good arm control.**

Josh uses his left hand to pull his right leg in tight on the back of Nikolay's head. Josh is swinging his left leg up to form the triangle.

Josh forms the triangle with his legs.

Josh tightens the triangle with his legs and adds pressure by using both hands to pull on Nikolay's head. This gets the tap out.

TRIANGLE TOP PIN AND CHOKE (DOUBLE TROUBLE FROM THE MOUNT)

Travis has Jon in the mount high on Jon's chest.

Travis uses his left hand to pull up on Jon's head.

Travis uses his left foot to step up so he can slide it under Jon's neck for the triangle.

Travis slips his left foot and leg under Jon's neck as shown.

Travis leans to his left to form the triangle with his legs.

Travis applies the pressure for the choke by using his left hand to pull down on Jon's left wrist as shown. Travis has Jon in a triangle pin and choke and can pound away with his fists if in an MMA match.

TOP TRIANGLE AND FLATTEN OPPONENT

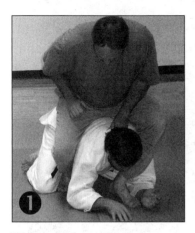

From a rodeo ride, Steve uses his left leg to step over Bill's left shoulder as shown.

Steve uses his right hand to hook under Bill's right arm as Steve drives forward.

Steve uses his right arm and hand to scoop under Bill's right arm to pull Bill forward. Steve uses his left hand to post out onto the mat for stability.

Steve forms the triangle with his legs as shown and uses his right hand and arm to scoop and pull Bill's right arm forward.

Steve leans forward and keeps pulling on Bill's outstretched right arm. Steve tightens the pressure with the leg triangle to get the tap out.

TOP TRIANGLE FROM A RODEO RIDE

Scott has Bret in the rodeo ride.

Scott uses his left leg to step over Bret's left shoulder.

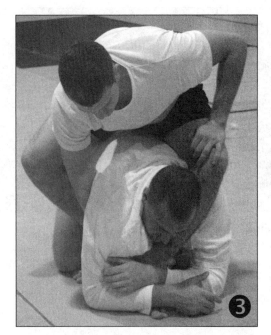

Scott uses his right hand to reach under Bret's right armpit and grab his left ankle.

Scott rolls to his left and uses his right hand to pull on his left ankle and place it under his right knee to form the triangle. As he does this, Scott tightens the triangle to get the tap out.

TRIANGLE TOP ROLL AND DRAG

Derrick uses his right leg to hook over Josh's right shoulder as shown.

Derrick uses his left hand to grab his right ankle and pull it in tight across Josh's shoulder and chest.

Derrick leans forward to his right forcing Josh to go to his right shoulder. This opens up Josh's left side so Derrick can form a triangle on that side.

TECHNICAL TIP: Look at how Derrick is using his left foot to wedge behind Josh's left side for better control and a tighter triangle.

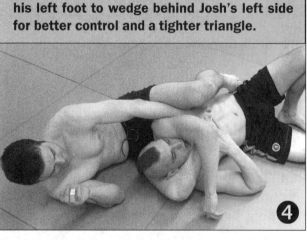

Derrick rolls Josh to the right as shown and forms a triangle with his legs as he does. Derrick is still using his right hand to pull his right ankle in tighter to form a better triangle.

Derrick rolls onto his buttocks and sits up tightening the triangle choke.

TRIANGLE FROM GUARD IF YOUR BENT ARMLOCK DOESN'T WORK

This is a classic case of "going to plan B" when one move doesn't work, so you go to another one that will.

Derrick has Trevor in his guard and is trying to secure a bent armlock from this position.

Derrick rolls to his right to try to secure the bent armlock.

Trevor senses the armlock and starts to pull his right arm down and away from Derrick.

As Trevor pulls his right arm down and free, Derrick uses his right hand to push Trevor's right upper arm and shoulder so Derrick can more easily wing his left leg over Trevor's right shoulder.

TRIANGLE FROM GUARD IF YOUR BENT ARMLOCK DOESN'T WORK

Derrick rolls to his right side and drives his left leg down hard on the back of Trevor's head and neck.

Derrick uses both hands to pull Trevor's left arm across Derrick's body as shown. This gives Derrick more room to form his triangle.

Derrick uses his right hand to position his foot in tight under his right knee as shown.

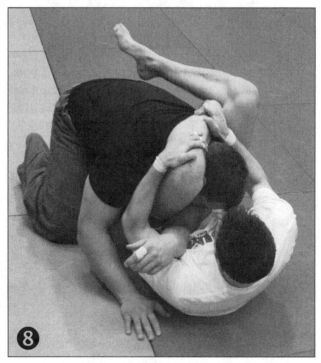

Derrick cinches in the triangle with his hands to get the tap out.

TRIANGLE FRONT ROLL

Bill is standing above Steve as shown.

Bill steps over Steve's right shoulder with his left leg and jams his right thigh onto the top front of his left shoulder.

Bill leans to his right and drives his right leg over Steve's shoulder and under Steve's body as shown.

Bill positions himself on his right side and hooks his right foot and leg under Steve's right armpit.

Bill forms the triangle with his legs.

Bill rolls to his left and pulls Steve with him. Steve rolls over his head as shown.

Bill rolls Steve over and applies the triangle. This is also a good hold-down. Look how Bill is using his right arm to control Steve's left leg. There are a lot of good triangle pins in my book GROUND-FIGHTING PINS AND BREAKDOWNS as well as many ways to put an opponent into this pinning position.

UPSIDE DOWN TRIANGLE CHOKE FROM THE TOP

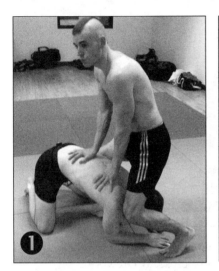

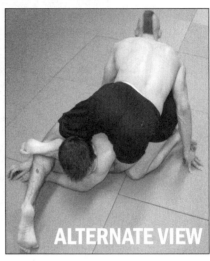

ALTERNATE VIEW

Josh is standing above Derrick who is on all fours. Josh hooks his right leg over Derrick's left shoulder and jams his left knee onto Derrick's right shoulder for control.

Josh uses his right leg to hook under Derricks' left armpit and under Derrick's neck and throat. Josh forms a triangle as shown.

Here's a top view of how Josh has formed the triangle with his legs and is leaning to his right.

Josh rolls onto his right side as shown.

Josh rolls onto his back, rolling Derrick with him and is now "upside down" applying the triangle choke.

UPSIDE DOWN TRIANGLE FROM THE GUARD

Jarrod has Drew in his guard.

Jarrod shrimps to his right and hooks his right hand and arm under Drew's left leg. This pulls Jarrod really close to Drew's left leg. As he does this, Jarrod uses his left leg to swing over Drew's head.

Jarrod swings his left leg over Drew's left shoulder and continues to pull himself in close to Drew with his right hand under Drew's left leg. This creates an "upside down" position for Jarrod.

Jarrod pulls himself and spins to his right and forms the triangle as shown.

Jarrod uses his left hand to pull Drew's right arm in tightly as shown making the choke tighter.

DOUBLE TROUBLE STRAIGHT ARMLOCK AND TRIANGLE FINISH: Jarrod can also use his left hand to push down on Drew's extended left arm as shown, creating a double trouble situation.

TRIANGLE FROM THE FRONT WHEN OPPONENT IS ON ALL FOURS

Ken is positioned above Bjorn, who is on all fours. Ken places his left knee of Bjorn's shoulder to isolate it and control it.

Ken uses his left hand to scoop up and under Bjorn's left arm as shown.

Ken uses his left hand to pull the apron of Bjorn's gi over his left wrist or forearm, trapping Bjorn's left arm to his side in a "judo keylock."

Ken sits on Bjorn's upper back and head as he uses his right leg to step over Bjorn. Ken sill has the judo keylock in place.

Ken rolls onto his left side and shoots his left leg out straight forming a pillow for Bjorn's head, while using his right leg to start to form the triangle and his right hand to reach out and grab Bjorn's right arm.

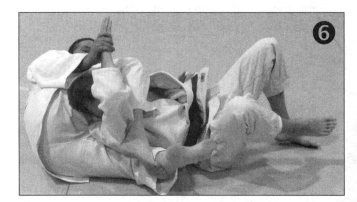

Ken uses his right hand to grab Bjorn's right lower arm or wrist and pulls it to tighten the triangle. Ken forms the triangle and applies the choke to get the tap out.

BENT ARMLOCK & TRIANGLE DOUBLE TROUBLE FINISH: Ken uses his right hand to push on Bjorn's right wrist and forearm to get the bent armlock. The triangle is still on tight, so this is a classic double trouble situation!

TRIANGLE FROM THE FRONT WITH LEG PULL

Scott is at the top of Bret who is on all fours. Scott jams his left knee onto Bret's shoulder for control and uses his left hand to and grab Bret's left leg above the knee to pull it out a bit so he can get a better grip on Bret's left ankle.

Scott grabs Bret's left ankle and pulls up on it.

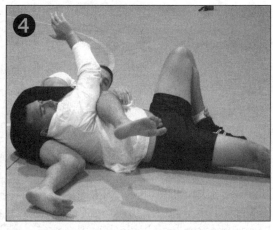

Scott pulls Bet over with his ankle grip and Scott lands on his lcft side.

Scott is on his left side and shoots his left (leg on the mat) leg out straight forming a "pillow" for Bret's head. Scott uses his right leg to hook under Bret's right armpit so he can form his triangle.

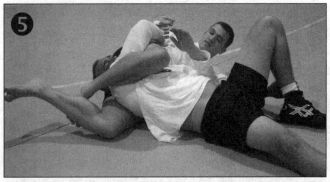

Scott forms the leg triangle and uses his right hand to grab Bret's right arm or wrist and pulls it to tighten the triangle. Scott squeezes the triangle tight to get the tap out.

CORNER TRIANGLE CHOKE AND FLATTEN HIM OUT

Steve is doing a standing ride on Bill.

Steve sits on the back of Bill's shoulders and neck as he places his left foot over Bill's right shoulder as shown. Steve's right knee is driving into Bill's left side and this tightens the leg control Steve has on Bill.

Here's another view of how Steve drives his left foot and leg over Bill's head and right shoulder. You can see how Steve drives his right knee deep and hard onto Bill's left side.

Look at the angle Steve is at relation to Bill. Steve places the top of his left foot behind his knee as he leans forward.

Steve drives his hips forward and arches his back so he flattens Bill out. Steve gets the tap out with the triangle from this position.

CORNER ROLLING TRIANGLE CHOKE

If Steve chooses not to flatten out to get the choke in the previous technique, he can use his right hand and arm to hook over Bill's right leg as shown. Steve will roll over his left shoulder to get momentum.

Steve rolls over his left shoulder. Look at how Steve's right arm is grabbing and controlling Bill's right leg as he rolls.

Steve rolls Bill onto his back and tightens the triangle for the tap out.

ROLLING DOUBLE TROUBLE TRIANGLE CHOKE & JUJI GATAME COUNTER TO SINGLE LEG TAKEDOWN

Bret shoots in and is grabbing Scott's left leg.

Scott uses his right leg to step over Bret's body and uses both hands to grab under Bret's right shoulder. Scott's left leg is positioned over Bret's left shoulder.

Scott rolls over his right shoulder. Scott uses his left leg (over Bret's shoulder) to form a triangle by placing his left foot under his right knee as he rolls.

Scott rolls onto his right side and uses both hands to pull Bret's right arm for the Juji Gatame. Scott tightens the triangle and gets the choke as well.

PULL HIS LEG TRIANGLE CHOKE COUNTER TO A LOW SINGLE LEG TAKEDOWN

Bret is grabbing Scott's right ankle. This move is useful if Bret has shot in for a low ankle pick or single leg takedown, but it can be done if Bret is simply in this position.

Scott quickly spins around to his left, over Bret and uses his left hand to grab Bret's left ankle.

Scott rolls back and uses both hands (if possible) to grab Bret's left lower leg, ankle or foot. Scott pulls Bret back as shown.

Scott rolls onto his left side and shoots his left leg (the one on the mat) out straight to form a "pillow" under Bret's head.

Scott forms the triangle with his legs as he uses his right hand to grab Bret's elbow (or forearm or wrist) to pull it in. Doing this helps Scott form a tighter triangle with his legs. Scott squeezes the triangle tight and gets the tap out.

FOOT PROP TRIANGLE (OPPONENT IS FLAT)

Sometimes, you can place your foot on your opponent's hip and use your foot to prop him over, rolling him into the triangle. Andy is flat on his front with Derrick above him. Derrick kneels on his right knee and places his knee (not shown) in front of Andy's left shoulder to block it and extends his left leg, using his left foot to prop the right side of Andy's hip. Often, when an opponent flattens out like this, the last thing he expects is a triangle from the front position. After some practice, you may prefer this set up for the triangle rather than wedging your foot in under your opponent's armpit. This is a good, fast and explosive way to roll your opponent into the triangle choke.

SOME FINAL THOUGHTS ON CHOKES AND STRANGLES

As in any phase of submission grappling, judo, jujitsu, sambo or MMA, your position and the position you put your opponent in is vital to being able to apply a submission technique. You have to create opportunities to be able to apply your choke (or armlock, leglock or any move). Your opponent won't lie there and let you choke him, so you have to put him there and keep him there until you get him to tap out. Then again, there are times when you can take advantage of your opponent's mistake, or take advantage of an opportunity that presents itself. In any case, always try to be in the best position for you and the worst position for your opponent.

Honestly, choking your opponent isn't the hard part. Getting him into position, breaking him down and controlling him are the hard parts of grappling or fighting. As you see in this book, time and again, there are a few ways to actually choke, armlock or leglock your opponent and an almost infinite number of ways to put him in a position so you can choke, armlock or leglock him. This is what makes all of this so interesting. Now, let's turn our attention to the next section: leg, knee, ankle and hip locks.

FOOT PROP TRIANGLE (OPPONENT IS BALLED UP ON ALL FOURS)

The foot prop can also be used when your opponent balls and doesn't give you an opening to wedge your foot in for your triangle. Andy is balled up tight on all fours. Derrick uses his left foot to prop Andy's right knee as shown to start his roll into the triangle.

Derrick rolls to his left with his left foot propping Andy's right knee, rolling Andy to his right (Derrick's left).

Derrick applies the triangle and gets the tap out.

SECTION THREE: LEGLOCKS
POSITION, THEN SUBMISSION

Leg and lower body submission techniques deserve serious attention from anyone. Even if you don't favor using them as an offensive weapon, somebody else will. Throughout this section, I'll refer to "leglocks" in a generic sense when speaking about any lower body submission techniques. In a lot of situations, there's a "flow" to applying leglocks and you can apply a heel hook from an ankle lock, or a toehold as a finishing move to a bent leglock or any combination of moves to get your opponent to tap out. For this reason, I'll use somewhat of a "shotgun" approach as to how I present leglocks and lower body submissions in this section. For another serious and in-depth look at lower body submissions, I recommend my book VITAL LEGLOCKS published by Turtle Press.

From my experience and observation, the three most often used foot submissions are the straight ankle lock, the toehold and the heel hook. For this reason, I'll start off with these techniques, and then go on to the other leglocks. Leglocks where you lock the knee joint are done as straight leglocks (also called legbars), bent knee locks, and leg (or knee) cranks, where you twist or manipulate your opponent's knee or leg out to the side and out of his normal (and comfortable) range of motion. Other lower body submission techniques are hip locks, where you pull your opponent's legs apart causing pain in his hips, grapevines (where you wrap your legs around his legs and stretch them causing pain in the upper legs and hips) and crabs (such as the old pro wrestling move, the Boston Crab) where you bend your opponent at his lower back and create pain in his lower back, hips and upper legs.

SAFETY IN TRAINING AND COMPETITION: TAP OUT IN TIME

If you've trained on leglocks very long, you'll discover that it usually takes a little more time to react to the pain you feel in a lower body submission than in an armlock or a choke. While this isn't always the case, I've observed (and experienced) the fact that grapplers don't tap out soon enough when a lower body submission has been put on them. Significant tendon or ligament damage can take place if you don't tap out or submit in a timely manner, especially when a heel hook or knee crank is applied. This is one of the reasons the sport of sambo recognizes a yell, shout or any verbal sign from a wrestler as a sign of submission as well as a tap out. As in any other type of submission technique, when in doubt, tap out to avoid an injury.

BASIC WAYS TO GRAB OR CONTROL YOUR OPPONENT'S FOOT OR ANKLE
Straight ankle locks may be the group of leg submissions that has the highest ratio of success. When I say "straight" I mean any ankle lock that is stretched and in a straight line with the leg. There are several basic variations of how to grab and control your opponent's ankle, foot and lower leg to secure the straight ankle lock, which are shown in the following photos.

FIGURE 4 GRIP ANKLE LOCK

There are several primary ways of controlling an opponent's ankle when applying a straight ankle lock. This is the figure 4 method and as you can see, Mike is using his hands in a figure 4 lock to hold Chris's left foot and leg. Mike places his left hand (palm down) on the top of Chris's left ankle. He uses his right forearm to reach under Chris's left ankle and his right hand to grab the top of his left wrist. As always in a straight ankle lock, it's important to cradle your opponent's foot in your armpit as Mike is doing with the top of Chris's left foot trapped on the backside of his armpit. This traps your opponent's foot in your arms, keeping his foot and leg in close and tight to your body. You can add more pressure and stretch the joint by arching up with your hips as well as rolling to one side for more leverage.

JACKET GRIP ANKLE LOCK

Jarrod is using his left hand to grab his left lapel after tucking Chris's right ankle up under his left armpit. Jarrod could have grabbed his other lapel as well. The important thing is that Jarrod has his other arm free.

REVERSE FIGURE 4 GRIP ANKLE LOCK

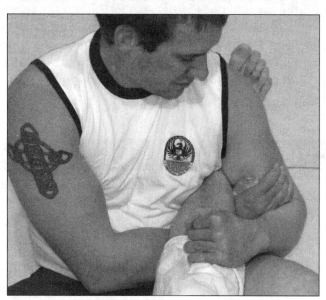

Here's a variation of the figure 4 hand position. Jarrod has moved his partner's right ankle and tucked it under his left armpit. Jarrod uses his right forearm to reach under his partner's left ankle and uses his right hand to grab his left biceps. He uses his left hand to grab the top of his partner's right shin. This is a strong grip that controls your opponent's ankle. Look at how Jarrod's right forearm is raking across his partner's Achilles' tendon on the back of the leg adding more pressure and pain.

SQUARE GRIP ANKLE LOCK

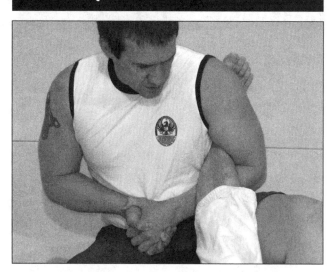

Jarrod is applying the square lock hand position on his partner's right ankle. The foot is trapped under Jarrod's left armpit. He is arching his hips forward as he applies the pressure to his partner's Achilles' tendon by using his left forearm to squeeze and roll against the tendon.

Shown here are a couple of other basic applications of foot or ankle locks that are generally used: the toehold and the heel hook. The ones shown here are the fundamentals of how to perform these joint locks. Different variations are shown later in this section. As with any subject, everything flows from a thorough understanding of the basics. The toehold and heel hook are no different, so make sure you practice the correct way to grab and manipulate your opponent's foot or ankle to apply these holds on a regular basis.

TOEHOLD

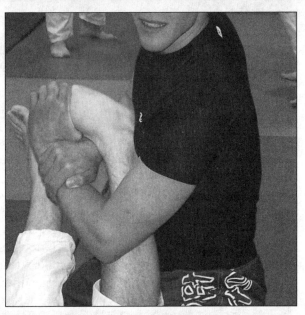

Basically, anytime you grab your opponent's toes or the side of his foot, and twist his ankle or foot (or in any way cause pain in his ankle or foot), it's a toehold. As shown in this photo, you grab his foot and twist the ankle, causing pain. As with the heel hook, it's important to cradle your opponent's foot between your body and arms and let the rotation of your body do the work for you. You can use the strength of your hands and arms to twist your opponent's foot, but you will get more power into the technique (and a better ratio of success) if you hug his foot, apply your hold and let the weight of your body do the work.

HEEL HOOK

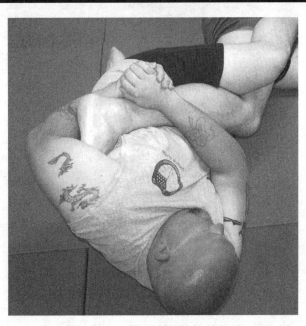

The heel hook is a common and effective leglock. When doing a heel hook, make sure you cradle your opponent's lower leg, ankle and foot tightly between your body and arms. When applying pressure, rotate your body and let the weight of your body do the work, not only your arms. When it comes to a strength match, your opponent's leg will usually beat out both of your arms, so use your body to make this move work. It not only does a real job on your opponent's ankle, it can cause severe damage to his knee as well! Heel hooks can be dangerous and many submission grappling events have made them illegal because of the severity of damage they inflict to the knee as much as to the foot or ankle. But even in spite of this, it's still an effective, hardcore submission technique and should be studied by anyone who is serious about lower body submissions.

BASIC LEG OR KNEE LOCK POSITIONS

Locking your opponent's leg or knee takes a bit more work than locking his ankle or foot but the results are usually pretty spectacular when you get the tap out from a big leglock.

From a tactical point of view, going for a knee lock can be a positive "time waster" in a tight match. Maybe this sounds like stalling but if you're in a tight match and have a small lead in the score, digging in and leg wrestling with your opponent, then making it all look like you're doing everything possible to get the ankle or knee lock is a great way to convince the referee you're the busier man on the mat and staying active. I've seen it used numerous times in sambo matches and it never fails to impress the referee. If for nothing else, use leglocks and leg wrestling as a tactical tool! However, I'm sure you wouldn't mind at all if, while you're "wasting time" working for a leglock, your opponent taps out from the pressure and pain you've put on him.

There are basically three types of knee locks. They are the bent knee lock, the knee crank and the straight knee lock (or knee "bar.") One application of the bent knee lock is when you jam a part of your body (or your opponent's body such as his own leg) behind his knee and bend it. Another is anytime you bend your opponent's knee and take it out of its natural range of motion. The straight knee lock takes place anytime you straighten your opponent's knee joint against a fulcrum (such as your crotch, hip or upper leg). Doing this "bars" the knee and causes pressure or pain in the joint. A knee crank occurs anytime you twist or turn the knee outside of its natural range of motion. A knee crank can either be done on a knee that is straight (or mostly straight) or bent.

BENT KNEE LOCK

There are pretty much two types of bent knee locks. The first (and most common) type is when you jam something on the inside of your opponent's knee joint (such as a knee as Chris is doing on Bob shown in this photo). You jam a part of your body inside of your opponent's knee and either pull on it or twist it, causing pain. The second type is shown in the next photo when you bend and twist the knee, causing the leg to go unnaturally out of its range of motion.

Sometimes, the different types of knee locks tend to run together. Here is a bent knee lock that could also be considered a knee crank. There's a blurred line between these types of joint locks, and really it's pretty much a matter of terminology. The bottom line is that it works. In both cases, you twist or crank your opponent's knee outside of its natural range of motion. Actually, Jarrod has Bret in a double trouble move by twisting his knee and starting to apply a toehold as well!

KNEE OR LEG CRANK	STRAIGHT KNEE LOCK (ALSO CALLED THE LEGBAR OR KNEE BAR)

Here's another photo of a knee crank. This one is a subtle, yet very painful knee crank. Often, the knee is cranked as a result of a heel hook, and this application shows this situation. John isolates Steve's upper leg as John rotates Steve's lower leg causing it to twist and crank outside of its natural range of motion. John's left leg is pushing down on Steve's right leg adding to the pressure and making the joint go out of the natural range of motion.

Sometimes referred to as a "knee bar" the straight knee lock is a very effective way of producing a tap out. This not only bars the knee joint against a fulcrum (in this case, Kyle is using his hips and crotch as a fulcrum to bar Ben's knee) but it also stretches the entire leg causing muscular pain as well.

HIPLOCKS, GRAPEVINES AND CRABS

When you catch your opponent in a hip lock, he usually gives up immediately because it hurts! Splitting a guy's hips apart often causes an immediate (and unpleasant for him) reaction. Hip locks can be dangerous. While the hip is a strong joint, it's possible to dislocate the hip joint or quickly tear ligaments and tendons with a hip lock.

The three primary hip and upper leg locks are:

1. The "Banana Split" or "Spladle," when you split your opponent's legs apart outside of his natural range of motion.

2. The "Grapevine," when you split your opponent's legs wide apart when he is either laying on his front or on his back.

3. The "Crab" or "Boston Crab," when you twist or manipulate your opponent's upper leg, hip and lower back using the weight of your body to apply pressure and cause pain to his lower back and hip areas. This is usually done when your opponent is on his front or front side.

GRAPEVINE

When you wrap or lace your legs around your opponent's legs, it's usually called a grapevine. Grapevines create pressure on your opponent's hips and are useful as a control position as much as a submission technique.

HIP LOCK (KNOWN AS THE BANANA SPLIT OR SPLADLE AND OTHER NAMES)

The banana split is commonly used in amateur wrestling as a pin, and we use it in jujitsu, sambo, submission grappling and MMA as both a control position and as a hip submission technique. It produces some severe pain and is called a "split" for good reason!

THE CRAB (BOSTON CRAB)

A nasty and painful hip, leg and lower back submission technique is the crab. The crab was made famous in the old days of legitimate professional wrestling by such great athletes as Lou Thesz and other wrestlers and is a dangerous, nasty lower body submission!

Okay, now that the groundwork has been laid, let's turn our attention to the many set ups, breakdowns and positions that result in leglocks and lower body submissions.

THE STRAIGHT ANKLE LOCK

Anytime you control your opponent's ankle and apply pressure in a straight line with his leg, this is a straight ankle lock. Often, the pressure you apply on your opponent's Achilles' tendon is the cause of the pain. Ankle locks are the workhorse of lower body submissions and used often in sambo and submission grappling matches. From my experience, the most reliable lower body and leg submissions are the ones aimed against the ankle or foot. It seems that the farther the part of the body is away from the chest area, the easier it is to control it and the foot is about as far away from the chest as a body part can get. When attacking the ankle or foot, the primary point to inflict pain is the ankle (and Achilles' tendon), either by twisting it or stretching it. An exception is the heel hook where you control and attack the heel of your opponent, but in reality, this is a variation of an ankle twist. John (on the left) and Mark are drilling on the straight ankle lock.

TECHNICAL TIP: An efficient way to learn the straight ankle lock is to do the "lacing" drill or "confidence" drill. These are the same drill, just different names. In this photo, Travis and Derrick each have a straight ankle lock and start the drill seated as shown in this photo. On the coach's command of "go" each tries to work in an ankle lock on the other. In the above photo with John and Mark, you can see how each grappler may arch back, roll or otherwise try to secure his ankle lock on his partner. You can do this drill on varying levels of resistance from total cooperation to 100% effort on the part of each athlete. It's important for an athlete to tap out if his partner sinks in the ankle lock for safety in training. Another drill is the "scramble" drill where each grappler is sitting on his buttocks on the mat facing each other and really close to each other, but does not have his partner's ankle grabbed. On the coach's signal of "go" each grappler works to get his partner's ankle and secure an ankle lock. For some more good drills on leglocks, read my book DRILLS FOR GRAPPLERS published by Turtle Press.

ANKLE LOCK FROM THE GUARD

Jarrod is on his back with Jeff in his guard. Jeff steps up with his right foot and leg to start to pass Jarrod's guard or trap Jarrod's left leg, which often happens in this position. When Jeff does this, Jarrod uses his left hand to grab Jeff's right ankle and his right hand to grab Jeff's left wrist for control.

Jarrod uses his left arm to trap Jeff's right ankle as he starts to roll to his right and use his left hand to pull on Jeff's wrist. Jarrod uses his left foot and leg to push Jeff over to Jarrod's right and Jeff's left. This starts Jeff rolling to his left as shown.

Jarrod continues to roll Jeff to the mat and as he does, tightens his hold of Jeff's right ankle with his left arm.

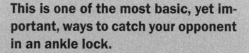

This is one of the most basic, yet important, ways to catch your opponent in an ankle lock.

Jarrod rolls Jeff over and secures a figure 4 grip on Jeff's ankle and gets the tap out.

STRAIGHT ANKLE LOCK FROM GUARD AGAINST A STANDING OPPONENT

This is a good ankle lock if your opponent is standing above you. Jarrod is on his back with both of his feet wedged in Jeff's hips as shown. Jarrod uses his right hand to hook Jeff's left ankle and uses his left hand to grab Jeff's left wrist. If Jarrod can't grab Jeff's wrist, that's okay, but it's important for Jarrod to get his hand on Jeff's ankle. As he does this, Jarrod uses both of his feet jammed on Jeff's hips to push Jeff down to his back.

Jarrod pushes Jeff onto his back as he uses his right hand to pull on Jeff's left ankle.

Jarrod pushes Jeff onto his back and hooks his right arm over Jeff's left ankle and secures a figure 4 straight ankle lock. Jarrod can use any ankle lock grip he wants.

ROLLING ANKLE LOCK AGAINST THE GUARD

TECHNICAL TIP: Positioning your knee in your opponent's crotch like this is a common set up for getting past your opponent's guard or to start a rolling ankle or leg lock from this position.

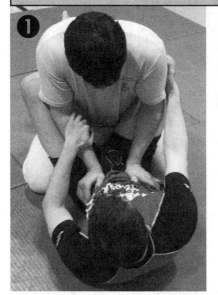

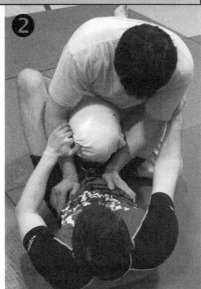

ALTERNATE VIEW

Jarrod is between Derrick's legs in his guard and is pressing down on Derrick with both hands to control him.

Jarrod drives his right knee between Derrick's legs and jams his shin on Derrick's crotch to create a diversion, but more importantly, to move his right leg over so he can roll Derrick into the gator roll and secure the ankle lock.

As Jarrod jams his right knee between Derrick's legs, he uses his left hand to reach back and hook his left arm over Derrick's right lower leg.

Derrick uses his left hand to grab Derrick's right ankle tightly, then rolls to his left as shown.

Jarrod rolls through and turns Derrick over as he rolls.

Jarrod had rolled over and rolled Derrick with him. Jarrod forms a secure grip to get the straight ankle lock as he rolls. Often, your opponent will tap as your roll him, so be ready to feel or listen for the tap or sign of submission as you roll.

STRAIGHT ANKLE LOCK FROM SAMBO CHEST HOLD OR OPPONENT'S GUARD (ROLL BACK VARIATION)

Steve has Bill held down but Bill has broken contact and is attempting to escape from the hold. As Bill pushes Steve away, Steve leans back, making sure his knees are wide for a stable base and opens the space between his body and Bill's.

Here's another view of how Bill has pushed Steve away. Notice that Steve is still holding Bill's sleeve with his left hand, but has started to uses his left elbow to slip back and hold Bill's right leg next to Steve's left side.

 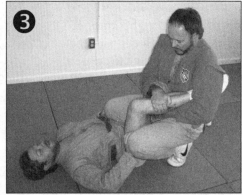 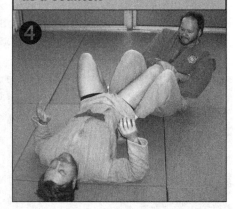

TECHNICAL TIP: Notice that Steve's feet are firmly tucked under Bill's buttocks to keep Bill from grabbing Steve's ankle as a counter.

Steve snatches Bill's right leg with his left arm as shown in this photo and pulls it in tightly to his left side. As Steve does this, he rises up and gets onto his right foot, jamming his right knee hard in Bill's crotch. This knee in the crotch provides Steve with some stability and creates a distraction, taking Bill's attention off his right leg. Notice how Steve has trapped Bill's right knee with both of his hands to his side.

Steve uses his left arm to hook under Bill's right leg and slides his left arm down to Bill's ankle as Steve leans back. Steve has now assumed a squatting position, keeping his knees pinched together around Bill's right leg. Steve makes sure to drive his left forearm directly under Bill's right Achilles' tendon Steve has controlled Bill's lower leg and ankle with a figure 4 hold and pulls Bill's right ankle in tightly to his left side. As he does this, Steve starts to roll backward.

Steve has rolled backward and arched his hips immediately, stretching Bill's right ankle and making sure to cinch tightly on Bill's right Achilles' tendon causing pain in the ankle. Steve keeps his knees squeezed together to trap Bill's right leg.

GATOR ROLL ANKLE LOCK FROM A ROLLBACK POSITION

As shown before, rolling an opponent to gain momentum and add pressure to the leg or ankle locks is a common skill that every grappler should know. Trevor has a straight ankle lock on Bryan's left ankle and has already rolled back to apply the pressure, but Bryan is resisting. Trevor will roll Bryan to create momentum and get the ankle lock as he rolls him.

Trevor keeps rolling to his left, all the while cinching in tighter on Bryan's left ankle. You can see how Bryan's left foot is trapped under Trevor's right armpit. This photo also shows that Bryan is trying to counter Trevor's ankle lock with one of his own.

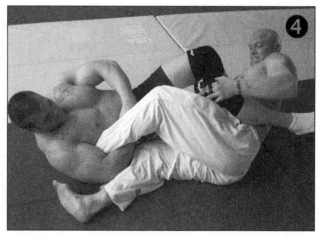

This shows a typical gator roll in action. Both grapplers are working for the advantage, but Trevor still has the upper hand with better control of Bryan's ankle. Bryan is actively going for his own ankle lock at this point.

Trevor keeps rolling and as he does, arches his hips to add more pressure to the ankle lock. Trevor has rolled Bryan over with his gator roll and the momentum of the roll has cinched the ankle lock in really tight, forcing the tap out.

ROLLING ANKLE LOCK COUNTER TO OPPONENT'S DEFENSE

If you've attempted a straight ankle lock and your opponent defends by jamming his foot forward and pulls on your jacket (or you) to ease the pressure, quickly start to roll to get the ankle lock. In this photo, Travis has jammed his right foot through Rusty's arms and has pulled on his jacket to ease the pressure of Rusty's ankle lock.

Rusty rolls to his left side which forces Travis's right foot up and deeper into Rusty's left arm. This rolling action also cranks Travis's right knee unnaturally.

Rusty continues to roll and the momentum of his rolling helps in securing Travis's right foot and leg and causes pressure on Travis's ankle and knee.

NORTH SOUTH GATOR ROLL

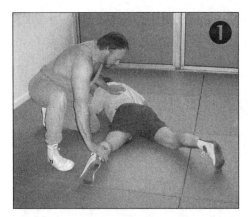

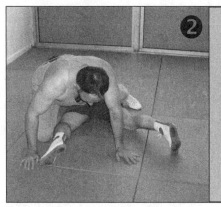

TECHNICAL TIP: Steve quickly gets to "the working end" of Bill to start his leglock. What this means is that in some cases, you will have to turn to your opponent's rear end or legs to start setting up the breakdown to secure your leglock or ankle lock.

Here's a pretty basic move, but one that will work for you when you need it. Bill is on his front in the chicken position and Steve is at his side. Steve quickly turns to face Bill's feet.

Steve is now in the north-south position and using his right knee to stabilize himself. Steve is starting to reach for Bill's left ankle.

Steve uses his right arm to hook over Bill's left foot and hug it tightly into his armpit as shown. Steve's left foot is posted on the mat wide and away from Bill's body so Bill can't reach for it very easily.

As Steve rolls to his left, he scoops Bill's left foot in even tighter and grabs his hands in a square lock. Steve uses his right forearm to place pressure on Bill's left Achilles' tendon. Notice how Steve's left knee has bent and he has swung it under himself to add momentum to his roll.

Steve is in the middle of the gator roll and arching his hips really hard to add pressure to the ankle lock. As Steve rolls, the momentum of the rolling action adds pressure to the ankle lock and gets the tap out.

NORTH SOUTH ANKLE LOCK

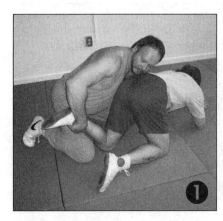

Bill is on all fours in a fairly stable position. Steve is breaking Bill down by using his left hand to hook under Bill's waist (Steve is using his left hand to grab Bill's far hip) and using his right hand to hook Bill's left ankle and pull it out.

Steve breaks Bill down to his front by pulling hard with his right hand on Bill's left ankle and driving into Bill with his left shoulder.

Steve keeps hold of Bill's left ankle with his right hand and quickly turns to face Bill's feet.

Steve posts on his right knee and left hand for stability as he hooks his right arm over Bill's left ankle and tucks it in his right armpit as shown.

Steve steps over Bill's body with his left knee and rests it on the mat. As he does this, Steve is in a direct north-south position with Bill. Steve uses a figure 4 arm position on Bill's left ankle. Notice that Bill's left leg is still bent. This makes Bill's leg a weaker target for Steve.

Steve can now either tripod out to apply pressure as shown here or start his gator roll.

DROP UNDER ANKLE LOCK OR HEEL HOOK

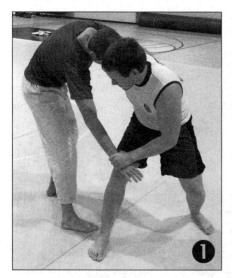 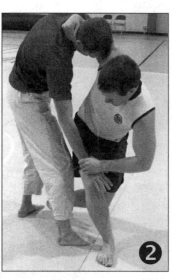 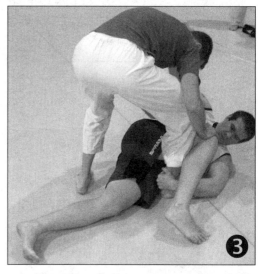

Jarrod has a head and arm tie-up on Bjorn and uses his right foot to step forward and to the outside of Bjorn's right side as shown.

Jarrod uses his left foot to backstep deep between Bjorn's legs.

As Jarrod backsteps between Bjorn's legs, he slides through Bjorn's legs and lands on his right side as shown, while using his left hand to grab Bjorn's right ankle.

Jarrod swings his right leg across Bjorn's right hip as uses his right hand to pull down on Bjorn's head as shown. Jarrod swings his right leg up as well.

Jarrod swings his legs over and hooks them together, lacing them, as he uses a heel hook on Bjorn's right heel.

ANKLE TO ANKLE (ANKLE PICK TO ANKLE LOCK)

I saw this used a lot in international sambo competition and even if you can't get the ankle lock, you get takedown points but it really is a good transition move from standing to the ground.

Jarrod shoots in with an ankle pick on Derrick. Jarrod is using his left hand to pick Derrick's left ankle.

Jarrod takes Derrick down with the ankle pick and uses his left hand and arm to hook tightly under Derrick's left ankle as shown. Jarrod pulls Derrick's left ankle to Jarrod's left hip.

STANDING ANKLE LOCK FINISH

Jarrod secures a figure 4 grip on Derrick's left ankle, uses his legs to trap Derrick's left leg and finishes with a standing straight ankle lock. For any number of reasons, Jarrod may not choose to finish with a standing ankle lock and can continue on to the ground.

ROLLBACK ANKLE LOCK FINISH

TECHNICAL TIP: Rolling onto your back like this really adds a lot of pressure to the ankle lock. As you roll back, make sure you have his ankle tucked tightly under your arm and arch forward with your hips for better leverage.

If Jarrod chooses to roll back, he makes it a point to squeeze his knees together on Derrick's leg, trapping it and starts to roll back.

Jarrod rolls back, arches his hips and applies pressure to the straight ankle lock. Look at how Jarrod's feet are tucked under Derrick's buttocks keeping them safely away from Derricks' reach for a counter leglock.

GATOR ROLL FINISH

Sometimes, rolling back isn't enough to make him tap out. In this cases, roll him over in a gator roll to gain momentum to secure the ankle lock.

Often as you roll your opponent, he'll tap out from the ankle lock. In some case, you may have to roll over and secure it from a belly down position like this to get the tap out.

CUBAN LEG GRAB TO ANKLE LOCK

The Cuban leg grab is one of the best throws or takedowns you will find. It's excellent for any type of combat sport or in a real fight and throws your opponent hard to the mat and sets him up for a leglock. The starting position is important. (As Nick Rothwell said to me once: "There's no submission without position.") For more information on the Cuban leg grab, refer to my book THROWS AND TAKEDOWNS published by Turtle Press.

Derrick uses his left arm to hook over Jeff's right upper arm. Derrick makes a point to move his left foot outside of Jeff's stance at Jeff's right leg.

Derrick lowers the level of his body by leaning forward and bending his knees and grabs Jeff's right leg immediately above the knee with his left hand. As he does this, Derrick drives his head into Jeff's chest and right front shoulder area and keeps firm control with his left arm overhook on Jeff's right arm.

Derrick uses his right hand to pull Jeff's leg to Derrick's right hip and throws Jeff to the mat. This isn't merely a takedown; it's a good, hard throw.

STANDING ANKLE LOCK FINISH

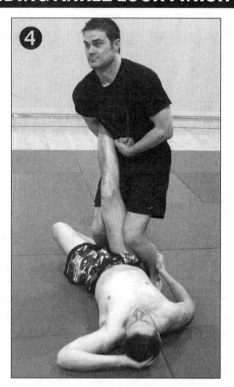

Derrick can finish and get the tap out with a standing ankle lock as shown. Often, you will have to finish with a rollback to an ankle or leglock.

ROLLBACK ANKLE LOCK FINISH

Derrick uses his right arm to firmly tuck Jeff's right lower leg and ankle in his right armpit. Derrick's knees trap Jeff's right upper leg as Derrick starts to squat and roll to his back. Look at how Derrick is hunching forward with his shoulders to stay round as he rolls back.

Derrick rolls back and secures the ankle lock for the tap out.

TECHNICAL TIP: WEAKEN HIS LEG BY CRANKING IT When you apply an ankle or foot lock on your opponent, try to always bend his leg outward at the knee, cranking it. A cranked or bent knee makes your opponent's entire leg weaker and more vulnerable to your ankle or foot lock.

ROLL BACK HEEL HOOK AND KNEE CRANK

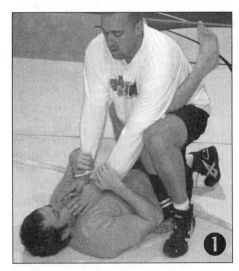

Bret is between Chuck's legs as shown and steps up on his left foot and leg to isolate Chuck's right leg.

Bret uses his left leg to step over Chuck's right upper leg and hip to the left side of Chuck's body. This traps Chuck's right leg. As he does this, Bret turns to his right to start to manipulate Chuck's right leg.

This view shows how Bret uses his left leg to step over Chuck's right leg and hip and start the knee crank.

Bret rolls back onto his left buttocks as he uses his right hand to scoop Chuck's right knee as shown. Bret uses his left hand to grab under Chuck's right lower leg to start the heel hook.

Bret rolls back and forms a triangle with his legs to lace Chuck's legs and applies the heel hook and puts downward pressure on Chuck's right knee for the tap out.

HEEL HOOK COUNTER TO STRAIGHT ANKLE LOCK OR LEG LACE

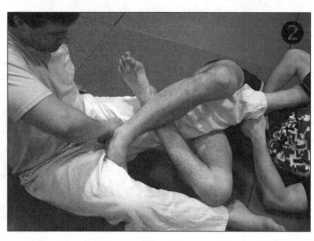

You might be able to surprise your opponent with this little heel hook when he's trying to do an ankle or straight leglock on you. Derrick is applying a straight ankle lock on Jarrod. Jarrod uses his right hand to grab Derrick's right heel and his left hand to grab Derrick's right ankle as shown.

Sometimes, Jarrod may be only able to use one hand. If that's the case, he uses his right hand to hook Derrick's right heel.

It's a surprise move, and might not always work, but Derrick's reaction shows that this "quick catch" technique can work suddenly, surprising your opponent.

HEEL HOOK COUNTER TO LEG SPLIT STRAIGHT ANKLE LOCK

Derrick uses his left foot to push on Jarrod's right leg to split him apart for control.

> **TECHNICAL TIP: A good way to control an opponent when applying an ankle lock is for Derrick to use his left foot and leg to push against Jarrod's right knee or leg to "split" Jarrod's legs.**

Jarrod uses his right hand to grab Derrick's left heel as Jarrod uses his left hand to control Derrick's right leg to prevent Derrick from lacing it.

Jarrod uses his right hand to twist Derrick's left heel and uses his right hand to add pressure to the twisting motion to get the tap out. Again, this may not always work, but if nothing else, it makes your opponent think about his heel and foot and takes his focus off locking yours.

QUICK CATCH HEEL HOOK AGAINST OPPONENT'S GUARD

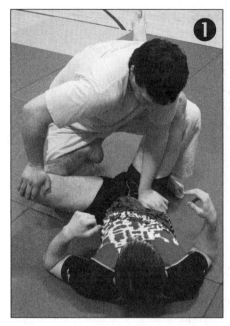

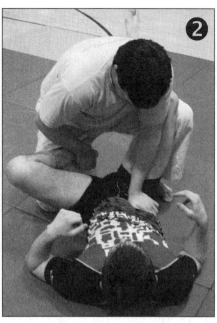

Another surprise move that may not always work, but can help you pass your opponent's guard. Jarrod is on his knees with Derrick using his left leg to control Jarrod. Jarrod uses his left hand to push down on Derrick's left leg and moves his left leg up as shown to prop Derrick's right leg.

Jarrod uses his right hand to hook Derrick's left heel as shown.

Jarrod uses his right hand to pull up on Derrick's left heel as Jarrod uses his right hand to push down on Derrick's right knee.

TECHNICAL TIP: GO "FISHING" FOR YOUR HEEL HOOK, ANKLE LOCK OR TOEHOLD
Often, when you and your opponent are in a scramble situation, both of you are actively working to get the other guy's ankle, heel or leg and the first one who establishes a strong hold gets the tap out. In a scramble situation, it is vital to aggressively "fish" for your opponent's foot to gain control and secure a joint lock.

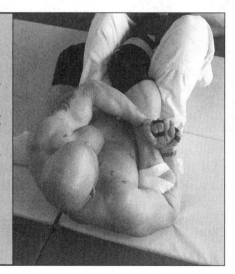

Jarrod leans back a bit to add pressure to his hand movements and gets a surprise tap out. As I said before, this isn't a high percentage move, but might catch an opponent off guard or can be used to get past his legs.

KOREAN ANKLE PICK TO STRAIGHT ANKLE LOCK

John has wrapped his right foot around Chance's right foot and is driving his right knee on the inside of the right lower leg, trapping Chance's right foot. As John does this, he reaches down with his left hand to scoop Chance's right ankle. John's right arm is hooked under Chance's left arm and shoulder.

John uses his left hand to grab Chance's right ankle and pull it to John's left hip. As John does this, he drives Chance down with his right hand, throwing Chance to the mat. This is more than a takedown and is a hard throw really.

John uses his left hand to swing Chance's right foot across his body as shown. As he does this, John is getting ready to hook under Chance's right leg with his right arm.

> This ankle pick was named the Korean Ankle Pick because it was popular among many Korean judo athletes in the 1960s and 1970s.

John hooks over Chance's right leg with his right arm and secures Chance's right foot in his right armpit. As John does this, he quickly moves his left leg by Chance's right hip and as John starts to sit back onto his buttocks, he jams his left foot in Chance's right hip.

John arches his hips really hard as he rolls backward using a square lock to grab his hands together. John has squeezed his knees together to trap Chance's right leg.

Here's a closer view of how John has grabbed his hands together in a square lock and is using his right forearm to wrench Chance's right Achilles' tendon.

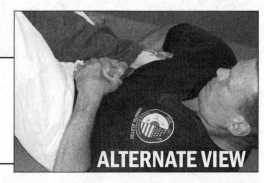

ALTERNATE VIEW

DOUBLE LEG TAKEDOWN TO ANKLE LOCK

Jarrod shoots in deep for a double leg takedown on Sean.

As Jarrod takes Sean to the mat, he keeps both of his arms tight around Sean's thighs. This keeps Sean from moving away or shrimping to try to pull Jarrod into his guard.

Jarrod quickly moves up and jams his left knee into Sean's crotch. As he does this, Jarrod used both of his arms to grab Sean's belt.

Jarrod keeps his left knee jammed in Sean's crotch as he uses his right arm to slide down Sean's left leg and grab the ankle. Jarrod maintains good control of Sean by keeping a firm grip with his left hand on Sean's belt. Jarrod uses his left arm to hook over Sean's left ankle as shown.

Jarrod quickly pinches his knees together to trap Sean's left leg and uses a figure 4 hand hold to secure Sean's left ankle for a straight ankle lock. Jarrod can either roll directly back onto his buttocks then onto his back or add more pressure by doing this, then rolling to his right hip as shown.

SCISSORS ANKLE LOCK (LEG TRIANGLE OR FIGURE 4 VARIATION)

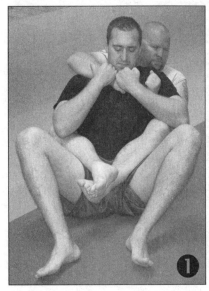

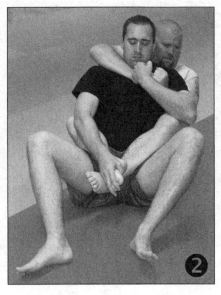

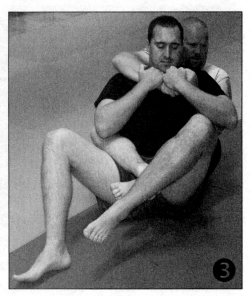

Here's why everybody tells you to never cross your ankles when you're behind your opponent in a seated rodeo ride! Eric is behind Bret in a rodeo ride and going for a choke. He's made the mistake of crossing his ankles to attempt to squeeze Bret to control him better.

As Bret fights off Eric's choke with his left hand, he uses his right hand to push down on Eric's right ankle. Bret may also pull Eric's right ankle out a bit to better set it up for the move to come.

Bret quickly uses his left leg to hook over Eric's right ankle as shown in this photo. Bret now can use both hands to fight off Eric's choke. Bret is using his left lower leg to push down on Eric's right ankle and this starts the ankle lock.

ALTERNATE VIEW

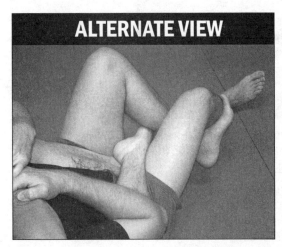

Here is a top view of the figure 4 ankle lock. You can see how Eric's right foot is trapped and being bent downward causing pain in the ankle joint.

Bret adds more pressure to the ankle lock by doing a triangle (also called a figure 4) leg position. Bret has jammed the top of his left foot under his right knee. As he does this, Bret uses his left lower leg to really put a lot of pressure on Eric's ankle. Bret can add more pressure by driving his right foot down.

SCISSORS ANKLE LOCK (FOOT PUSH VARIATION)

Here's a nasty little move that really hurts. Kyle has Ben in a rodeo ride and has crossed his ankles. Kyle's left ankle is on top. Ben uses his hands and arms to pull Kyle's knees into him for better control.

Ben uses his left leg to hook over the top of Kyle's left ankle and his right hand to pull his left foot up and over Kyle's left ankle. Ben uses his left hand and arm to scoop Kyle's left leg in tighter to his body for more control.

Ben uses his right foot to push down on his left foot just above his ankle. By doing this, Ben exerts a great deal of pressure on Kyle's left foot as shown and causes pain in the ankle.

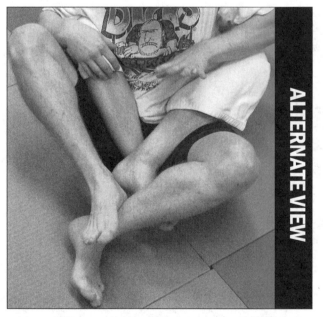

ALTERNATE VIEW

Here's a closer view of how Ben is using his right foot to push down on his left ankle and lower leg to trap Kyle's foot. You can se how this wrenches Kyle's left foot to the left and produces pain in the joint.

TAP OUT TEXTBOOK

BENT KNEE LOCK FROM THE BOTTOM

Jarrod grapevines Bret from his bottom guard position.

Jarrod rolls to his left hip and side, using his right knee and foot to push Bret away. Jarrod quickly uses both hands to grab for Bret's right foot and leg. Jarrod makes sure to leave his left leg jammed behind Bret's bent right knee.

Jarrod uses both hands to grab Bret's right foot and pull up on it creating a bent knee lock. If Jarrod wants, he can finish with a toehold.

GRAB AND TOEHOLD FROM THE BOTTOM

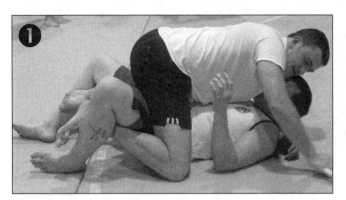

Scott has Jarrod is a grapevine and Jarrod wants to escape, or even better, slap a leg or foot lock on Scott.

Jarrod pulls his right leg free of Scott's left leg.

Jarrod slides his right leg to his left under Scott and uses his left leg to hook over his right knee as shown.

Jarrod bends his right knee and places his right foot on the mat as shown and uses his left leg to cross over his right knee. Doing this pulls Scott's right foot upward.

Jarrod uses his right hand to grab Scott's right foot and twist is downward. This twists the ankle for the tap out.

HEEL HOOK AGAINST OPPONENT'S GUARD

Chad is on the bottom and has Jarrod in his guard. Jarrod uses his left hand to grab Chad's right leg.

Jarrod passes Chad's right leg over across his head and body and uses his right hand to trap Chad's right heel as shown. Look at how Jarrod tucks Chad's right foot in his right armpit for good control. Jarrod might be able to surprise Chad with a heel hook at this point.

Jarrod moves to his left (to Chad's right) as he uses his right hand to pull Chad's right foot.

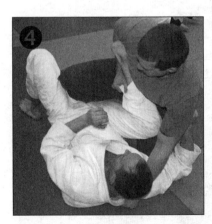

Jarrod uses his right knee to jam into the inside of Chad's left thigh. Jarrod will keep hold of Chad and roll to his back.

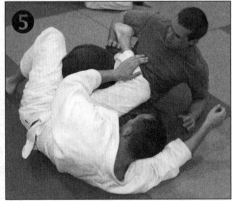

Jarrod rolls back as he squeezes his knees together trapping Chad's right leg. Jarrod quickly uses his right hand to start the heel hook.

Jarrod forms his hands to secure the heel hook on Chad's right foot, leans back and applies the heel hook for the tap out.

HEEL HOOK GUARD PASS TO SIDE HOLD OR POSITION

Jarrod has moved to his left and used his right hand to hook Chad's right heel as shown.

Jarrod keeps moving to his left to get to Chad's right side and uses his left hand to hook over Chad's head to secure the side position.

TRIANGLE PULL OUT AND GUARD PASS TO KNEE CRANK AND HEEL HOOK

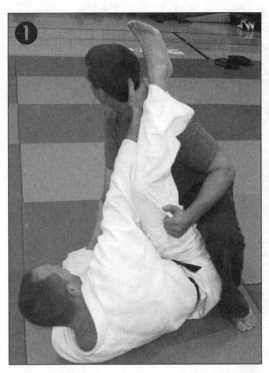

Chad is trying to start a triangle choke from his guard and Jarrod pulls up and away from it as shown.

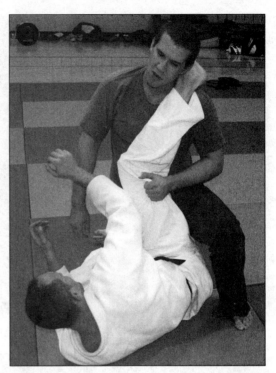

Jarrod moves his head and traps Chad's right foot with his head and left shoulder. Jarrod uses his left hand to grab Chad's right knee and upper leg as shown.

Jarrod uses his right hand to grab Chad's right heel and trap it between his head and left shoulder.

ALTERNATE VIEW

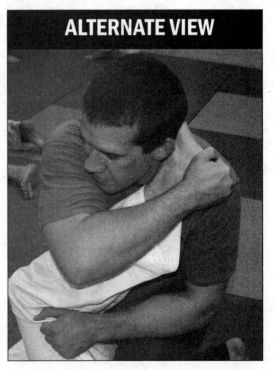

Here's a closer view of how Jarrod grabs Chad's heel as he traps it with his head and left shoulder.

TRIANGLE PULL OUT AND GUARD PASS TO KNEE CRANK AND HEEL HOOK

Jarrod pulls in Chad's heel and leg close in to his body.

As Jarrod pulls in on Chad's right leg, Jarrod twists to his right and uses his right leg to step over Chad's right upper leg. This creates a leg crank and Chad doesn't like it.

Jarrod forms a triangle with his legs to lace Chad's right leg and control it. As he does this, Jarrod rolls back and twists to his right creating both a heel hook and a knee crank.

Here's another view of how Jarrod finishes the move to get the tap out.

GATOR ROLL ANKLE LOCK FROM GUARD CRUSH

Jarrod is jamming Sean into the mat using the weight of his body and driving into him, arching with his hips. He is holding Sean's jacket with both of his hands and driving him into the mat, pinning him so Jarrod can apply an ankle lock.

Jarrod uses his left hand to hook under Sean's left Achilles' tendon and ankle, resting his left forearm under Sean's Achilles' tendon.

Jarrod quickly uses the figure 4 grip to control Sean's lower right leg as he continues to bear his weight down on Sean pinning him to the mat. Jarrod could arch his hips forward as he cradles Sean's right ankle in his armpit and finish the ankle lock here, but if Sean hasn't tapped out, Jarrod can add momentum by starting a gator roll.

Jarrod immediately starts his gator roll to his right side to gain momentum on the ankle lock. Jarrod will roll to his right and as he does, cinch the ankle lock in tighter.

FAR ANKLE BREAKDOWN TO ANKLE TRAP

John has grabbed Eric's far (left) lower leg with both hands. His left hand is hooking Eric's left ankle and his right hand is trapping Eric's left lower leg. John is driving his right shoulder into Eric's left side and hip.

John drives hard with his right shoulder into Eric's left side as he scoops Eric's left lower leg up and in to his body with his left hand. Notice how John is driving off his left foot to get extra power.

John has broken Eric down on Eric's left side and immediately uses his left arm to hook under Eric's left foot. Look at how Eric's left leg is bent. John is grabbing Eric's jacket with his left hand, trapping his foot. John continues to drive Eric over onto his back.

John has broken Eric down on his back. John maintains control of Eric's jacket with his left hand trapping Eric's left foot as shown. Look at how the top of Eric's foot is resting inside the crook of John's left elbow.

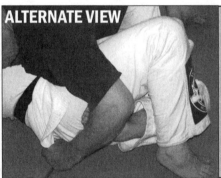

ALTERNATE VIEW

Here's a closer view of how John has trapped Eric's left foot and is cranking it upward and into Eric's buttocks. This stretches Eric's ankle and causes pain.

TECHNICAL TIP: This is a good breakdown to get your opponent on his back, so even if his ankle is made of rubber and he won't tap out, you still have him in a strong hold or ride from the side.

John adds more pressure to the hold by using his right forearm to jam under Eric's neck (by holding onto Eric's collar). John is driving his right elbow upward and forcing Eric's head to turn to Eric's right. This cranks the neck and adds pressure to the entire move getting the tap out.

LEG LACE TO HEEL HOOK

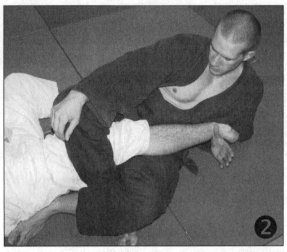

From the scramble position, Jarrod has laced Sean's right leg with a triangle. Once he has Sean's right leg isolated with the lace, Jarrod quickly uses his left arm to start to scoop Sean's right heel into the inside of his left elbow.

Jarrod maintains control of Sean's right leg with his lacing action (using a triangle hold) as he slides his right forearm under Sean's right heel to set up the heel hook. Sean's right foot is wedged in the inside of Jarrod's right arm and Jarrod is hugging Sean's foot tightly to his body.

Jarrod applies the heel hook, pulling Sean's right leg in tight to his body as he rolls to his back. Notice that Jarrod's left wrist is immediately under Sean's right Achilles' tendon as Jarrod applies the heel hook. Jarrod continues to keep the triangle hold on Sean's right leg to isolate it.

Notice that Jarrod's right leg is hooked over Sean's right upper leg to form the triangle that laces Sean's leg tightly. Jarrod is hugging Sean's right foot in tight to his body and arching and turning to his right, allowing the weight and turn of his body to do the work.

LEG BUNDLE (DOUBLE LEG) ROLL TO HEEL HOOK

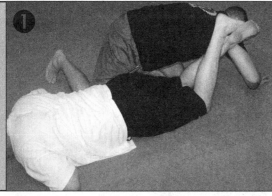

TECHNICAL TIP: A "bundle" or "bundling your opponent's legs or feet" refers to grabbing both of his legs or feet and capturing them as Bret does here.

Greg is in the chicken position with his legs hooked together. Bret turned to Greg's feet and is hooking his right arm under Greg's feet.

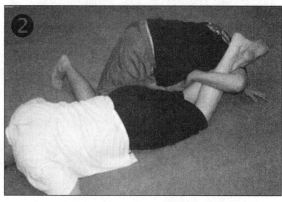

Bret hooks under Greg's ankles with his right arm as shown and scoops them both in tightly to his body.

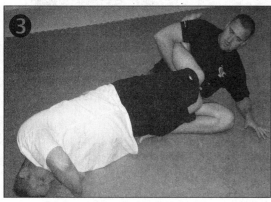

Bret has scooped both of Greg's ankles in tight to his body and trapped them with his right arm. As he does this, Bret rolls to his left side and rests on his left hip. Bret pulls Greg's legs really tight to the right side of Bret's body for maximum control of both of Greg's legs.

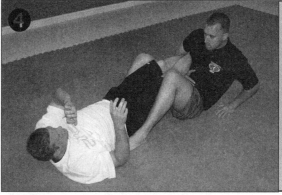

TECHNICAL TIP: Bret makes sure to tuck both of his feet under Greg's buttocks to keep Greg from countering by grabbing Bret's ankles.

Bret rolls over his left side and onto his buttocks as shown as he scoops Greg's legs and feet up under his right armpit and into the right side of his torso. Notice that by rolling, Bret has Greg's legs and body between his legs.

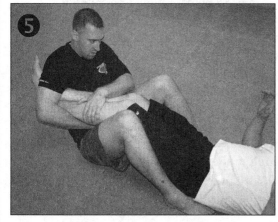

Bret sits up and pulls Greg's feet in tight to his body. Bret squeezes his knees together, further trapping Greg's legs and pinching them together.

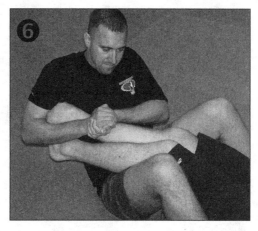

Bret quickly applies a heel hook on Greg's top foot by sliding his right forearm under Greg's top (right) heel. Bret applies a square lock and hugs Greg's right foot tightly into his left side. Bret will get the tap out by twisting his upper body to his left.

TAP OUT TEXTBOOK

STAND AND STEP OVER HEEL HOOK

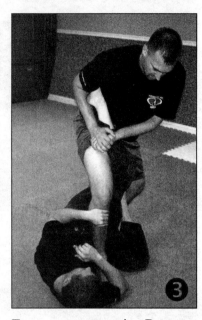

Bret is standing up as Bill is trying to either keep him away with his feet or pull him back down into his guard. As Bret stands, he uses his right hand to grab Bill's left ankle.

Bret uses his right hand to pull Bill's left foot up into Bret's right armpit. As he does this, Bret uses his right hand to hook under Bill's left heel. Bret grabs his hands together to form a square lock to secure the heel hook. Bret twists to his left as he cradles Bill's left foot in his right side forcing the tap out. Notice how Bret has used his right upper thigh and hip to help cradle Bill's left foot and secure it tightly.

To cause more pain, Bret can step over Bill's left leg as shown causing both a heel hook and a knee crank on Bill's left leg.

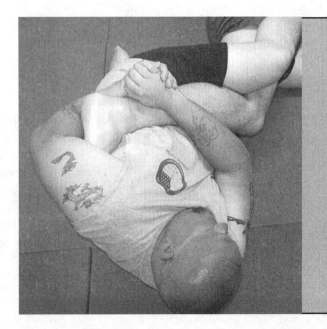

TECHNICAL TIP: HEEL HOOK ARM POSITION
For a heel to hook to be effective, you must cradle your opponent's foot tightly in your side as shown in this photo. Eric is using his hands (locked together in what's called the "square" lock) to pull Bret's foot and lower leg tightly to his left side. Eric applies pressure to Bret's foot, ankle and leg by turning to his right as he hugs Bret's foot. Eric is allowing the turn and weight of his body to do the work which makes the lock tighter and more effective.

LEGLOCKS 383

CROSSOVER KNEE CRANK AND HEEL HOOK

Alan is in Caleb's guard and uses his right arm to trap Caleb's left lower leg.

Alan rolls to his left buttocks as he swings his right leg over Caleb's left upper leg and hip as shown. Alan wedges the top of his right foot under Caleb's right upper leg and hip.

TECHNICAL TIP: When you're first learning knee cranks, this is a good one to start with.

Alan rolls back to his right and applies a knee crank on Caleb's left leg. The knee cranks gets the tap out.

If Alan chooses, he can slide in a heel hook on Caleb's left foot to give Caleb some double trouble with a knee crank and a heel hook. This is the kind of move that can ruin your day if you're on the wrong end of it.

LEG LACE FROM GUARD TO HEEL HOOK

John is on his back in the guard position making sure both of his feet are wedged in Steve's hips. John uses his left hand to grab Steve's right heel and uses his right hand to pull Steve's right wrist to John's right side.

John shoots his left leg through Steve's legs, pulling himself through using his left hand on Steve's ankle. John makes sure to keep Steve's right arm pinned to his chest as he does this. Notice that Steve's right foot is next to John's left hip.

John starts to lace his left leg around Steve's right leg and over Steve's right hip as shown in the photo. As he does this, John uses his right foot to hook into Steve's left knee just above the knee joint.

ALTERNATE VIEW

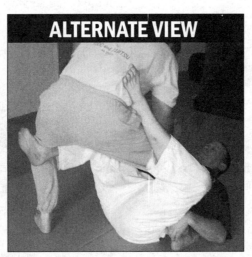

Here is another view of how John is starting to lace his left leg around Steve's right leg. Notice John's right foot wedged immediately under Steve's left knee.

ALTERNATE VIEW

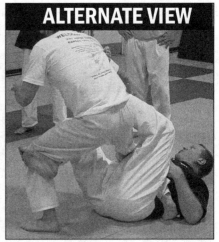

Here's another view of how John controls his opponent's lower body. In this photo, John is sideways to Frederic and using his left foot to jam in Frederic's right hip. The action of jamming his right foot in Frederic's left knee and hooking his left foot on Frederic's hip causes Frederic to fall backwards.

LEG LACE FROM GUARD TO HEEL HOOK

This is a good way to get your opponent to the mat if he's standing above you. It's also a nasty "double trouble" move where you can get a heel hook and a bent knee crank.

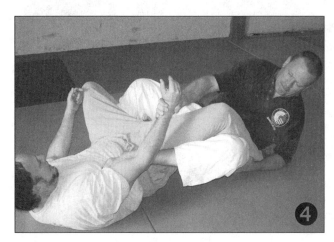

John takes Steve down to his back and using his right hand, starts to slide down Steve's right leg to grab his heel.

ALTERNATE VIEW

Sometimes your opponent will land more on his side as Frederic has done here. When this happens, it puts Frederic's right foot in the perfect position to get heel hooked as well as get a sideward crank on his right knee. John's right arm can immediately hook under Frederic's right heel. John uses his right leg to press down against Frederic's right knee (that is bent sideways) to apply pressure on both the right heel and right knee. Having your opponent land on his side doesn't always happen, but be ready when it does as you can slap on the heel hook and knee crank immediately!

John laces his left leg over Steve's knee (just above the knee joint) and uses his left forearm to trap Steve's right heel as shown. John is using his left hand to grab Steve's right lower leg. This sets up the heel hook and isolates Steve's right leg to crank the knee.

John applies the heel hook on Steve's right foot by using his right hand to cup over Steve's right heel and pull it to John's right.

SCRAMBLE TO HEEL HOOK IF OPPONENT PULLS HIS LEG OUT OF THE LACE

If John fails to control Steve well enough with his legs in the lacing move, Steve may be able to pull his right leg up and step over John's body as shown. Steve will do this to either simply get his leg free and out of trouble or he may actually do this step over to try to lace John's right leg as a counter. If that's the case, a scramble will take place between the grapplers to get the dominant position. You can see how Steve has moved his right leg over John's body and is sitting up to try to stabilize his position and lace John's right leg if possible.

John moves his right arm over Steve's right foot and places his right forearm under Steve's right heel as shown. By doing this, John captures Steve's right heel again to try another heel hook. Look at how John is using his right hand to scoop up and under Steve's right lower leg to control it.

John grasps his hands together in a square lock and secures the heel hook on Steve's right heel.

John rolls to his left side and uses his right leg and knee to drive downward. As he does this, John squeezes his knees together to trap Steve's right leg. By rolling to his left, John adds a lot of pressure to the heel hook and gets the tap out.

THE SAYLOR HEEL HOOK

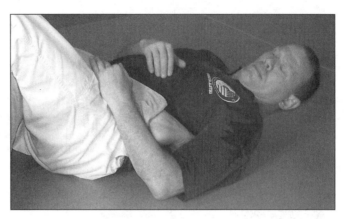

Here's a photo of the unique way John Saylor has trapped Frederic's heel. Notice that John is grabbing his pants at his left hip to anchor the heel hook in his left forearm. If it's a no gi situation and John is in a singlet or shorts, he can place his left hand (palm down) on his left thigh instead of grabbing his pants. John was the first person that I've seen to do this heel hook application back in the early 1990s. This variation really cranks the heel and adds a tremendous amount of pressure.

Here's another variation of how John Saylor does his heel hook.

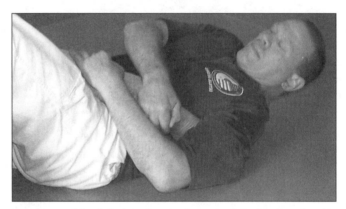

John cups his right hand over Steve's right heel and pulls it in very tightly to his chest making sure the top of Steve's right foot is placed firmly in John's left ribcage or side. As John does this, he starts to turn his body to his right, wrenching Steve's right foot.

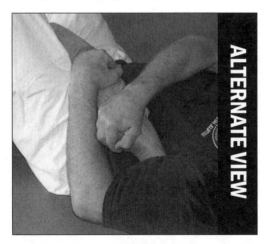

Here is a closer view of how John cups his right hand on Steve's right heel and firmly holds it in his left side. You can see that John will be able to really exert a lot of pressure on Steve's foot as John turns and rolls to his right side. John won't have to roll very much.

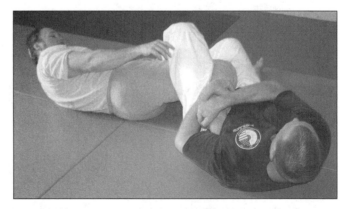

As John rolls to his right, he not only cranks Steve's ankle but Steve's right knee as well. Believe me, this hurts!

HEEL HOOK LACE COUNTER TO SINGLE LEG TAKEDOWN

Alan grabs Bret's right leg to take him down. If you get taken down or thrown, the fight isn't over. Do your best to keep your wits about you and turn the table on him!

Alan takes Bret to the mat and as soon as Bret hits onto his back, he uses his left leg to swing over Alan's right leg.

TECHNICAL TIP: This move can also be started if you are the bottom grappler in the guard and your opponent stands up or if he's standing above you.

Bret swings his right leg over Alan's right leg and laces his legs together, trapping Alan's right leg. Bret readies his hands to start to grab Alan's right foot.

Bret rolls to his right a bit to turn Alan forward. As he does this, Bret sinks in his heel hook on Alan's right heel.

LEG PULL AND SHIN TRAP

TECHNICAL TIP: A "quick-catch" is a technique that you surprise your opponent with suddenly and without too much set up.

A "quick catch" move, but it might work. If not, it's still a good way to control your opponent's legs when he's fighting you from his guard. Jarrod turns to his side and grabs Bjorn's right leg as shown in this photo.

Jarrod pulls Bjorn's right leg out and to the mat and as he does this, he drives his right knee down onto Bjorn's right calf or shin.

STEPOVER ROLLING HEEL HOOK

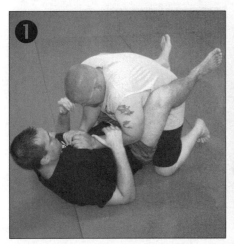

Eric is between Bret's legs in the guard position. Eric starts to pull his body backwards to give himself space to work the leglock.

Eric rises up on his left foot as shown, cradling Bret's right leg on Eric's left knee. Eric quickly grabs the outside of Bret's right foot (by Bret's toes) and as he does this, Eric uses his right hand to reach over to grab Bret's right heel.

Eric grabs his hands together to form the square lock and applies the heel hook on Bret's right foot. As he does this, Eric jams his left leg over Bret's right leg at Bret's right thigh as shown.

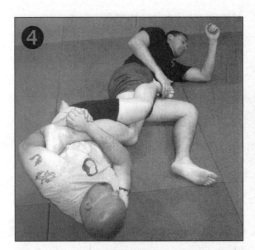

Eric rolls to his right side, keeping the heel hook in effect as he does. Eric makes sure to hug Bret's right foot tightly to his left side as he rolls to his right side and hip. This applies a lot of pressure to Bret's heel and knee and creates even more pressure with the knee crank.

Eric has trapped Bret's right heel with his hands and arms and is applying added pressure by rolling to his (Eric's) right and clamping in tighter with his hands on Bret's ankle. As he does this, Eric is using his left elbow to lift Bret's heel and turn it to Eric's right. Also notice how Eric has Bret's ankle and foot tucked firmly in his left rib cage, trapping it.

ROLLING TOEHOLD FROM STANDING START

1. Jarrod is standing above Sam and uses his left hand to grab Sam's right foot. Jarrod makes it a point to have his right leg and foot on the inside of Sam's left foot as shown.

2. Jarrod turns to his left to start to roll.

Jarrod uses his hands to form a toehold grip on Sam's right foot as he starts a right shoulder roll. Look at how Jarrod uses his right leg to kick up and lift Sam's left lower leg.

Jarrod does a right shoulder roll, forming his toehold grip on Sam's right foot.

Jarrod finishes his roll and secures the toehold. It may be a flashy move, but it takes your opponent by surprise.

ROLLING TOEHOLD FROM THE GUARD

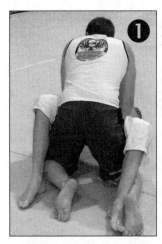

Jarrod is on top of Bjorn in the guard.

Jarrod turns to his left and props up Bjorn's right leg by posting up high with his left leg. As he does this, Jarrod uses his left hand to grab Bjorn's right foot.

Jarrod starts to roll over his right shoulder as he forms a toehold grip with his hands on Bjorn's right foot.

Jarrod rolls over his right shoulder securing the toehold as he rolls.

Here's the roll midway through the movement.

As he finishes his shoulder roll, Jarrod sinks in the toehold.

Jarrod finishes the roll and gets the tap out from the toehold.

TRIANGLE AND BUNDLE OPPONENT'S LEGS INTO THE ROLLING TOEHOLD

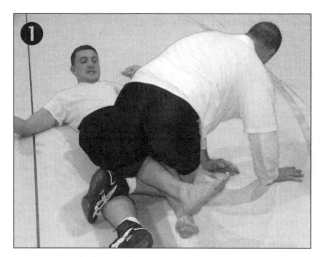

Bret controls Scott from the top position by forming a triangle with his legs to trap both of Scott's legs.

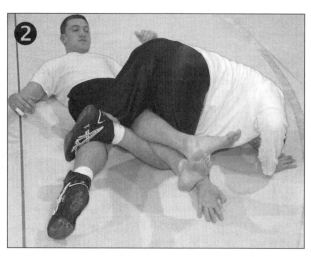

Bret rolls forward over his left shoulder. Look at how this controls Scott's legs.

Bret rolls over his left shoulder bringing Scott's legs up with him as he rolls.

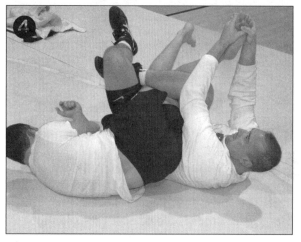

Bret completes his shoulder roll and rolls Scott over onto his back, while starting to grab his left foot.

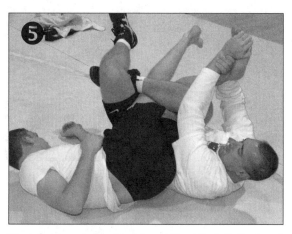

Bret forms a toehold grip on Scott's left foot and secures the toehold for the tap out.

NORTH SOUTH ROLLING TOEHOLD

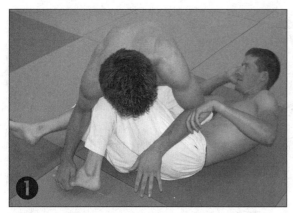

Vince is on top of Travis and moves to his left and to Travis's right. As he does this, Vince uses his right hand to grab Travis's left foot.

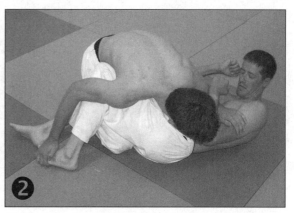

Vince uses his right hand to pull in on Travis's left foot for control.

Vince continues to move to his left and swings his feet over Travis as shown. As he does this, Vince starts to secure the toehold on Travis's left foot.

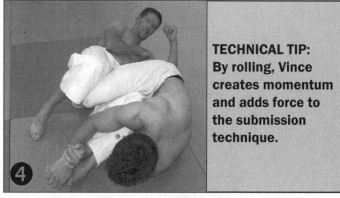

TECHNICAL TIP: By rolling, Vince creates momentum and adds force to the submission technique.

Vince rolls over his left shoulder securing the toehold.

As Vince rolls, he sinks in the toehold and gets the tap out.

ALTERNATE VIEW

Here's another view of how Vince has rolled in this north south position.

ANKLE TRAP AND TOEHOLD

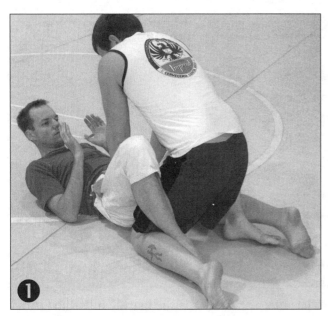

Jarrod uses both hands and arms to pin Bjorn's hips flat on the mat for control.

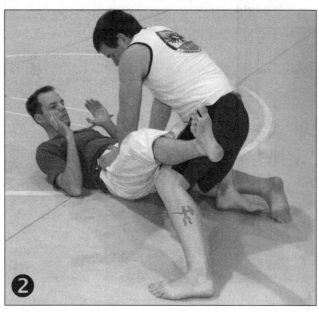

Jarrod moves his left leg up and back, pulling Bjorn's right leg up as shown. Jarrod makes it a point to use his right foot and lower leg to trap Bjorn's left foot.

Jarrod moves his left leg back and drops on it. This traps Bjorn's left foot between Jarrod's right upper leg and calf. Jarrod uses his left hand to grab Bjorn's left foot.

Jarrod sits on Bjorn's left leg and uses both hands to twist Bjorn's left ankle and foot.

TOEHOLD ESCAPE FROM LEG PRESS

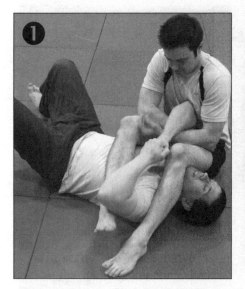

Derrick has Jarrod on his back in the leg press position.

Jarrod uses his left hand to grab Derrick's right foot as shown.

Jarrod quickly rolls into Derrick and swings his left leg up and over Derrick.

Jarrod swings his left leg up and over Derrick's body and slides out of the leg press. Jarrod keeps hold of Derrick's right foot with his left hand.

Jarrod uses his hands to form a toehold grip on Derrick's right foot to get the tap out.

QUASIMOTO FROM OPPONENT'S CLOSED GUARD

Bjorn has Jarrod in his closed guard. Jarrod uses his hands and arms to push down on Bjorn's hips for control and to keep Bjorn flat on his back and hips. Doing this limits Bjorn's movement from the bottom position.

Jarrod quickly turns to his left and uses his left hand to hook over Bjorn's left foot. This often breaks open Bjorn's guard.

To create pressure on Bjorn's left ankle, Jarrod hunches forward and he uses his left hand to hook Bjorn's left foot.

QUICK CATCH TOEHOLD NECK WRAP

Sometimes, when you pass under your opponent's guard, you can use your hand to grab his foot and wrap it behind your head and neck as Jarrod is doing in this photo.

TAP OUT TEXTBOOK

NEAR LEG TOEHOLD FROM A SIDE RIDE

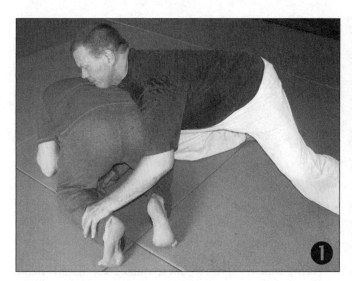

John is riding Chance from the side.

John uses his left hand to grab Chance's right foot and uses his right hand to slide under Chance and between his legs as shown. John will use his right hand to grab onto the top of Chance's right foot.

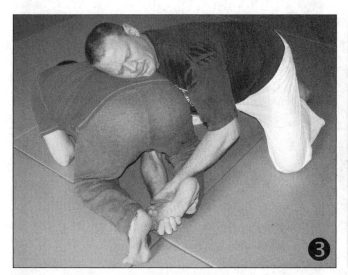

John secures the toehold by using his right hand to grab the top of Chance's right foot and uses his left hand to grab his right wrist.

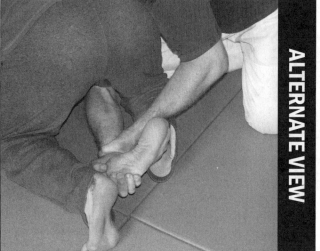

Here's a closer view of how John has secured his toehold on Chance. John uses his left hand to pull up and twist Chance's right foot.

TOEHOLD FROM A SCRAMBLE

Often, when grappling on the mat, both athletes will "scramble." This is when each of them are sitting on their buttocks and grabbing for their opponent's ankles or feet in an effort to secure an ankle lock, heel hook or toehold. In this situation, Chris has managed to secure an ankle lock on Jarrod and Jarrod will use a toehold to counter. Chris has his feet scissored around Jarrod's right leg.

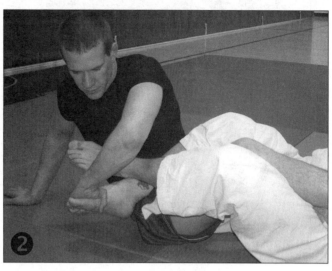

Jarrod uses his left hand to reach over and grab Chris's right (bottom) foot. Notice how Jarrod is grabbing Chris's toes and lower foot. As he does this, Jarrod makes it a point to use his right forearm to pull Chris's left (top) foot in close to his body to trap it.

Jarrod has used his right hand to reach up and under Chris's right ankle and has grabbed his left wrist forming a figure 4. This bundles Chris's feet and lower legs up to control him better. Jarrod's left hand is pushing down on the top of Chris's right foot and toes, trapping and twisting it. As he does this, Jarrod pulls both of Chris's feet in closer to him and pulls his left elbow back to his left. Doing this really adds pressure to the toehold.

ALTERNATE VIEW

Here's another view of how Jarrod is using his left hand to push down on the top of Chris's right foot and how Chris's right ankle is being twisted.

ANKLE PICK TO TOEHOLD

Jarrod and Chris are locked up and working for a takedown.

Jarrod shoots in with an ankle pick using his left hand to scoop Chris's right ankle.

Jarrod makes sure to pull Chris's right ankle to his left hip with his left hand, so he can use this position to work on Chris's right foot.

Jarrod steps into Chris with his left foot as he plants Chris's right foot on his left hip for control.

ANKLE PICK TO TOEHOLD

Jarrod quickly reaches over and under Chris's right ankle with his right arm. As he does this, Jarrod slides his right hand toward Chris's right lower foot (at the toes) and uses his right hand to grab the outside of Chris's right foot. Then Jarrod uses his right hand to grab his left wrist forming a figure 4 hand hold. Also, notice how Jarrod has stepped forward with his right foot with his right toes pointing outward.

Jarrod uses his right leg to step over Chris's right leg, trapping that leg to isolate it. Jarrod then uses his left hand to push down on Chris's right foot. He also pulls his right elbow toward his own body, trapping Chris's right lower leg.

TOEHOLD AGAINST OPPONENT'S SPINNING JUJI GATAME

Jarrod rolls to his left hip, keeping control of Chris's right foot as he does, to secure a stronger toehold. Jarrod can finish this move any number of ways, but rolling back and sinking it in works well.

A toehold is a good counter to a spinning cross-body armlock. Sean has Jarrod in his guard and has hooked his right hand under Jarrod's left knee as he attempts to start a spinning cross-body armlock. Jarrod senses the danger and quickly uses his left hand to reach under Sean's right leg and grab the top outside of his right foot. Jarrod then uses his right hand to grab his own left hand and adds pressure by pulling down.

CRUSH HIS GUARD AND APPLY A TOEHOLD

Chris is on his back with Jarrod standing above him. Jarrod makes it a point to bend his knees and move in close to Chris. Jarrod uses both of his hands to grab Chris's legs and pull them onto his upper thighs.

Jarrod quickly squats directly down on the back of Chris's legs, driving with his hips. Jarrod uses his left hand to grab the outside of Chris's right foot at the toes and pull it in close to his chest. Notice how Jarrod is using his left forearm to trap Chris's left ankle to his chest for better control.

Jarrod uses his left hand to tightly secure Chris's right foot and his left hand to pull it around as close to his chest as possible. As he does this, Jarrod uses his right hand to grab his left wrist for a figure 4. Jarrod draws his right wrist and forearm close to his body to crank Chris's ankle tightly. Notice how Jarrod is driving down with his hips and bodyweight onto the back of Chris's thighs and buttocks to control him.

Sometimes, when your opponent has you between his legs in his guard, you can stand up to try to create distance. Other times, you might have thrown your opponent and he ends up rolling around and placing his feet in your hips.

Jarrod can exert more control and get more leverage in his toehold if he jams his left knee in Chris's right side at the ribs and chest area as shown in this photo. While he's doing this, Jarrod cranks hard on the toehold.

TOEHOLD AGAINST OPPONENT'S ELEVATOR FROM THE GUARD

If Chris is attempting to use the elevator rollover from the guard position, Jarrod can counter with a toehold. Chris is using his right leg and foot to hook under Jarrod's left leg as shown.

Jarrod pulls back and squats low on his right knee to create space. Jarrod also makes sure to draw his left foot in closer to his left hip to trap Chris's right foot.

Jarrod uses his left hand to grab the top of Chris's left foot at his toes as Jarrod turns his body to his left.

Using his right hand, Jarrod reaches on the outside of Chris's right leg and knee and then under Chris's right lower leg to grab his own wrist. This creates a figure 4 with his hands. Jarrod pushes down on Chris's right foot using his left hand. Jarrod's right wrist is the lever that Jarrod is using to create pain in the ankle.

TOEHOLD FROM THE HALF GUARD OR SIDE POSITION

Jarrod is on top of Chris in a side hold and Chris has scissored Jarrod's left leg as shown.

Jarrod shifts his body to his left and rests on his right hip and upper leg. Jarrod also posts on the mat with his right elbow and left hand for stability. As he does this, Jarrod places his left foot on the mat to create space and gain a more stable position.

Using his left hand, Jarrod reaches for and grabs the top of Chris's left foot, pulling it in close.

Jarrod now turns to his left and uses his right hand to also grab Chris's left foot as shown in this photo. Jarrod pulls hard on Chris's foot and as you can see, Chris's right leg is trapped and is being used as the fulcrum creating the joint lock.

SIDE RIDE TO TOEHOLD

Jarrod is riding Chris and has quickly turned to the "business end" and is using his left hand to scoop Chris's right ankle. Jarrod is in a stable position, having posted with his left leg as shown.

Jarrod now turns completely to face the back end of Chris and has continued to scoop up on Chris's right ankle with his left hand. At this point, Jarrod grabs the bottom of Chris's right foot and starts to pull it in and around to Jarrod's right toward Chris's right hip.

Jarrod quickly turns his left hand over and is pulling up on Chris's right foot as shown while continuing to use his right hand to pull up on Chris's right foot.

ALTERNATE VIEW

Here's another view of this toehold. You can see how Jarrod is using his right hand to pull Chris's right foot up and toward his buttocks. Jarrod is using his left hand to pull on Chris's foot as well creating a painful toehold.

TAP OUT TEXTBOOK

KNEE CRANK AND TOEHOLD FROM A SIDE HOLD

This is a pretty simple and straightforward move, but one that comes in handy. Jarrod is holding Chris in a side hold and Chris is bending his near (right) leg to keep Jarrod from going over the top to mount him.

Jarrod takes advantage of this situation by using his right hand to reach for Chris's right ankle.

Jarrod hooks his right hand on the top of Chris's right. foot, while jamming his right elbow on the inside of Chris's right knee and his right shoulder on the inside of Chris's right inner thigh. As he does this, Jarrod uses his right hand to pull Chris's right foot toward him.

Jarrod has now used his right hand to reach over Chris's body and grab the top of Chris's right foot as shown. Jarrod now pulls Chris's foot toward him with a lot of force.

ALTERNATE VIEW

Here's another view of how Jarrod is pulling on Chris's right foot with both of his hands and has created both a toehold and knee crank to get the tap out.

TECHNICAL TIP: Ed is applying the toehold using the figure 4 grip. The important thing is that the knee crank sets up the toehold. Twisting and cranking your opponent's near leg makes him focus in on that and not the toehold that you slap on as a follow up.

STRAIGHT KNEE LOCK TO THE TOEHOLD

Jarrod has rolled Chris into a cross-body leglock and is making a real effort to get the lock to take effect.

Chris has managed to get onto a more stable position on his right hip and pulled away, lessening the effect of the leglock. As Chris does this, Jarrod quickly uses his right hand to grab Chris's right ankle really close to the heel of the foot. Jarrod also uses his left hand to grab the top of Chris's foot as shown in this photo.

Jarrod forms a figure 4 with his hand to secure Chris's foot and ankle in a toehold. Jarrod rests his right elbow on the mat for stability as he uses his right hand to grab his left wrist. Jarrod's left hand is holding the top of Chris's foot and pushing it downward creating pain in the joint.

NEAR LEG RIDE TO BENT KNEE LOCK AND TOEHOLD (SAYLOR BENT KNEE LOCK AND TOEHOLD)

John has Steve in his guard and is up on his buttocks as he uses his right hand to reach over Steve's right shoulder to grab his belt. John also has also used his left hand to hold Steve's right elbow and pull it close to John's body. John's right leg is between Steve's legs and his left leg is positioned as shown.

John rolls hard to his right side as he scoots his body out from beneath Steve's. As he does this, John starts to uses his right leg to hook on the inside of Steve's right inner thigh and upper leg.

John now laces his right leg hard inside Steve's right leg in a near leg ride. As he does this, John uses his right elbow to jam in Steve's right rear end and uses his right hand to grab Steve's right foot as shown.

John now mvoes to the outside of Steve's body and is seated on his buttocks as shown. Notice that John has laced his right leg on the inside of Steve's right leg and is using his right foot to draw Steve's right leg in as tight as possible. John is pulling on Steve's belt with his right hand and driving Steve forward.

NEAR LEG RIDE TO BENT KNEE LOCK AND TOEHOLD (SAYLOR BENT KNEE LOCK AND TOEHOLD)

BENT KNEE LOCK FINISH: John does a near leg bent knee lock by pulling with both hands on Steve's right foot. John uses his left foot to push on his own right ankle or heel to help create a powerful bent knee lock on Steve's right leg. Notice that John has rocked back onto his back and forced Steve to flatten out onto his front.

TOEHOLD FINISH: John can use a toehold from this bent knee lock position by shifting his right hand and forearm onto the inside of his opponent's right foot as shown. Look at how John is using his right forearm to push against Jim's right heel and using his hands to pull in on Jim's upper foot and toes. This crates a nasty ankle twist variation of the toehold.

TECHNICAL TIP: SWITCH FROM ONE LOCK TO AN-OTHER AND KEEP CONTROL
A good point to remember is that you can slap on a heel hook instead of a straight ankle lock or a toehold. Any of these ankle and foot locks are interchangeable. Another thing to consider is that you can quickly switch to a heel hook if your straight ankle lock doesn't work. Don't hesitate to switch to another foot lock if the initial attack doesn't work.

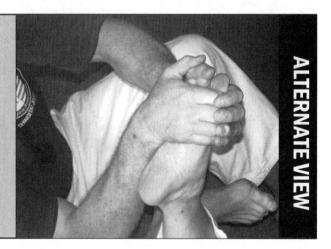

ALTERNATE VIEW

Here's a closer view of this toehold. You can see how both of John's hands are pulling on his opponent's upper foot and toes and John's right wrist and forearm are pushing on the inside of the right heel creating a twisting movement and a lot of pain!

TOEHOLD FROM THE HEAD AND ARM PIN

Jarrod has Chris in a head and arm hold.

Chris starts his escape by turning his body into Jarrod and kicking his left leg over in an attempt to hook Jarrod's left leg.

As Chris does this with his left leg, Jarrod catches Chris's left leg with his own left leg and foot, stopping Chris's leg hook.

Jarrod uses his left leg to push down on Chris's left leg and Jarrod uses his left hand to grab the top of Chris's left foot.

Jarrod uses his left hand to hook over Chris's left lower leg and ankle and has grabbed his right wrists as shown to form a figure 4 handhold. Jarrod continues to hold the top of Chris's foot with his left hand and pushes down on Chris's left foot to create the toehold.

ANKLE CRUSH

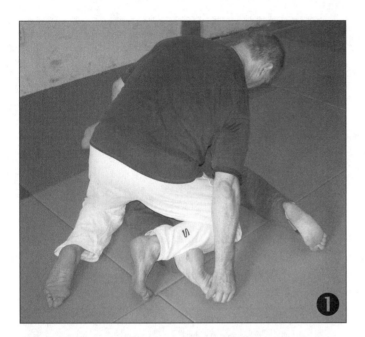

Here's a sneaky little move to use on your opponent when you are riding him. John is riding Chance and has used his right knee to trap Chance's left lower leg and ankle as shown. As he does this, John uses his right hand to reach down and grab Chance's left foot at the toes.

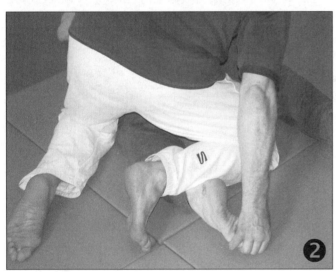

John has used his right knee and lower leg and trapped Chance's left leg. Notice that John's right shin is driving down directly against Chance's Achilles' tendon (which creates a lot of pain) and John is using his right hand to grab and pull Chance's left upper foot at the toes inward. This twisting and crushing action really hurts!

SPIN AND STRETCH TO STRAIGHT LEGLOCK

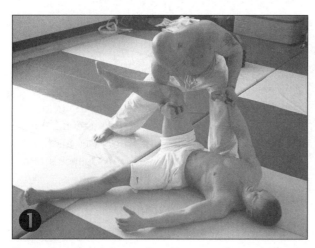

Bryan has thrown or taken Drew to the mat. Bryan immediately hooks his right hand and arm under Drew's right knee, pulling it as close as possible to his body. Also, Bryan quickly bends his knees after throwing Drew to lower his level so he can be closer to Drew to apply the leglock.

Bryan uses jams left knee across and over Drew's right hip, while using his right arm to pull Drew's knee close to his chest. Bryan turns to his right, facing Drew's feet.

> This is a quick way to follow up with a leglock from a throw or takedown and is one of my personal favorites.

Bryan shoots his left knee hard across Drew's right hip and rolls to his left side as shown in this photo. As he does this, Bryan pulls Drew's right leg in tight to his chest, grabbing it like a baseball bat.

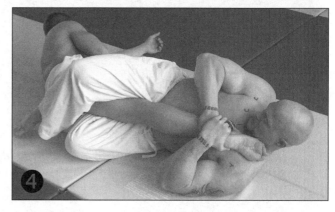

Bryan lands on his left hip and stays in that position so he can exert a lot of pressure when he arches his hips. As he pulls Drew's right leg in tight to his chest, Bryan arches hard with his hips. Notice how Drew's right knee is jammed in Bryan's crotch, to "bar" Drew's knee and straighten it. Bryan uses both of his legs and feet to hook around Drew's buttocks as he pulls on his right leg.

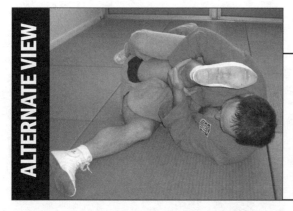

ALTERNATE VIEW

This photo shows a top view of Steve pulling Bill's foot and ankle tightly to his chest and arching his hips into Bill's straightened knee to add more pressure to the knee bar. Look at how Steve has jammed his left knee and shin tightly into Bill's crotch and hooked his right leg around Bill's buttocks to make sure there is no space between the bodies, making the leglock tighter and more effective.

INSIDE TO OUTSIDE LEGLOCK AGAINST THE GUARD

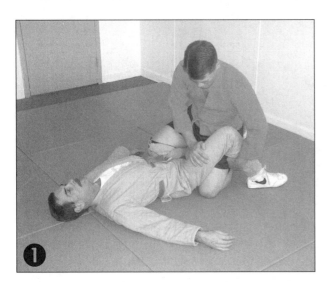

This is a good move is you're between your opponents legs in his guard. Bob has Chris in his guard, but Chris has pulled back to create distance. Chris then uses his right knee to jam in Bob's crotch. As he does this, Chris uses his left hand to grab Bob's left lower leg.

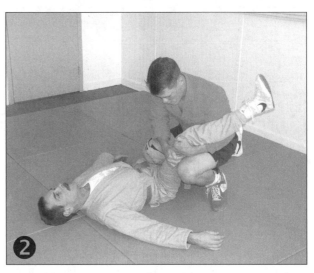

Chris jumps up into a squatting position keeping his right knee jammed in Bob's crotch. Chris makes sure to pinch his knees together to trap Bob's right leg. Chris uses both hands to grab Bob's knee and starts to pull up on it a bit.

Chris quickly slides his right knee across Bob's crotch and right hip and inner thigh and he hugs Bob's right knee to his chest holding on with both hands as shown in this photo.

Chris keeps driving his right knee through and lands on his right hip. As he does this, Chris continues to hold onto Bob's leg and pulls it tight to his chest creating a knee bar. Chris pinches his knees together to trap Bob's outstretched right leg and Chris can use his left lower leg and foot to hook into Bob's left knee to help split Bob's legs apart and control them better.

FAR HIP ROLL TO LEGLOCK AGAINST A FLAT OPPONENT

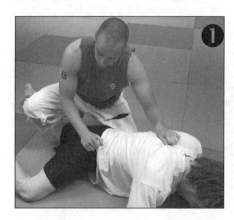

Kyle is riding Ben, who is flat in the chicken position. Kyle jams his right shin and knee on Ben's left upper leg to trap it. This keeps Ben flat and prevents him from moving away.

Kyle places his right knee on the mat as shown and hooks under Ben's right upper leg with his right hand as shown. Kyle might have to use his left hand to post on the mat for stability.

This is another view of how Kyle has trapped Ben's left leg and hooked under his right upper leg to start the move. Notice how Kyle has his knees wide and hips low for a solid base and has his right foot trapping Ben's left leg immediately above his knee to keep Ben from moving.

> Your opponent most likely won't expect you to try a leglock if he's lying on the mat flat. This is a good leglock from the top ride position.

Kyle steps over Ben's right hip and upper leg with is left knee as he scoops Ben's upper right leg to his chest as shown in this photo. As Ben rolls to his left, driving his left knee through, he makes sure to pull Ben's right leg to his chest.

Kyle has driven his left knee through and landed onto his left hip as shown. As Kyle has rolled onto his left hip, he has continued to pull Ben's leg to his chest and has stretched it out straight. He pinches his legs together, trapping Ben's outstretched right leg. Kyle pulls hard on Ben's lower leg and for extra control, Kyle uses his left arm to hook over Ben's ankle and trap it.

Kyle has used his left hand to grab behind his head to secure Ben's right leg even more and this photo shows how Kyle has used his crotch as the fulcrum and has barred Ben's right knee. This also stretches the entire leg really hard and hurts more than only the knee.

NEAR KNEE TRAP AND HEAD HOOK

Jeff is flat on his front and Jarrod is at his side. Jarrod may have just broken Jeff down to this position or Jeff may be flat on his front for a lot of reasons (most of them bad for Jeff).

Jarrod uses his left arm to hook Jeff's right foot and bend Jeff's knee as shown.

Jarrod uses his right hand to grab Jeff's left shoulder or upper arm or even hook around Jeff's head. As he does this, Jarrod continues to use his left arm to hook Jeff's right foot.

Jarrod gets the tap out by using his left hand or hooked arm to pull Jeff's right foot up as shown. By using his right hand to hook around Jeff's head or his right shoulder, Jarrod gets more leverage. This is a knee crank and causes pain in Jeff's right hip and upper right leg as well. This usually works, but even if your opponent is made of rubber and he doesn't tap out from the knee crank or hip pain, you work him over pretty good and can dampen his enthusiasm to fight you as hard as he did before.

THE ENGLISH PRETZLE (BENT KNEE TRIANGLE FROM THE SIDE POSITION OR SIDE HOLD)

Scott has Bret in a side hold and makes it a point to uses his left hand to hook under Bret's near (left) leg.

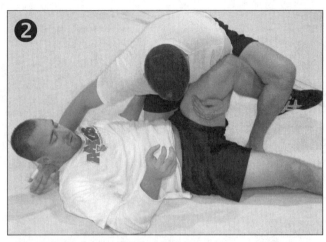

Scott moves to his left (toward Bret's feet) and positions his left leg over Bret's left leg as shown. Scott uses his left hand to pull in on Bret's leg.

Scott places his right hand on Bret's right knee and uses his left hand to grab his right upper arm for support. As he does this, Scott moves his left foot closer to Bret's right leg.

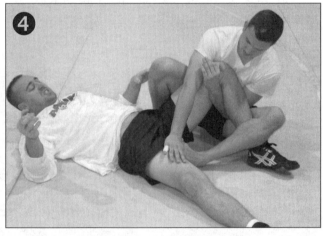

Scott rolls onto his left hip and uses his left hand to pull Bret's left knee close to his chest. Look at how Scott's left foot is starting to move over Bret's right thigh. Scott will move his left leg up and over Bret's left upper leg.

Scott moves his left leg up and over Bret's left thigh and forms a triangle with his legs. You can see how Scott's leg triangle traps Bret's left leg and creates both a great bent knee lock and a hip split.

RISKY ROLL TO STRAIGHT LEG TRIANGLE

Bret slides back onto his stomach as shown stretching out both him and Eric. As he does this, Bret hooks Eric's upper legs in tightly.

This is a gutsy move and a risky one, but if you work on it, it can surprise your opponent. Bret is in Eric's guard and uses his left hand to hook under Eric's right leg as shown. Bret uses his right hand to hook over Eric's left leg.

Bret rolls to his left using his left hand and arm to hook and scoop up on Eric's right leg. Bret uses his right hand to hook over Eric's left leg. As Bret rolls to his right, he uses his right leg to hook over Eric's left, outstretched leg.

Bret rolls over onto his back and bends his right leg to trap Eric's extended leg. Bret uses his left leg to hook over his bent right leg forming a triangle with his legs. As he does this, Bret arches his hips up and forward, creating a knee bar on Eric's left leg.

DIVE AND ROLL TO STRAIGHT LEGLOCK

Jarrod and Bjorn are facing off at a far distance. Jarrod wants to close the gap and surprise Bjorn with a leglock.

Jarrod drops low and dives on his right side to close the distance between his body and Bjorn.

Jarrod rolls over his right shoulder and uses his hands to grab Bjorn's left leg. As he does, Jarrod climbs up on Bjorn's left leg. Look at how Jarrod places his left foot on Bjorn's left hip.

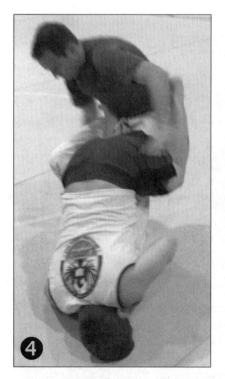

Jarrod continues his shoulder roll and uses his hands and arms to pull Bjorn's left leg in tight to Jarrod's chest.

Jarrod's roll forces Bjorn to the mat. Jarrod pulls hard on Bjorn's left extended leg and arches his hips forward and drives his hips into Bjorn's left knee, creating a knee bar.

HEAD TRAP TO LEG CRANK

Jarrod uses his left hand to grab Bjorn's left leg and traps Bjorn's right foot with his head and left shoulder. Jarrod uses his right knee to drive into Bjorn's left leg as he uses his right hand to push down on Bjorn's left leg and knee.

Jarrod uses his right hand to grab Bjorn's right heel, trapping his foot with his head and left shoulder.

Jarrod turns to his right trapping Bjorn's extended right leg wit his hands.

Jarrod swings his left leg over Bjorn's right upper leg and rolls to his right back securing both a heel hook and a knee crank.

LEG HOOK ROLL TO TRIANGLE BENT KNEE LOCK

Jarrod uses his right leg to hook on the inside of Bjorn's right leg as shown. Jarrod reaches over Bjorn's right shoulder with his left hand and arm.

Jarrod reaches over with his right hand and grabs Bjorn's right foot as Jarrod bends forward.

Jarrod does a right shoulder roll and takes Bjorn to the mat.

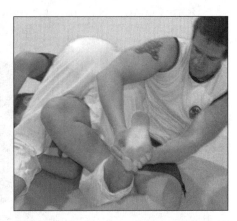

Jarrod quickly uses both hands to grab Bjorn's ankle as shown as Jarrod forms a triangle with his legs on Bjorn's right leg.

The momentum of the forward roll rolls both grapplers over as shown. As he rolls, Jarrod applies pressure on Bjorn's right knee by using both of his hands to pull Bjorn's right ankle and foot to Jarrod.

Jarrod finishes the move and gets the tap out.

ESCAPE FROM MOUNT TO THE STRAIGHT LEGLOCK

Bret is on his back with Chuck on top of him. Bret uses both hands to grab Chuck's hips and push him forward (toward Bret's left shoulder).

As Bret uses his hands to push on Chuck's hips pushing him to Bret's left shoulder, Bret bridges.

Bret quickly shrimps to his right side and wedges his left leg and knee to against Chuck's midsection and torso as shown. As he does this, Bret uses his right hand to move under and starts to hook Chuck's left leg.

Bret moves sideways to Chuck as shown and swings his right leg over Chucks' extended left leg. Bret starts to use his hands to trap Chuck's lower left leg to his chest.

TECHNICAL TIP: Immediately upon trapping Chuck's leg to his chest with his hands and arms and lacing his legs, Bret arches his hips forward hard into Chuck's extended leg. Bret wastes no time in "grabbing, lacing and arching" to get the tap out.

Bret uses his legs to lace Chuck's extended left leg to control it. Bret uses his hands and arms to trap Chuck's left leg to his chest and arches his hips (this is the fulcrum that bars Chuck's left knee) and gets the tap out.

UNDERHOOK AND ROLLOVER MOUNT ESCAPE TO STRAIGHT LEGLOCK

Jeff is on top of Derrick and has control with his mount.

Derrick uses his right arm to hook under Jeff's left upper leg as shown. Derrick uses his left hand to hook around Jeff's head. Derrick now has "high and low" control working for him. His right hand hooked under Jeff's left leg is the low control point and Derrick's left hand hooked on Jeff's head is the high control point. This "high and low" control is useful in many situations, especially this one.

As Derrick uses his right hand to scoop up and under Jeff's left leg and hip, Derrick bridges to his left shoulder. Derrick's feet are firmly planted on the mat and he drive off of them for a good bridge over his left shoulder. As Derrick does this, he uses his left hand that is hooked behind Jeff's head to pull Jeff down to Derrick's left shoulder as shown.

Derrick bridges and rolls over as shown.

UNDERHOOK AND ROLLOVER MOUNT ESCAPE TO STRAIGHT LEGLOCK

Derrick rolls over and is now between Jeff's legs in his guard. Derrick has escaped from the mount and has the top position. Derrick continues to use his right hand and arm to hold onto Jeff's left upper leg.

Derrick moves his left knee up between Jeff's legs and jams it on Jeff's crotch. Derrick will slide his left knee over Jeff's lower torso to start his leglock.

Derrick slides his left leg across Jeff's torso and right hip as Derrick uses his arms to grab Jeff's left leg and pull it to his chest as he rolls to his left as shown.

Derrick rolls to his left and ends up on his left side as shown. He uses his hands to trap and pull Jeff's extended left leg to his chest.

Derrick arches his hips forward as he uses his hands to pull Jeff's left leg to his chest creating a knee bar and getting the tap out.

CROSS BODY STRAIGHT LEGLOCK AGAINST OPPONENT'S HALF GUARD

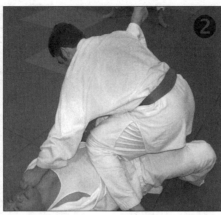

ALTERNATE VIEW

The bottom grappler, Kirt, has trapped Chris's right leg in a scissors hold. Chris lessens the control of the scissors on his leg by placing his right foot on the mat and working Kirt's scissor lock as far down his leg as possible, eventually getting it to Chris's lower leg and ankle. It's important for Chris to have his right foot on the mat for a solid base to work from.

Chris jams his left knee in Kirt's near side (in this case right) ribs and torso. Chris makes sure to really put a lot of pressure on Kirt's torso with his left knee as he pops up and scoops Kirt's left leg with his right arm.

Here's another view of how Chris has jammed his left knee in Kirt's torso and scooped Kirt's left leg. Chris has also posted his right foot on the mat for better balance and control. Chris has used his right arm to scoop Kirt's left leg and is pulling the leg to his chest.

Chris grabs Kirt's lower leg like he would grip a baseball bat and pulls Kirt's leg to his chest as tightly as possible. As he does this, Chris drives his left knee across Kirt's midsection and then rolls onto his left his with his left knee pointing toward where Kirt's feet were.

Chris has driven his left knee across Kirt's midsection and rolled onto his left hip as described in the previous photo. As he does this, Chris hugs Kirt's leg to his chest, arches his hips and applies pressure to Kirt's knee and upper leg. Chris makes it a point to stay on his left side and not roll onto his back so he can exert more pressure by arching his hips. Kirt's knee is barred across Chris's crotch.

NEAR KNEE CRANK FROM SIDE POSITION OR HOLD

Jarrod has the side control on Bret and Bret crosses his right (near) leg over his left leg to keep Jarrod from moving over on top of him for a mount.

Jarrod uses his right hand to hook over, then under, Bret's right ankle and lower leg.

Jarrod uses his right hand to grab Bret's far (left) hip. This cranks Bret's right knee and upper leg and gets the tap out.

DOUBLE LEG BREAKDOWN TO STRAIGHT LEGLOCK

This is another one of my favorites and my sambo athletes drill on this move a lot. Steve has moved to the side of Greg who is on all fours. Steve uses both hands to reach through and grab Greg's far knee (in this case, Greg's right knee). Notice that Steve's left hand is down by the knee and his right hand is a bit higher. Make sure not to lace your fingers together.

Steve drives hard into Greg's left (near) hip with his upper chest and body as he uses both hands to scoop Greg's knees and drive Greg onto his right side. Steve has now broken Greg down from a stable to an unstable position.

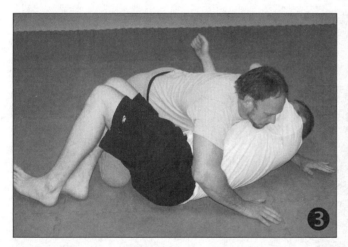

Steve moves up on Greg's body and gets chest-to-chest contact for greater control.

Steve quickly rises up and jams his left lower leg and knee on the top of Greg's torso at the stomach. Steve also makes sure to use his right arm and hand to control Greg's legs. Steve turns to his right as he does this.

DOUBLE LEG BREAKDOWN TO STRAIGHT LEGLOCK

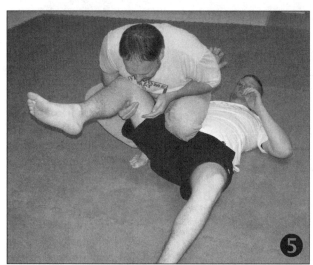

As Steve continues to turn to face Greg's lower body, he continues to slide his left knee down Greg's near (right) hip. As he does this, Steve bends forward and uses both hands to grab Greg's right upper leg and pull it to his chest.

Steve keeps driving forward with his head down and hugs Greg's right leg to his chest. The momentum of Steve driving forward with his left knee jamming between Greg's legs makes Steve's body roll to Steve's left.

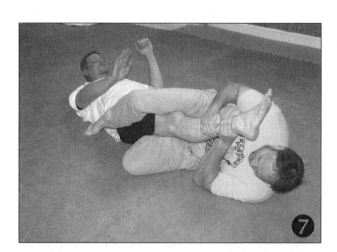

Steve rolls forward and onto his left side as shown. Notice that Steve has pulled Greg's right leg to his chest and is holding it like a baseball bat. Steve is squeezing both of his legs together to trap Greg's right leg. Steve's right leg is hooked over Greg's upper leg and hip.

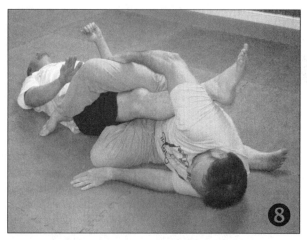

To create a barring action against Greg's right knee and upper leg, Steve uses his right arm to hook over Greg's right lower leg and uses his right hand to grab his right thigh as shown. Steve arches really hard with both of his hips as he does this.

SINGLE LEG SCOOP TO LEGLOCK

Bret uses a left jab to set Alan up.

Bret shoots in with a single leg takedown immediately after delivering his left jab. Bret uses both hands to grab Alan's right leg.

Bret stands and uses his hands and arms to pull Alan's leg up to Bret's chest.

Bret uses his right hand to grab the outside of Alan's right foot and twists it forward as shown.

SINGLE LEG SCOOP TO LEGLOCK

Look at how Alan's right foot is twisted and how Bret moves it forward. Doing this upsets Alan's balance and will take him to the mat.

Bret takes Alan to the mat.

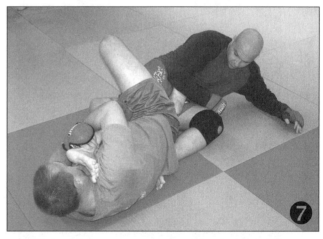

Bret rolls forward to his left, hugging Alan's extended right leg to his chest with both hands. Bret drives forward with his hips onto Alan's right knee. This creates a strong straight leglock.

Bret swings his left leg over Alan's right hip and upper leg bending his knee as shown. Bending his knee like this helps Bret slide his left leg over Alan more effectively. Bret will roll forward over his left side.

LEG TRAP AND LEGLOCK

Jarrod traps Chad's right foot with his legs as shown and sits on Chad's trapped right leg.

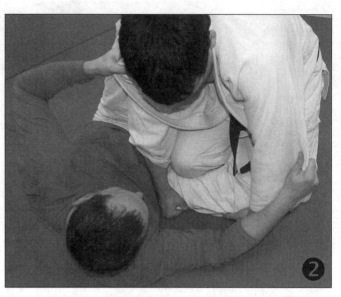

Jarrod jams his right knee across the inside of Chad's right inner thigh. Jarrod uses his right hand to grab Chad's right thigh. Jarrod will use his left hand to grab Chad's right knee and pull up.

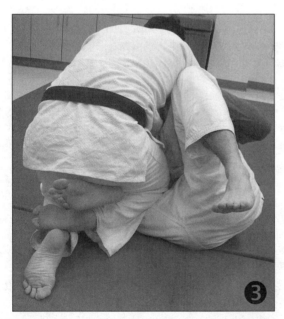

Doing this hurts Chad's right inner thigh. Jarrod crosses his feet as shown to trap Chad's right foot and ankle in tighter. Jarrod sits down harder on Chad's trapped right foot and ankle.

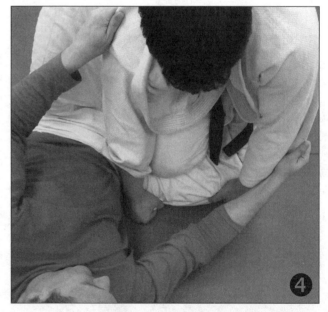

As Jarrod uses his right hand to grab Chad's right leg near his hip, Jarrod jams his right knee down onto the inside of Chad's right thigh as shown. Jarrod uses his left hand to pull up on Chad's knee to create pressure and get the tap out.

LEG LACE FROM THE GUARD TO TRIANGLE STRAIGHT LEGLOCK

Bret is fighting off his back from the guard with Scott standing above him.

Bret moves to his right, and as he does, he rolls to his right hip and slides his right leg up and under Scott's left leg to start his leg lace.

Bret continues to roll to his right and swings his right leg over Scott's left leg. As he does this, Bret uses his right hand to grab Scott's left ankle.

Bret forms a triangle with his legs and uses his legs and feet to drive Scott forward. Bret keeps hold of Scott's left ankle with his right hand.

This is a good move when you are on your back with your opponent in your guard and he stands up to get past your legs. This is also good if your opponent is standing and trying to pass your guard.

Bret pushes Scott down forward and sinks in his leg triangle on Scott's extended left leg. Bret uses both hands to secure and pull on Scott's left ankle as he drives his hips upward and into Scott's left knee creating a knee bar to get the tap out.

SPINNING LEG LACE FROM THE GUARD TO LEGLOCK

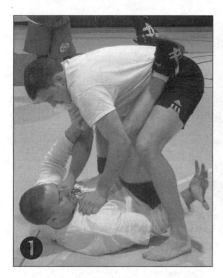

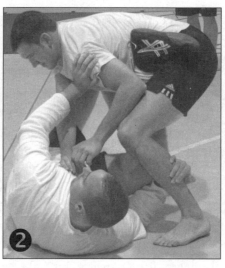

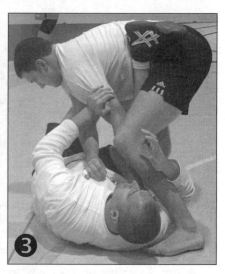

Bret has Scott in his guard and Scott is standing. Bret starts to shrimp to his right and uses his right hand to hook under and grab Scott's left leg.

Bret shrimps to his right and grabs Scott's left leg with his left hand. Bret can pull himself in really tight so that his head is close to Scott's left leg.

Bret is shrimped in under Scott on his right side and uses his left hand to push Scott's left arm down and out of the way. Bret does this so he can swing his left leg over Scott left side.

This is what I consider to be an essential leglock from the guard position and one of the first things you can do if you are in this position. It's not complicated and can be done quickly and effectively. Even if you don't get his leg, you may be able to work in an ankle lock or heel hook. If not that, you can use this move to control him and get a better position for another technique.

Bret swings his left leg over Scott's left side and jams it on Scott's left buttocks. Look at how Bret is using his shrimping movement and his right hand to control Scott's left leg. Bret will roll to his left and over his left shoulder to pull Scott down to the mat.

Doing this forces Scott to the mat and splits him wide. Bret finishes with a straight leglock as shown.

LEG JAM FROM A SCRAMBLE

Jarrod has Bjorn laced with his legs and is attempting a heel hook from this position.

Bjorn has slipped out of Jarrod's heel hook. Jarrod follows up by placing his right knee across Bjorn's left leg as Jarrod uses his left hand to trap Bjorn's left foot to his body.

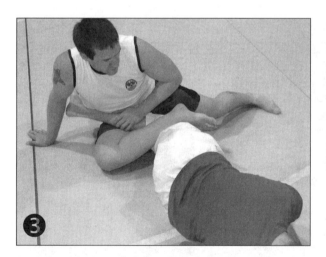

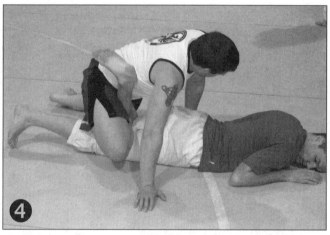

Jarrod scoots up closer to Bjorn. Notice how Jarrod uses his left leg to post out wide for stability. Jarrod jams his right leg across the back of Bjorn's left knee.

Jarrod crawls up and onto Bjorn. Jarrod leans forward trapping Bjorn's left leg in a bent knee lock.

KNEE JAM AND HEAD HOOK

Jarrod breaks Jeff down flat on the mat as shown.

Jarrod uses his left hand to grab Jeff's right ankle and pulls up on it. Jarrod slides his left foot and leg over Jeff's bent right knee as shown.

Jarrod moves his left foot in deep and jams his left lower leg over the back of Jeff's right leg. As Jarrod does this, he drives his left hip forward into Jeff's right lower leg. Jarrod leans forward hard to add pressure to the bent knee lock.

As he does this, Jarrod reaches forward with his hands and arms and hooks Jeff's head as shown. Jarrod grasps his hands together and pulls Jeff's head back as he leans forward with his body and traps Jeff's bent right knee. This move really hurts! Not only does his right knee, upper leg and hip hurt, Jeff's head is being pulled back resulting in tap out time for anybody in this position.

KNEE JAM BENT LEGLOCK WITH ARM HOOK

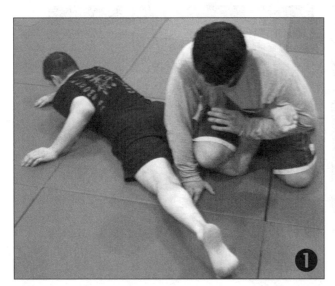

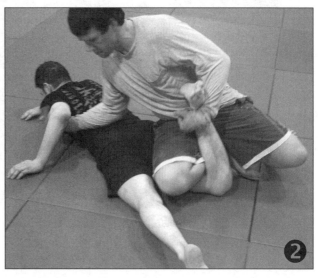

Jarrod has broken Jeff down flat and jammed his right knee onto the back of Jeff's right knee as shown. Jarrod uses his left hand and arm to hook Jeff's right foot.

Jarrod leans to his right toward Jeff's upper body and uses his right hand to hook under Jeff's left upper arm or armpit.

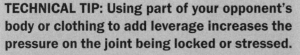

TECHNICAL TIP: Using part of your opponent's body or clothing to add leverage increases the pressure on the joint being locked or stressed.

Jarrod leans heavily forward to his right onto Jeff as he uses his left hand and arm to hook and pull Jeff's right foot up. Jarrod's right knee jammed on the back of Jeff's bent right knee is working Jeff over pretty good by now. Grabbing with his right hand onto Jeff's left upper arm and pulling himself forward onto Jeff adds pressure to the knee lock and gets the tap out.

TOEHOLD AND KNEE JAM DOUBLE TROUBLE FINISH: Jarrod can use his hands to grab Jeff's foot and secure a toehold along with the knee jam leglock to get the tap out. Look at how Jarrod slides his left hand and arm under Jeff's right heel and grabs his left hand which he has already placed on Jeff's foot. This is a powerful toehold.

NEAR ANKLE SNATCH FROM RIDE TO LEG JAM BENT KNEE LOCK

Steve turns to Chris's back from his ride and uses his right hand to grab Chris's left ankle.

Steve pulls Chris's left leg out straight and breaks him down.

Steve quickly turns in and slides his right leg over Chris's left knee as shown.

Steve leans forward with his right leg jammed in behind Chris's left bent knee. To add pressure, Steve uses his hands to grab Chris's belt or any part of his clothing. If Chris isn't in a gi, Steve leans forward more and uses one of his arms to hook around Chris's head or under his arms.

ALTERNATE VIEW

This view shows how Chris's left foot is trapped on Steve's chest.

NEAR ANKLE SNATCH TO BENT KNEE CRANK

Jarrod uses his left hand to pull Derrick's right ankle and foot back. Notice how Jarrod is using his right hand to reach under Derrick's waist and hook onto Derrick's far (left) hip for control.

Jarrod uses his left hand to pull Derrick's right ankle back and straightens Derrick's right leg. Doing this breaks Derrick down onto his front as shown.

Jarrod secures a figure 4 grip with his hands and arms and posts his left leg out wide to his left for stability. As he does this, Jarrod starts to pull Derrick's right lower leg into his chest and to Derrick's right, starting it to bend outward to Derrick's right.

Jarrod sits through with his right leg and positions himself on his right hip as shown. Doing this forces Derrick's right knee inward. As he does this, Jarrod leans back, cranking Derrick's right knee out to Derrick's right and getting the tap out.

LEG LACE AND KNEE JAM FROM THE SPINNING JUJI GATAME

Jarrod is doing a spinning Juji Gatame on Sean from the bottom and has shrimped to his right side. Sean resists the technique and attempts to stand up.

As Sean stands, Jarrod uses his right hand to grab Sean's left ankle or leg and pulls himself in closer to Sean's left leg as shown.

Jarrod uses his right leg to start to hook under Sean's left hip and leg as he pulls himself in closer to Sean's left leg.

Jarrod loops his right leg under and around Sean's left leg and uses his left leg to push down on Sean's left shoulder. Look at how Jarrod is collapsing Sean and bending him over. This allows Jarrod to form his legs in a triangle.

LEG LACE AND KNEE JAM FROM THE SPINNING JUJI GATAME

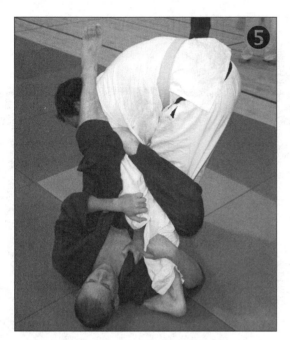

Jarrod forms his legs into a triangle and is locked on firmly to Sean. Jarrod drives his left leg and foot forward onto Sean's neck and head to knock him over. Look at how Jarrod is using his right arm to hold firmly onto Sean's left leg.

Jarrod forces Sean to the mat and rolls up on top of him. Look at how Jarrod's right leg is hooked over Sean's left knee.

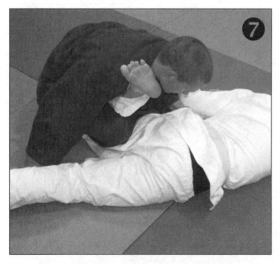

Jarrod uses the momentum of Sean falling forward to carry himself up and onto Sean. Notice how Jarrod is trapping Sean's left leg and bending it.

Jarrod finishes the move by rolling up and onto Sean, trapping Sean's left knee as shown. Sean's left foot is trapped on Jarrod's chest.

TAP OUT TEXTBOOK

ROLLING LEGLOCK THROW (IN A GI)

ALTERNATE VIEW

Josh (right) is using his right hand to grab over Ben's left shoulder in a back grip for maximum control. This pulls Ben in close to Josh's body so he can quickly attack without having to close the space between his body and Ben's.

Josh fits in for a forward throw.

Here's a view of the powerful grip Josh has with his right hand over Ben's left shoulder and straight down Ben's back, grabbing his jacket.

Josh starts to roll forward over his left shoulder and as he does, he uses his right hand on Ben's jacket to grab the outside of Ben's left ankle as shown.

Josh rolls over his left shoulder as he uses his left hand to scoop Ben's left ankle. Josh uses his left hand to pull hard on Ben's jacket.

ROLLING LEGLOCK THROW (IN A GI)

ALTERNATE VIEW

5 Josh rolls over his left shoulder bringing Ben with him.

Here's another view of this throw showing how Josh uses his right leg to sweep between Ben's legs and how Josh uses his left hand to control Ben's left ankle.

6 Josh rolls Ben over, keeping control of Ben's left ankle with his left hand.

7 Josh immediately applies a cross-body straight leglock.

ROLLING LEGLOCK THROW (NO GI)

This is a good "no gi" version of the rolling leglock. Bret uses his right hand to hook over Scott's left arm and shoulder.

Bret places his right leg between Scott's legs as shown and wedges his right foot high on Scott's right inner thigh.

Bret starts to roll forward over his left shoulder as he uses his left hand to scoop under Scott's left leg. Bret keeps control of Scott with his right arm hooked over Scott's left arm.

Bret rolls over his left shoulder and brings Scott with him as he rolls.

Bret's forward roll forces Scott to roll over as well.

ROLLING LEGLOCK THROW (NO GI)

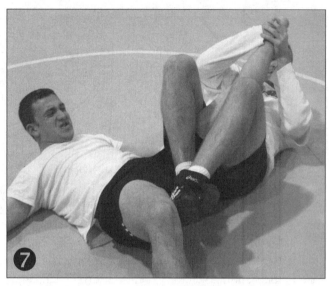

Bret finishes his roll and comes up using his left hand to trap Scott's left leg and pull it to his chest. Look at how Bret's right leg is hooked over Scott's left hip and upper leg.

Bret uses both hands to grab Scott's left leg and hooks his left ankle over his right ankle as he rolls back to apply the leglock.

TECHNICAL TIP: When you have a straight knee bar applied on your opponent here are some ways to stretch it out more and give yourself a better angle to apply it. Will has both of his feet hooked around John's buttocks as he pulls hard on John's left leg and arches his hips to get the leg bar. Will is grabbing John's leg at the ankle like a baseball bat.

To add more pressure to the straight knee lock, Will has hooked over John's left ankle and lower leg with his left arm and wedged John's left foot in his right armpit. This allows Will to arch harder into the action of the leglock.

Here's a back view of how Will has hooked over John's leg and trapped it in his armpit. Notice that Will is on his left hip and not flat on his back so he can drive harder with his hips into the arch and create more pressure to the knee lock.

ROLLING KNEE LOCK FROM BOTTOM RIDE POSITION

ALTERNATE VIEW

This is really the same move as done in the standing version except that the grapplers are not standing. Eric is on all fours and Bret is riding him. Eric makes it a point to look around from his position so if Bret posts his left leg as in the photo, he can take advantage of the situation and grab his leg.

Eric reaches through his legs with his right hand and grabs Bret's leg just above the knee. Eric makes sure to pull it in tight for control.

Eric is grabbing Bret's left leg just above the knee with his right hand.

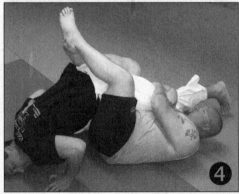

As Eric pulls Bret's left leg in tight to his body, he quickly rolls over his right shoulder. As he does this, Eric uses his left leg to whip over in a kicking motion across Bret's left side at the ribs.

Eric has completed his right shoulder roll and quickly grabs Bret's left leg with both hands as shown in the photo. Notice that Eric's legs are hooked over Bret's left buttocks.

Eric grabs Bret's left leg with both hands and pulls it tightly to his chest. As he does this, Eric arches hard with his hips directly into Bret's straightened knee. This creates a knee bar and cause pain in Bret's outstretched knee. Eric makes sure to keep both his feet tightly hooked on Bret's buttocks.

STRAIGHT KNEE LOCK FROM THE TURK

A rule when stuck on the bottom is to get your head out and get out of trouble. This method is called the "Turk" and it is a useful move to get from the bottom position to the top or even lift your opponent up to create a scoring position for yourself.

Bret is on the bottom and Eric is riding him from the top.

Bret drives hard into Eric and jams his head in Eric's crotch. As he does this, Bret uses his right hand to grab Eric's left leg above his knee. Bret is using his left hand to post on the mat for stability.

Bret drives into Eric and rises up with his head between Eric's legs. Bret is using his right hand to hold onto Eric's left upper leg and is using his left hand to stabilize Eric's lower left leg.

Bret turns to his right and slams Eric onto the mat on his back, while moving to the outside of Eric's left leg, pushing his head hard on Eric's left inner thigh. Notice that Bret still has control with His right hand on the upper leg and his left hand on the lower leg. Bret is hugging Eric's left upper leg with his right arm, shoulder and head making sure to control it.

Bret steps over Eric's left leg with his right foot and leg and hooks Eric's left leg as shown. Bret continues to hug Eric's right upper leg to him.

TECHNICAL TIP: If you get stuck on the bottom with your head pinned under your opponent's hips, work like crazy to get out of that position. If your opponent controls your head, he can control your body easier.

Bret now sits through with his leg and hip and rests on his right hip. Bret uses his left foot to hook Eric's left lower leg and ankle and his left leg to really draw Eric's leg back. Bret is using his crotch as the fulcrum and using his left leg to pull Eric's outstretched leg hard. Bret holds on tight with both his hands and arms to continue to trap Eric's upper right leg isolating it and keeping it straight. The pain is in Eric's knee from the knee bar.

NEAR LEG RIDE TO BENT KNEE LOCK

This is a standard sambo leglock and has stood the test of time on mats all over the world. I believe this is one of the fundamental leglocks any grappler should learn and be able to perform well.

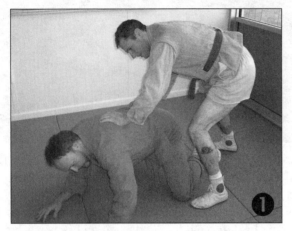

Shawn is behind Steve in a standing ride.

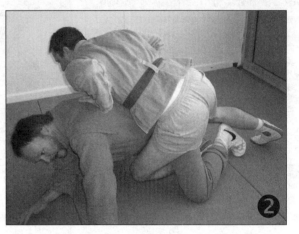

Shawn uses his left leg to hook in over Steve's left leg for a near leg ride.

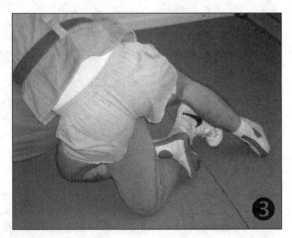

Shawn secures the near leg ride by lacing his left leg and foot around Steve's left leg as shown. Make sure to trap his leg and control it so you can work your leglock in better.

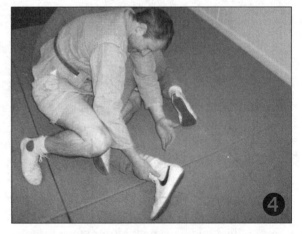

Shawn quickly turns to Steve's rear and starts to grab Steve's left ankle with his hands.

NEAR LEG RIDE TO BENT KNEE LOCK

Shawn pulls up on Steve's foot and ankle as shown as he sits back. Shawn's left leg is still wrapped around Steve's left leg.

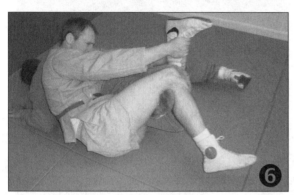

Shawn forms a triangle with his legs to isolate Steve's left leg as he pulls Steve's left foot toward himself

Shawn may also use his right foot to push against his own left leg (that is lacing Steve's left leg) to add pressure to the lock.

TECHNICAL TIP: This photo shows Bryan pushing on his left heel with his right foot to add more pressure to the bent knee lock. The combination of Bryan pulling up with his hands on Drew's foot and pushing with his foot on his own foot that trapped Drew's knee gets a quick tap out.

ROLL BACK TO ADD PRESSURE ON THE NEAR LEG BENT KNEE LOCK

Alan has laced his left leg onto Caleb's left leg and is about to apply the bent knee leglock.

As Alan rolls back, he starts to form the triangle with his legs to secure Caleb's left leg.

TECHNICAL TIP: If you roll far back onto your shoulders in a backward somersault, make sure to keep your leg triangle in tight on your opponent's leg and keep pulling on his foot and ankle to apply pressure and get the tap out.

ALTERNATE VIEW

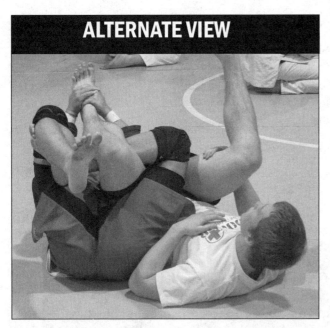

From this view, you can see how Alan secures the triangle with his legs and uses his hands to pull on Caleb's foot to secure the leglock. Alan rolls completely onto his back to get more pressure on the leglock.

Alan rolls back as far as he can onto his back and shoulders so he can swing his legs into the triangle easier and add pressure to the leglock. Alan may even roll over backward if necessary to sink in the leglock.

NEAR LEG RIDE TRIANGLE TO BENT KNEE LOCK

Jeff sinks in a near leg ride with his left leg on Derrick's left leg.

Jeff places his left foot in the back of his bent right knee and forms a triangle with his legs, trapping Derrick's left leg as shown.

Here's another view of how Jeff traps Derrick's left leg with his leg triangle from this ride.

After Jeff secures the leg triangle, he uses both of his hands to grab Derrick's left ankle.

Jeff pulls up on Derrick's ankle driving Derrick forward and breaking him down flat.

Jeff turns to his left (toward Derrick's head) and uses his left hand and arm to hook around Derrick's head. As he does this, Jeff uses his left hand to pull Derrick's foot, bending Derrick's left knee and getting the tap out.

TAP OUT TEXTBOOK

OUTSIDE KNEE JAM FROM WRESTLER'S RIDE

Steve has Eric in a ride from the side.

Steve turns to Eric's rear end and uses both hands to grab Eric's left ankle and foot.

Steve pulls up on Eric's left ankle collapsing him on his front.

Steve slides his left bent knee over Eric's left hip and jams in behind Eric's bent left knee. Steve has firm control of Eric's foot as shown and pulls it to his chest.

Steve drives his left knee behind Eric's bent knee and uses both hands to pull back on Eric's left foot.

LEG BUNDLE INTO DOUBLE LEG KNEE JAM

Sometimes an opponent may lie on his front. In many of these cases, he's hoping his rigid position will keep you from doing something to him. Also, for some reason that doesn't make sense to me, some guys will cross their ankles, thinking that doing this stops you from applying a leg or ankle lock.

Steve is at the side of Chance, turned to Chance's rear.

Steve uses his right hand to hook under Chance's ankles, while posting with his left hand on the mat as he moves his left knee across Chance's left hip.

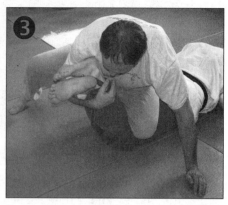

Steve jams his left knee behind Chance's knees as he uses his right hand to hook Chance's crossed ankles and pull them to his chest.

Steve drives his left knee in hard behind Chance's knees and starts to lean back pulling with his right hand on Chance's crossed ankles.

Steve grasps his hands together in a square lock and pulls back on Chance's ankles. This gets the tap out.

To add pressure sideways making it a nasty knee crank, Steve leans heavily to his left side and wraps Chance's ankles in his right biceps as shown in this photo. Steve makes sure to squeeze Chance's ankles to his chest as he wraps the ankles in tightly. Steve actually moves his left shoulder back and drives forward with his right hip, making a quick rotation as he cranks Chance's entangled ankles to Chance's left.

INSIDE BENT KNEE LOCK AGAINST OPPONENT'S GUARD

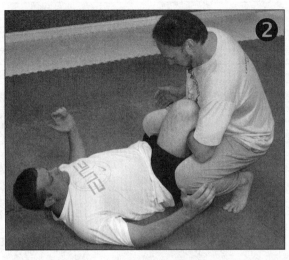

Steve is in Greg's guard and Greg attempts to control Steve with his right leg in an elevator or butterfly control from this position. Steve might have also taken Greg to the mat and ended in this situation.

Steve quickly comes to a squatting position and jams his right knee between Greg's legs on his crotch. Steve uses his left arm to hook under Greg's right knee, jamming his left forearm deep into the back of Greg's right knee.

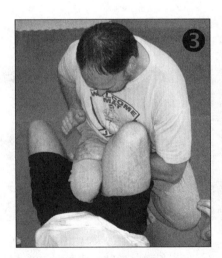

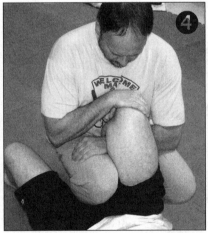

Steve places his left hand (palm down) on his right upper leg as shown. Look at how Steve's left forearm is tightly wedged behind Greg's right bent knee.

Steve uses both of his knees to pinch Greg's right leg. Steve uses his right hand to grab Greg's right knee. Steve makes sure to move his body in as close as possible to Greg at this point, completely trapping Greg's right leg.

Steve rolls back and arches his hips forward as he does. You can see how Greg's bent right leg is trapped. This is a pretty painful move and often gets an immediate tap out.

LEG STRETCH FROM THE LEG PRESS POSITION

Erik has Sam in the leg press position.

Erik moves his right leg over and uses his foot to hook Sam's far (left) leg. This controls Sam's left leg for the time being.

Erik rolls to his right a bit and uses his right hand and arm to hook under Sam's near (right) leg and pull it in toward Erik.

Erik quickly slides his right arm toward Sam's ankle and extends it out as shown. Erik uses his left hand to grab Sam's right outstretched leg for better control. Erik uses his hands to pull Sam's right leg to him and gets the tap out.

LEGLOCK COUNTER TO TRIANGLE CHOKE FROM OPPONENT'S GUARD

Chuck is on his back and has Bret in his guard. Chuck has his right leg on Bret's left shoulder and is trying to start a triangle choke on Bret. Bret moves to his left (Chuck's right) and moves his hands in to grab Chuck's head to start a can opener.

If the can opener doesn't work, Bret moves to his left around toward Chuck's head. Bret moves his left leg over Chuck's head as shown. Bret uses his left arm and shoulder to trap Chuck's right leg as shown.

Bret continues to move over Chuck's head and sits on Chuck's body as shown. Bret uses both hands to pull Chuck's extended leg to his chest.

Once Bret has good control of Chuck's extended leg, he rolls to his left hip, stretching Chuck's right leg and applying a straight leglock.

STRAIGHT LEGLOCK FROM KNEE ON CHEST

Jarrod is riding Chad with a knee on chest ride. His right knee is on Chad's torso and his left leg and foot are posted out wide for stability. Jarrod is controlling Chad's head with his left hand.

Jarrod uses his right hand to hook under Chad's left leg.

This shows how Jarrod pulls Chad's left leg to his chest. Jarrod's right knee is on Chad's torso. Jarrod moves his left leg toward and over Chad's head.

Jarrod swings his left leg over Chad's upper body and places it on the mat by Chad's left hip, as he starts to hug the left leg to his chest.

Jarrod squats low and is now facing away from Chad as shown here. Jarrod squats and starts to roll back.

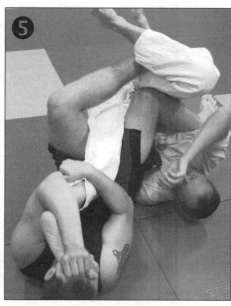

Jarrod firmly grasps Chad's left leg and rolls back. This stretches Chad's leg out and creates a straight leg lock to get the tap out.

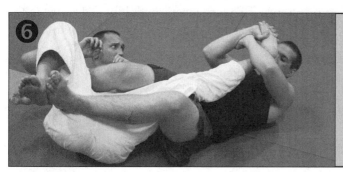

**THE FOBES FINISH
(TOEHOLD FINISH IF YOU WANT)**
Jarrod stretches Chad's leg out straight for the leglock and can finish with a toehold if he chooses. Jarrod says it's always a good day when he can finish a guy with a toehold.

FAR ANKLE SNATCH AND ROLLBACK TO STRAIGHT LEGLOCK

Bret is riding Scott and moves to Scott's backside using both hands to grab and control Scott's far (right) ankle. Bret uses his left hand to reach over and under Scott's right hip and uses his right hand to grab low on Scott's right ankle as shown.

Bret uses his right foot to trap Scott's leg by stepping over it as shown. Bret uses both hands to firmly grab Scott's right ankle and rolls to his right buttocks bringing Scott with him.

Bret rolls back onto his right hip and buttocks and uses his left arm to slide up and hook Scott's right leg to his chest as shown. Bret starts to use his feet to push Scott's body and legs away and will hook his legs together.

Bret rolls back and ends up on his right side as shown. As he does this, Bret uses both hands to trap Scott's extended right leg to his chest, hooks his ankles together and arches forward with his hips to bar Scott's right knee. This looks similar to a banana split but places more pressure on Scott's right knee than on his hips and crotch (although they get stretched pretty well and hurt a lot too).

NEAR KNEE TRAP AND CRANK

It looks complicated but isn't really. Play around with it and you'll like it. Alan has attempted a straight ankle lock on Caleb and has Caleb's left foot tucked under his right armpit. Caleb starts to roll out and escape the ankle lock. Alan moves his right leg over Caleb's left upper leg as shown. You can see that Alan already has Caleb's left ankle tucked under his right armpit. Alan places his right foot under Caleb's right leg at the knee.

Alan moves his body to his right and this traps Caleb's left leg, bending it against Alan's right side. To move his body into this position, Alan uses his hands to grab Caleb's right leg and pulls himself toward Caleb's upper body.

Alan has trapped Caleb's left bent leg to his right side and he rolls back cranking Caleb's left knee.

For more control and to add pressure to the knee crank, Alan uses his hands to grab Caleb's left arm and pulls himself to his right toward Caleb's upper body. Alan is using his right foot and leg to hook Caleb's right knee for control. This is a nasty knee crank from the side.

SPINNING STRAIGHT LEGLOCK FROM THE GUARD

Bret is on his back and Chuck is standing.

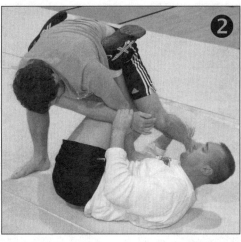

Bret shrimps to his right and uses his right hand to hook Chuck's left ankle. Bret slides his right foot under Chuck's hips as he shrimps to his right.

Bret slides his right leg under Chuck's hip and between his legs and uses his left foot and leg to kick over and control Chuck's buttocks and hips. Bret has spun around to his right and uses both hands to grab Chuck's left lower leg.

Bret uses his feet and legs to push Chuck forward and to the mat. Bret laces his legs, arches his hips upward into Chuck's knee and uses his hands to pull Chuck's leg to his chest. This creates a straight knee bar and gets the tap out.

ACHILLES' HEEL PRESSURE TO ADD TO THE STRAIGHT KNEE LOCK: To add pressure to the straight knee bar, Bret rakes his forearms along Chuck's extended leg at the Achilles' heel to add pressure.

ROLLING ANKLE SNATCH TO A STRAIGHT LEGLOCK

TECHNICAL TIP: This is a similar set up to the far ankle snatch and rollback to the straight leglock.

Bret is at Scott's side controlling him with a ride. Bret moves his body and uses both hands to reach over Scott's lower back and grab Scott's right ankle.

Bret does a shoulder roll over his left shoulder.

Bret completes the roll and rolls Scott over with him. As he completes the roll, Bret starts to hook his legs together and manipulate Scott's right leg to set him up for the leglock.

Bret wraps his legs together and pulls Scott's right leg to his chest as he rolls back and arches his hips forward creating a straight leg bar on the knee.

TECHNICAL TIP: LACING THE LEGS AND LEG WRESTLING

Controlling your opponent's legs is vital in immobilizing him so you can initiate your leg, ankle, knee or hip lock. Knowing how to control your opponent with your legs and breaking him down to set him up for any move (but in this case a leglock) is what is known as "leg wrestling." Specifically, when you wrap your legs around your opponent's legs to control him, it's called "lacing" the legs. Much in the same way you would lace up your shoes or boots, you "lace" your legs around your opponent's legs to control him better for a leg or foot lock. Some people call it "wrapping," "snaking," or simply "riding." Shown in these photos are several examples of how you can lace your opponent's legs.

Derrick is working to lace Roman's left leg and work in an ankle lock.

Jarrod is starting to lace Bjorn's legs by "climbing" up his lower body and will quickly wrap his legs together to control Bjorn's left leg and break him down to start his leglock. Manipulating your opponent with your legs is necessary to set him up for an effective leglock (or any technique). Think of your feet as if they are hands and use your legs as if they are arms to effectively control an opponent.

Bret has laced Scott's left leg from his back in the guard position and is about to break him down to start his leglock. Bret will continue to use his legs to wrap and control Scott and work the leglock into place.

Shawn is using his left leg to lace Steve's left leg in this near leg ride to set up a leglock. This shows how you can lace your opponent's legs from about any position.

BENT KNEE CRANK FROM THE HEAD AND ARM HOLD

TECHNICAL TIP: Alan's legs provide the solid base he needs when doing this move, so he makes sure to keep his legs wide and feet planted on the mat.

If you are holding your opponent and feel confident that you can finish him off, this is a good one to do it. Once your opponent has been caught in it and you are cranking on his knee, it's too late for him. This photo shows Alan holding Caleb with a head and arm hold.

Alan keeps his right arm around Caleb's neck and head as he rolls across his buttock to his left (toward Caleb's feet) and uses his right hand to reach for Caleb's right leg as shown.

Alan uses his left hand to hook under Caleb's right lower leg and pulls it forward as shown. Alan is lying with his back to Caleb and a wide leg base for maximum stability and power in the move. Alan keeps hooking with his right hand around Caleb's head.

Alan is cranking on Caleb's right knee with his left arm, pulling to Caleb's right side and using his right arm to hook under Caleb's neck and head forcing Caleb to bend to his right in a very unpleasant situation. Alan is trying to bring his hands together in front of him and doing this cranks Caleb's body sideways. The knee crank along with the upper body punishment makes Caleb tap out.

BENT KNEE CRANK FROM THE SIDE

Here's a punishing move if you have the side position or are in a side or chest hold controlling your opponent. John has Jim in a side hold and uses his right hand to reach over Jim's body to grab the top of Jim's left foot. As he does this, John pulls it toward Jim's left arm and shoulder. This causes the knee to bend outside of its normal range of motion and is a nasty knee crank. John has good control of Jim's upper body by hooking under his neck with his left arm.

THE BACK ROLL BANANA SPLIT

This is pretty much the standard banana split many of us learned in wrestling. The emphasis is not only to break him down or tilt and control your opponent, but also to apply a hip lock on him.

Bret sinks in a near leg ride on Eric, lacing his right leg on Eric's right leg.

Bret reaches over Eric's hips and uses his left hand to hook under Eric's left leg and hip.

Bret rolls back onto his buttocks as he grabs his hands together and pulls Eric up toward him as shown. Bret keeps his right leg laced onto Eric's right leg, trapping it.

Bret continues to roll back, extends his right leg and splits Eric open as shown. Bret uses his hands to pull Eric's left leg open wide and close to Bret's chest.

LEG TRIANGLE FINISH:
Bret forms a triangle with his legs and drives his legs downward to the mat. This splits Eric open and gets a quick tap out from the pain in the hips.

FOOT PUSH FINISH:
If Bret chooses not to triangle his legs for control, he can use his left foot to push down on his right lower leg to create a lot of pressure and get the tap out.

FAR SIDE ROLL TO THE BANANA SPLIT

Bret sinks his right leg in on Eric's right leg for a near leg ride.

Bret uses his left hand to grab Eric's left ankle.

Bret reaches with his right hand and arm over Eric's left hip and under his left leg as he starts to do a left shoulder roll over Eric.

Sometimes rolling into a banana split works well because the rolling action builds momentum.

Bret grabs Eric's left ankle with both hands as he rolls over, forcing Eric to roll. Bret's right leg is hooked and laced around Eric's right leg.

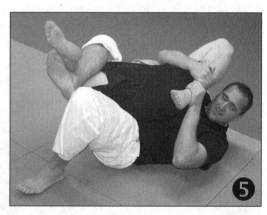

Bret completes his roll over Eric with his right leg still controlling Eric's right leg, resulting in this split open position.

OPEN LEGS AND PULL WIDE FINISH: Bret can extend his right leg to pull Eric's right leg open further and pull on Eric's left leg for a quick tap out.

LEG TRIANGLE FINISH: Bret can get a quick tap out by forming his legs into a triangle as shown and splitting Eric open.

NEAR SIDE ROLL TO THE BANANA SPLIT

Steve sinks in his near leg ride on Chance with his left leg laced on Chance's left leg.

Steve uses both hands to reach around Chance and grab Chance's right ankle and lower leg as shown. As he does this, Steve leans to his left and starts to tilt Chance to Chance's left shoulder.

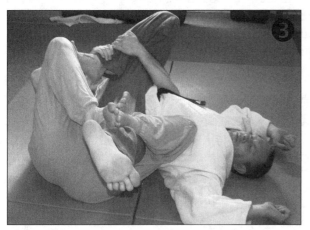

Steve scoops Chance's right leg and rolls to his left shoulder. Look at how Steve keeps his left leg laced onto Chance's left leg and is starting to form a triangle with his other leg.

DOUBLE HOOK TRIANGLE FINISH ON LEG: Steve rolls back and finishes the banana split forming a triangle with his legs on Chance's left leg. Look at how Steve has looped his right leg over Chance's left lower leg for more power to get the tap out.

TRIANGLE FINISH ON LEG: Steve finishes the banana split using a standard leg triangle on Chance's left leg.

DOUBLE LEG GRAPEVINE (BASIC)

Scott has the top position and is holding Jarrod to the mat. Scott uses his legs to grapevine Jarrod's legs as shown. To add pressure to the grapevine, Scott drives his hips forward and uses his legs to split Jarrod's legs out wide. Even if Jarrod doesn't tap out from the pressure of this grapevine, Scott is pinning, riding and generally controlling Jarrod to set him up for another submission technique.

KNEE PUSH COUNTER TO OPPONENT'S GRAPEVINE FROM THE GUARD

When you have your opponent in your guard, a good way to control your opponent's lower body is to grapevine his legs. Jarrod is using the grapevine to control Bret, but Bret counters by leaning forward with his hips and using his hands to push down on Jarrod's knees. This splits Jarrod's legs out wider and causes pain in his hips. It may be all it takes for Bret past Jarrod's guard.

GRAPEVINE FROM A FLAT RODEO RIDE

You may not make your opponent tap out from this grapevine, but it's still an uncomfortable place for him to be. Riding your opponent as Eric is doing to John controls his lower body really well and sets him for a variety of submission techniques.

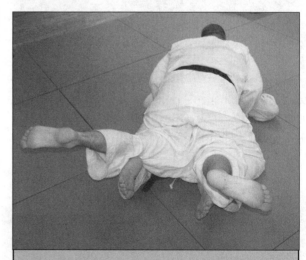

TECHNICAL TIP: This view from the back shows how Eric is driving John forward and driving his hips in on John to add pressure and control into the ride.

GRAPEVINE SPRAWL OR RIDE

Brian has laced his legs onto Jorge's and secured a good grapevine. To keep Jorge on his back for a while, Brian leans forward driving his hips onto Jorge's midsection and stomach. Brian leans forward, toward the to of Jorge's head and uses one or both of his hands and arms to extend out and post on the mat for more stability in the ride. This upper body stability can allow Brian to spread Jorge's legs wider creating more pressure and allows Brian plenty of time to hold Jorge to the mat, getting points or a win for a holddown or giving Brian more time to work in an armlock or choke on Jorge.

BOSTON CRAB (ONE LEG) FROM A TAKEDOWN

Will has taken Bret down to the mat and forms a figure 4 grip on Bret's left lower leg. Will's left foot is situated between Bret's legs.

Will steps over Bret with his right leg.

Will has stepped over Bret and has the crab securely in place.

BOSTON CRAB (BOTH LEGS)

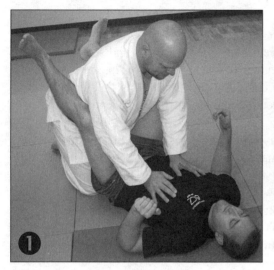

Will is between Bret's legs.

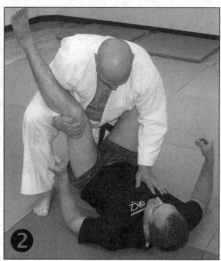

Will uses his right hand to hook under Bret's left leg and starts to stand using his right leg to stand on initially.

Will stands up and forces Bret onto his shoulders. This is an important step. Bret needs to be pretty high up on his shoulders so Will can roll him more easily.

Will tilts Bret over toward Will's left as shown. Will is now grabbing both of Bret's knees with his hands as shown.

Will uses his right foot and leg to step over Bret and finish the crab. Will has good control of Bret's knees and legs with both of his hands. Will sits down a bit and bends Bret. Be careful when applying these. Crabs are effective because they hurt and can do serious damage to your opponent's back.

BOSTON CRAB (ONE LEG)

If Will prefers, he can let go of one of Bret's legs (in this case Bret's left leg) and apply the crab on one side only.

Will immediately grabs his hands together with Bret's right leg tucked under his armpit as he sits back on Bret getting a quick tap out.

A FEW WORDS TO WRAP UP THIS SECTION

The leglocks and lower body submissions shown in this book (as well as quite a few of the techniques in the first two sections) come from two primary sources as different in origin as they are in the cultures that produced them. The first source is the legitimate professional wrestling that flourished in the late 1800s through the early to middle 1900s in the United States as well as the rest of the world. The philosophies, theories and techniques from America's professional wrestling stayed alive in the catch wrestling that became so popular in Japan as well as in the United States in the late 20th Century. Frank Gotch, Farmer Burns, George Hackenschmidt, Joe Stecher, Lou Thesz, Stanislaus Zybysko, Jimmy Londos, Billy Robinson, Gene LeBell, Vern Gagne, Ed "Strangler" Lewis, Karl Gotch, Pat O'Connor, and many other great wrestlers were household names in many parts of the world for many years. Leg submissions were an integral part of professional wrestling and these great wrestlers and technicians were the first, at least from my knowledge, to systematically teach and perform leglocks, ankle locks and other lower body submissions to the public. In fact, the man considered by many to be the greatest professional wrestler of all time, Frank Gotch, perfected the toehold and won many matches with it.

The second source used in this section on leglocks is the sambo of the former Soviet Union. Sambo's influence on leg submissions is immense and my study and practice of sambo opened my eyes and my mind to an entirely new way of not only doing, but thinking about judo, jujitsu and submission grappling. Sambo's utilitarian, no-frills and functional approach to grappling and fighting certainly changed the Olympic sports of judo and wrestling; and because of that, changed the way people think about and perform a myriad of skills in every form of grappling done today including leglocks. The leg and lower body submissions developed and taught in sambo are technically sound and have been proven effective on mats all over the world by athletes in a variety of grappling and fighting sports.

There's actually a third source of inspiration that contributed to this section on leglocks. It's that innovative attitude seen on mats in a lot of places where somebody who will always remain anonymous, comes up with a great technique. Then somebody else, equally as anonymous, will see it work, modify it and pass it along to somebody else who continues the chain of innovation, coaching and learning. I hope this has been a link in that chain.

SOME PARTING COMMENTS

Jujitsu, judo, submission grappling, sambo, MMA and every combat sport known to mankind are just plain fun to do. Fun, not in the giddy sense, but the "serious" kind of fun that keeps you interested all your life and makes you stay up at night thinking about new ways to manipulate another human's body and get him to tap out from it. This book contains a lot of techniques that can make an opponent tap out and I hope what you've seen on these pages will keep you up at night from time to time, thinking of how to perform a move you saw in this book or how you can improve on it and make it work better for you.

As always, after this book comes out in print, I'll think of something I forgot to put in here and say to myself, "I should've included that move in the book!" It's happened with every book I've written, but not every book can include everything so it's hoped that you use the information provided here and improve or enhance your skills and find it useful as a valuable resource for years to come. This book's focus has specifically been on the submission techniques of armlocks, chokes and leglocks and I've tried to include moves that are practical and effective. Additionally, you can see on every page how your position, and controlling your opponent's position, is vital to success in making any submission technique work. As stated in several places in this book, please refer to my other books published by Turtle Press for more on what I have to say about a variety of subjects connected to submission grappling. It may sound as though I'm only trying to sell books, but each and every one of the other books can offer you more insight and instruction on everything seen in this book, plus on other subjects not covered in this book. Additionally, there are other good sources of information available from other people, so don't hesitate to explore them.

The basic concept of this book is that function dictates form and a technique that works for you on a steady basis against opponents of all levels with a high ratio of success is a good technique. It doesn't matter where you learned it, what you call it or who you learned it from, as long as it works for you and works when you need it to work. No single philosophy or approach to training, school, style or even country or culture has all the answers on the subject of submission grappling, martial arts or fighting of any type. Submission grappling, combat sports and martial arts are "result oriented." In the final analysis, as a grappler or fighter, it's what you do on the mat that is remembered.

I'm sure you will use this book as one of many sources to improve your skills, expertise and technical knowledge on how to manipulate the human body and make an opponent or adversary submit to you in a sporting context or in a real fight. No single book can provide everything, other than provide you with a desire to continue your study and improve your personal skills and knowledge of the subject. If this book has done that, then as a coach and author, I'll consider it a success.

One final thing…always keep in mind that if you make your opponent submit to you and tap out, he'll never forgive you and most certainly, he'll never forget you! Keep training and best wishes.

INFORMATION ON SHINGITAI JUJITSU

What's been presented in this book is how we approach jujitsu and grappling in Shingitai Jujitsu. If you would like more information on Shingitai, contact John Saylor, Director, Shingitai Jujitsu Association, P.O. Box 428, Perrysville, Ohio 44864. E-mail him at sjahq@aol.com or visit www.JohnSaylor-SJA.com.

If you would like to contact Steve Scott, e-mail him at stevescottjudo@yahoo.com or visit www.Welcome-MatJudoClub.com.

ABOUT THE AUTHOR

Steve Scott holds advanced black belt rank in both Kodokan Judo and Shingitai Jujitsu and is a member of the U.S. Sombo Association's Hall of Fame. He first stepped onto a mat in 1965 as a 12-year-old boy and has been training, competing and coaching since that time. He is the head coach and founder of the Welcome Mat Judo, Jujitsu and Sambo Club in Kansas City, Missouri where he has coached hundreds of national and international champions and medal winners in judo, sambo, sport jujitsu and submission grappling. Steve served as a national coach for USA Judo, Inc., the national governing body for the sport of judo as well as the U.S. Sombo Association and the Amateur Athletic Union in the sport of sambo. He also served as the coach education program director for many years with USA Judo, Inc. He has personally coached 3 World Sambo Champions, several pan American Games Champions and a member of the U.S. Olympic Team. He served as the national team coach and director of development for the under-21 national judo team and coached U.S. teams at several World Championships in both judo and sambo. He was the U.S. women's team head coach for the 1983 Pan American Games in Caracas, Venezuela where his team won 4 golds and 6 silvers and the team championship. He also coached numerous U.S. teams at many international judo and sambo events. Steve conducted numerous national training camps in judo at the U.S. Olympic Training Centers in Colorado Springs, Colorado, Marquette, Michigan and Lakes Placid, New York. He also serves as a television commentator for a local MMA production and conducts submission grappling clinics for MMA fighters. As an athlete, he competed in judo and sambo, winning 2 gold medals and a bronze medal in the National AAU Sambo Championships, as well as several other medals in smaller national sambo events and has won numerous state and regional medals in that sport. He was a state and regional champion in judo and competed in numerous national championships as well. He has trained, competed and coached in North America, South America, Europe and Japan and has the opportunity to train with some of the top judo and sambo athletes and coaches in the world.

Steve is active in the Shingitai Jujitsu Association with his friend John Saylor (www.JohnSaylor-SJA.com) and has a strong Shingitai program at his Welcome Mat Judo, Jujitsu and Sambo Club. He has authored several other books published by Turtle Press including ARMLOCK ENCYCLOPEDIA, GRAPPLER'S BOOK OF STRANGLES AND CHOKES, VITAL LEGLOCKS, GROUNDFIGHTING PINS AND BREAKDOWNS, DRILLS FOR GRAPPLERS and CHAMPIONSHIP SAMBO, THROWS AND TAKEDOWNS, as well as the DVD, CHAMPIONSHIP SAMBO. He has also authored COACHING ON THE MAT, SECRETS OF THE CROSS-BODY ARMLOCK (along with Bill West), THE JUJI GATAME HANDBOOK (along with Bill West), PRINCIPLES OF SHINGITAI JUJITSU (along with John Saylor), INSIDE JUJI GATAME and THE MARTIAL ARTS TERMINOLOGY HANDBOOK, as well as the DVD, SECRETS OF THE CROSS-BODY ARMLOCK. Steve is also active in training law enforcement professionals with Law Enforcement and Security Trainers, Inc. (www.lesttrainers.com) and is a member of ILEETA (International Law Enforcement Educators and Trainers Association).

Steve is a graduate of the University of Missouri-Kansas City and teaches jujitsu, judo, submission grappling and sambo full-time as well as CPR and First-aid. For over thirty years, he worked as a community center director and coached judo, jujitsu and sambo in various community centers in the Kansas City area. He has conducted over 300 clinics and seminars across the United States and can be reached by e-mailing him at stevescottjudo@yahoo.com or going to www.WelcomeMatJudoClub.com. For many years, he was active as an athlete in the sport of Scottish Highland Games and was a national master's champion in that sport. He is married to Becky Scott, the first American woman to win a World Sambo Championship. Naturally, they met at a judo tournament in 1973 and have been together ever since.

Steve's first coach, Jerry Swett, told him as a teenager that he had a God-given gift for teaching and this impelled Steve to become a coach, and eventually, an author. Steve's second coach, Ken Regennitter, helped him start his judo club and loaned him the first mat ever used at the Welcome Mat Judo, Jujitsu and Sambo Club. Steve owes much to these kind men. His life's work and most satisfying accomplishment has been his effort as a coach to be a positive influence in the lives of many people.

TAP OUT TEXTBOOK

Index

Symbols

A

B

C

D

Also Available from Turtle Press:

Kung Fu Grappling
Street Stoppers:
Sendo-Ryu Karate-do
Power Breathing
Throws and Takedowns
Drills for Grapplers
Vital Point Strikes
Groundfighting Pins and Breakdowns
Defensive Tactics
Secrets of Unarmed Gun Defenses
Point Blank Gun Defenses
Security Operations
Vital Leglocks
Boxing: Advanced Tactics and Strategies
Grappler's Guide to Strangles and Chokes
Fighter's Fact Book 2
The Armlock Encyclopedia
Championship Sambo
Complete Taekwondo Poomse
Martial Arts Injury Care and Prevention
Timing for Martial Arts
Strength and Power Training
Complete Kickboxing
Ultimate Flexibility
Boxing: A 12 Week Course
The Fighter's Body: An Owner's Manual
The Science of Takedowns, Throws and Grappling for Self-defense
Fighting Science
Martial Arts Instructor's Desk Reference
Solo Training
Solo Training 2
Fighter's Fact Book
Conceptual Self-defense
Martial Arts After 40
Warrior Speed
The Martial Arts Training Diary for Kids
Teaching Martial Arts
Combat Strategy
The Art of Harmony
Total MindBody Training
1,001 Ways to Motivate Yourself and Others
Ultimate Fitness through Martial Arts
Taekwondo Kyorugi: Olympic Style Sparring

For more information:
Turtle Press
1-800-77-TURTL
e-mail: orders@turtlepress.com

http://www.turtlepress.com